Stuyvesant Fish Morris.

Pelham *1857.*

Anna Ella Carroll

OF MARYLAND

THE

STAR OF THE WEST;

OR,

National Men and National Measures.

BY

ANNA ELLA CARROLL,

AUTHOR OF THE "GREAT AMERICAN BATTLE," ETC.

"Our country's glory is our chief concern:
For this we struggle, and for this we burn;
For this we smile, for this alone we sigh;
For this we live, for this would freely die."

THIRD EDITION, REVISED AND ENLARGED.

NEW YORK:
MILLER, ORTON & CO.
1857.

W. H. TINSON, PRINTER & STEREOTYPER.

TO

COMMODORE CHARLES STEWART,

OF THE AMERICAN NAVY.

When the honor, the rank, the commission, or the subsistence, of any class of Americans is at stake, the Constitution does not allow secret proceedings to be instituted against them; because an act so perpetrated directly interferes with their inalienable and fundamental rights. It forbids all conclaves, or cabals, which are invested with power, to make deductions upon the accusations they themselves have made when, unseen by the public eye, the parties so arraigned have been denied the means of personal explanation or defense!

As Americans, we claim to belong to a nation distinguished for its freedom, its justice, and its intelligence; and to deprive a citizen of all that is dear in life, while absent and unconscious; to malign his reputation, without opportunity of defense, and thus bring upon him shame or destitution, is a crime by the laws of God and the country, and cannot but endanger the safety of the people! Whatever proceeding, under our institutions, tends to elicit truth and justice, requires the sanction of religious obligation, the examination of witnesses, and a faithful record!

The board of officers that have recently sat in judgment upon the reputation, fortune, and happiness, of the entire naval corps, have exercised just such discretionary power as we know to be at war with the Federal Constitution, and at variance with the spirit and intent of the law of Congress.

No class of citizens in our land are more tenacious of their rank than officers of the navy; and the desire for honorable promotion is cherished with an interest that no suffering nor sacrifice can remove. Is it for the mere consideration it confers, or the additional pecuniary advantage it involves? No; but because of the voluntary surrender of a life-service to the honor, usefulness, defense and glory of their country. And hence, no apparent rank, however high, no compensation, however adequate to his personal ease and comfort, ever atones, in the estimation of a right-minded and gallant officer, for the sullied honor which has destroyed equality with his associates in the service.

To the integrity, the talents, the distinguished services, and the lofty patriotism of the senior post-Captain, the highest and the oldest officer of the navy, of whose record the whole country is proud, the author now respectfully dedicates these pages.

The noblest motives that could actuate an American belong to him. The great exploits of the navy belong to him. The most enduring and substantial benefits of this great arm of the public service have been conferred by him! No greater glory, therefore, has been shed upon our country's history than that reflected by its distinguished citizen, Commodore Charles Stewart. He surrendered a lucrative and honorable position in the commercial marine, and, under the commission of lieutenant, entered the service of the navy the 9th of March, 1798. In 1800, during our hostilities with France, he commanded the small schooner Experiment, of twelve guns, with which he captured several armed vessels of the enemy! He subsequently secured the *La Diane* from his adversaries, a three-masted ship, and, with his small force, put to flight a brig of eighteen guns, which ordinary sagacity would have assumed to be an impossibility.

In 1801, when the reduction of the navy was made, under Mr. Jefferson, this brave officer was retained to reflect his own heroism upon the service, and, like the stars he displayed in so much triumph, to add new lustre to the American name! When the war was waged against Tripoli, the gallant Stewart was in the squadron of Commodore Preble, and was ready to enter the *second* conflict with a hostile power. We find him commanding the *Siren*, and actively engaged in burning the Philadelphia in the very harbor of the enemy, and afterwards received upon his deck the illustrious officer to whom that achievement was especially committed! The naval encounters of the subsequent four years won for the young lieutenant a reputation which has grown brighter ever since; while the navy acquired for the fame of our country, under her flag, so gallantly borne by him, a halo of light which has never been overshadowed!

Very early after the cessation of these hostilities, Commodore Stewart was tendered the commission of Captain, bearing date the 22d April, 1806, a position under which he has sacrificed every personal consideration to the honor of the American flag and the fair fame of his own pure and beautiful name. In order to become familiarized with the ocean and the practical arts and habits of navigation, Captain Stewart, with the permission of the Government, entered several private expeditions for exploration and trade; thus enlarging his experience for the service during the seven years interval which preceded our war with Great Britain in 1812; so that imbued with every quality to defend the honor and glory of his country, he was prepared to rush into action on the first summons to the battle! President Madison, supposing there was no other way to save our armed vessels but by drawing them into the docks for protection, would have adopted that policy to shield them from the foe, but for the timely counsel of Commodore Stewart! To him, therefore, are we indebted for the fresh pride and exultation that was awakened for our country on the ocean in the last war with England, as every note of victory from that scene of action sent a new throb of joy, which was consecrated to the just and glorious interests of our nation!

Commodore Stewart commanded the frigate *Constitution*, and while cruising on the Portuguese coast, he engaged in a conflict with the *Cyane* and *Levant*, two English vessels, and conquered both! At the close of this war, it was at once seen that our ocean victories, so important in their national bearing, had resulted from the wisdom of Commodore Stewart, to whom the administration of Mr. Madison had deferred! And the Congress of the United States in 1816—February 22d, passed a resolution requiring the President to present this illustrious officer with a gold medal, expressive of the high sense the country entertained for his character, conduct, and services; and the Legislatures of New York and Philadelphia likewise tendered similar exhibitions of praise. He then followed our pennant upon the shores of South America, in behalf of liberty, and watched the condition of these new born republics; where, from 1821 to 1824 he commanded the squadron of the Pacific. When science and humanity demanded, we found him penetrating the ices of the poles; when despotic vengeance demanded, we found him there too, nobly executing the mission of this great nation!

And now, with what indignation and shame do we recall the fact, that Commodore Stewart was made the distinguished *victim* of that irresponsible cabal, whose judgment the President of the country, without a single disinterested channel of explanation or enquiry, adopted! But the verdict of the people *rejects* the decision of that President and Board! And grateful for the eminent public services, which have given prestige to the Navy, and elevated and adorned the history of the country in the sight of all mankind, the Author, as an humble representative of millions of her countrymen, re-affirms the truth of history, and inscribes this evidence of her admiration and confidence to Commodore Charles Stewart.

CONTENTS.

THE FIRST AMERICAN EXPLORING EXPEDITION.

CHAPTER I.

CHAPTER II.

THE PACIFIC RAILROAD.

CHAPTER I.

CHAPTER II.

CHAPTER III.

CHAPTER IV.

CHAPTER V.

LOSS OF THE SLOOP OF WAR ALBANY, COMMANDER GERRY, OFFICERS, AND CREW.

CHAPTER I.

CHAPTER II.

CULPABILITY INVOLVED IN THE LOSS OF THE ALBANY.

CHAPTER I.

CHAPTER II.

CHAPTER III.

THE AMERICAN NAVY.

CHAPTER I.

CHAPTER II.

CHAPTER III.

CHAPTER IV.

AN AMERICAN HERO THE VICTIM OF A CONSPIRACY. CAPTAIN BARTLETT'S VINDICATION.

CHAPTER I.

CHAPTER II.

CENTRAL AMERICA.

CHAPTER I.

CHAPTER II.

CHAPTER III.

CHAPTER IV.

THE ROMISH SYSTEM A POLITICAL CORPORATION.

CHAPTER I.

CHAPTER II.

CHAPTER III.

Engraved by J.C. Buttre.

K. Rayner

OF NORTH CAROLINA

THE

FIRST AMERICAN EXPLORING EXPEDITION.

CHAPTER I.

WHATEVER tends to increase the stimulus to commercial or maritime research, adds to our national resources, and becomes an important element to the foundation of our national power.

For fifty years after our independence as a nation had been acknowledged by the civilized powers of the earth, and more than forty after our present matchless form of government had been adopted, we remained, for maritime and scientific knowledge, wholly pensioners upon foreign governments.

We had not given a single impetus to a national enterprise; we had not contributed a single dollar for the promotion of scientific intelligence; we had not taken a step to advance navigation as a science; our ships sailed by charts which we had no part in making; and not a mathematical instrument had we then constructed. Even Spain, with her exclusive system of monopoly, had shamed us by contributions to geographical knowledge, in the form of numerous charts. The Italians and Portuguese had ventured into unknown seas and made important discoveries. The Danes and Norwegians had pushed into the Arctic regions and planted colonies on the ice-bound shores of Greenland. The torrid zone, supposed to have nothing but sandy deserts and a vertical sun, had been found to teem with organic life, and with a denser population than the temperate zone. The frigid, too, no longer lay under perpetual snows, and navigators had seen plants grow, and flowers bloom, in its partial summer. Russia had made discoveries in every part of the globe. Her expeditions had penetrated into Tartary, north of Thibet, and under the snow-capped ranges of the Himalaya and Imans, and the northwest portion of our own continent. While in the Southern Ocean, she had gone as far as the 70th parallel of latitude, and boasted of having discovered islands that Cook never saw.

England, however, had been preëminent in her scientific explorations. Under her auspices the whale-fishery was transferred from East to West Greenland. She had sent Owen to the southeastern coast of Africa, King to the Straits of Magellan, and constructed charts for that almost unknown passage to the Pacific; while, for three centuries, she had persevered in her attempt to find a northwest passage, no generation having yielded to its supposed impracticability.

Thus were we occupying a national position which humiliated the American character in the sight of the whole scientific world, when the first man, who was a citizen of our country, a son of our soil, appeared, to elevate by his efforts, the scientific intelligence of the people, and to equalize our condition, in this repect, with every foreign government of the Old World. Hon. J. N. Reynolds, of New York, was the projector of the first exploring expedition in the United States. An expedition which, though shorn of much of the magnitude of its original design by the scandalous action of weak, incompetent, and unfaithful officials of the government, has, nevertheless, been pregnant with beneficial results to this nation—the greatness or limit of which no human eye can foresee? This American, then, conceived and accomplished for his country, what the most undaunted navigator had not before imagined, or had the moral courage to propose. And he stands alone, at an unapproachable distance, possessing a claim to this distinction, not merely for having attempted, but having actually accomplished his purpose!

SECTION I.

The act of Congress which passed the 14th of May, 1836, authorizing the First Exploring Expedition, was the result of the arduous labors of that single individual. No one within the precincts of Congress ignored that fact; while he received from the scientific professions and the country, the highest evidences of honor it was in their power to bestow. And when we consider the immense public benefit which has resulted to the country in its commerce, science, literature, and arts, by the services of Mr. Reynolds, we cannot but invoke the judgment of the American people to these results.

His labors have become to all the subsequent expeditions which we have accomplished, what the "tamping bar" of England is to miners.

They have guided our men of science in their explorations, as that bar guides the miner through inflammable gases, without the fear of being fired by the rocks. Nor was the effect of that first efficient action of our American Congress confined to our exclusive national benefit. The governments of France and England very soon appropriated the valuable information elicited by Mr. Reynolds in maturing out that expedition. The Geographical Society of England was in session when the news of our contemplated exploration reached Europe, and the deepest interest was so instantly awakened, that similar expeditions were at once fitted out by both England and France. And soon the Lion, the Lily, and the American Eagle appeared in the same constellation; and, what is more singular, the ensigns of France and the United States made the Southern Continent the same day!

Americans will remember that it was under

the administration of President Jackson that this exploring expedition obtained the sanction of Congress, and in the success of which Jackson felt the deepest solicitude.

Mr. Reynolds having been early distinguished for excellence and eminence in classical attainments among his contemporaries, soon became noted not only for science, but for literary distinction ; and, with all his acknowledged ability, he seems to have singularly striven for that modest *incognito* which, fortunately for his country, he has not been able to maintain. His love of wild adventure, and his travel around the circumference of the earth, had given him extraordinary experience as a navigator, and his enthusiasm in the cause of science had brought him into notice through his works at an early age. While his address in the Hall of the House of Representatives, on the 3d of April, 1836, on the subject of the surveying and exploring expedition to the Pacific Ocean, and South Seas, with his inimitable discussions upon the *manner*, that expedition was finally dispatched, will ever remain among the classical productions of the English language in this country, and wherever that tongue is spoken or read.

It is not wonderful that when this American surveyed the earth in its magnitude, and beheld the natural greatness of his native land, her unequalled institutions, the genius, enterprise, and energy, of his countrymen, that he should have mourned to see American libraries filled with the maps, charts, and histories, of what science had done in other nations, and that he made the resolution of the boy, voluntarily acted out in the man, his purpose to stimulate and develop these national resources. The only wonder is, that this had not been done before! For, although the survey of the coast had been recommended by Mr. Jefferson, the work had but then been commenced. And much of its merit was, therefore, neutralized by such national neglect.

SECTION II.

In the meantime, we had more tonnage than all the nations of Europe together when Columbus discovered America, and owned a navy larger than was all the effective force of the Old World at that day.

Americans, do you wish to know what made

you so early able to compete with England in familiarity with the ocean? It was the severe hardships to which the early settlers of our country were inured. Six years before the Pilgrims landed on Plymouth Rock, John Smith had coasted from the James River to Portsmouth, and surveyed all the islands and harbors of New England. This was in 1614. When the Pilgrims came, in 1620, they went to work and built ships at once, in order to survey the southern coast, and traffic with the natives. In less than fifty years after that, the American tonnage was great enough to excite the jealousy of England! Even when, in 1665, Massachusetts had a militia of but four thousand, she owned one hundred and forty vessels of between twenty and one hundred tons burden. So of New York, at that time in British power. The very first thing her colonists did was to hollow out a tree, to cross the adjacent waters, and commune with the settlers. Indeed, maritime enterprise has been the earliest characteristic of the American people. And this drew the seafarer and emigrant to the Atlantic shores. The Indians, at the dawn of the seventeenth century, prowled around the dwellings of the emigrants, and the necessaries of life were raised in scanty supplies, because these sagacious adventurers were busied in fitting out expeditions to ascertain the indentures on our coast, its rivers and harbors. The fisheries, then, were more ardently pursued than any other enterprise, and from them, in connection with lumber, and the fur trade, the nation received its first impulse, and its first resources.

Very soon this maritime enterprise of America excited the envy of France against England, and this was the primary and efficient cause of the first and second French wars, in which America became the common battle-ground. The American privateers displayed, at that crisis, naval skill which rendered them the pride of the mother country, while they added wealth to their own enterprise. These French wars then made the trying ordeal by which the American people were trained for the battle of Independence. We took, by these means, a step from base subserviency to England to the rank of a maritime nation, of no small account! Nearly two thousand vessels were captured by American enterprise, from the enemy, in the War of the Revolution. It was by this success solely, that ammunition and clothing were obtained for our cause, in the darkest and most critical periods of that contest. General Washington declared that this saved him from a retreat, and from the possible necessity of being obliged to disband the American forces. At one time, when besieging Boston, there were but two barrels of gunpowder for twenty thousand men; two English ships, laden with military stores, came in sight just at that crisis, which were captured by Captain Manly, and appropriated to American use.

The maritime affairs of the country, after the War of Independence, were managed by a *Committee*, and we had no navy until 1794, several years after the present Constitution was adopted. In 1798, four years after its organization, our little navy humbled the fierce corsair in the Mediterranean, and gave promise of the future glory which it achieved for the country in 1812.

SECTION III.

It is remarkable that, as *Colonists*, more genuine American spirit was discoverable in behalf of commerce, than after we attained our nationality. Then it penetrated into dangerous shoals and sand-banks. It sent men of science twice into distant parts to observe the transit of Venus over the sun, and which duty, in consideration of the imperfect construction of instruments at that period, was performed with astonishing accuracy. But, from the Declaration of Independence to the Second War with England, in 1812, not a dollar was expended by government to aid a scientific exploration, with the exception of the small amount appropriated for an expedition to the Rocky Mountains.

The Americans enjoyed the entire carrying trade during the French Revolution, when all Europe was in arms, and this gave our country an impetus to greatness, and an increase in wealth, without a modern parallel.

This, as might have been anticipated, awakened jealousy on the part of France and England, and, in 1806, led to exactions on our commerce. The Berlin and Milan decrees followed in 1807, and caused non-intercourse, which resulted in the war of 1812. Our navy had not been then properly increased, and though it won imperishable glory on the seas, we merged from the conflict with a weak commercial marine. But, after the war, commerce again took its onward march, our fisheries extended themselves from our own coasts to the shores of Brazil, around all the capes of the Pacific and Indian oceans to the Maldives and Islands of Japan.

Cotton, which had been several years before introduced into the country merely as a botanical experiment, now became an article of primary importance, and took rank over all else, while the machinery of the North was at once ready to fabricate it, and millions of the race were soon clothed in this material.

From that period manufacturers began to influence national economy. The *sugar* of the South, and *flax* of the West, were then brought into general use. Internal improvements soon developed new markets for both agricultural and manufacturing articles; the necessaries of life were at the command of all; the inhabitants of the interior sought the commerce of the seaboard, while the traveller from the seaboard penetrated into the interior. Thus was the great impulse given to individual labor, which indirectly opened the resources of the nation. In laboring for themselves they benefited their neighbors, and soon, almost by intuition, concluded that this labor, divided among the three great interests of the nation, would best subserve the happiness of the whole. This called for the merchants. They sent their keels into unknown seas, and, in a sober business spirit, they sacrificed to utility. They caused the national industry to combine all the elements of productiveness, so that every atom should bear its fair proportion in the great result.

Our fathers, in the midst of gloom and adversity, saw with prescience the rising glory of the western orb. They beheld afar the gardens they planted and the treasures which would be unfolded to their children through the shedding of their blood!

The knowledge of the most enlightened nations was confined to a circuit of but a few thousand miles, several years after Galileo had taught the sublime doctrine, that the eighty millions of fixed stars seen through a telescope were centres of other systems. The mere existence of the Pacific ocean was unknown until 1513. Then Balboa, a Spanish commander, crossed the ridge, which divides the Andes Mountains at the Isthmus of Darien. Immediately it became a desideratum to open a passage, by sea, to this unexplored ocean, and thus to reach the Moluccas and East India possessions of the Spanish crown.

SECTION IV.

Charles the Fifth sent Magellan, in 1520, for that purpose, and the straits of his name bear witness how he fulfilled the trust!

He ascertained the southern limit of this western continent; and is said to have wept in triumph, as this mighty ocean appeared before him. And while the Pacific was traversed and the Spice Islands reached, Magellan fell ingloriously by the spear of a native. His labors and successes were second to no voyager, save Columbus. And he must ever bear the palm of immortality, because he opened the pathway to a new hemisphere! which was soon penetrated by others, who found New Holland, New Zealand, and numerous other islands in the Indian, Pacific and Southern oceans. When the fact became known, as to what Magellan and his successors had done, the greatest excitement prevailed among commercial nations. The Court of Seville tried to keep secret this new route to the Moluccas. But this only roused other nations; the Hollanders soon doubled Cape Horn, and with incredible energy the extent of the southern hemisphere, in this western world, was made known. The history of the enterprise of our own land teaches the impossibility of computing the results of scientific research in advance.

We know that England's efforts for a northwest passage to India led to the discovery of the North American continent. We know that the Hudson Bay Company was opened by the same means. And neither Cabot, Hudson, Davis, or Baffin dreamed of the Newfoundland cod fisheries and the whale fisheries of Davis' Straits, which were opened in the same unexpected manner. Mr. Reynolds declared that no insuperable obstacle remained to prevent the final and complete success of English enterprise for this northwest passage. He showed that nearly the whole extent had been traced on a map, and that the effort was commended by all men of sense. "Let her have it," said the true American, "a nobler field and a wider range has opened the South to us," as he pressed upon the attention of Congress the necessity of a voyage of discovery, with scientific appliances, to increase our national knowledge of the Southern and Pacific oceans.

In 1826–7, Mr. Reynolds first brought the

importance of this subject before Congress, accompanied by petitions from inhabitants of the several States, praying the aid of the government to carry the same into effect. Among these were a memorial from the State of New York, dated October 19th, 1827, signed by the Lieutenant-Governor, Speaker of the House of Representatives, and almost the entire Legislature. One from North Carolina, with the high officials of that State, and its House of Commons. A third from Virginia, dated Richmond, January 1, 1828, sustained by the Speaker of the House of Delegates, and most of the members of her Legislature. And a very earnest appeal from the Maryland Legislature, accompanied by a cogent preamble and resolutions.

The House appointed a Committee to consider the application, who entertained a favorable opinion of Mr. Reynolds' *novel* project; and who, desirous to promote inquiry, moved its special reference to the Navy Department. During the interval between the first and second sessions of that Congress, the proposed expedition was much discussed in the public journals, and it is a significant fact that *not a solitary press in the country opposed the measure.* While the commercial community, and particularly such as were interested in the fishery, whale, or fur interest, came to the support of Mr. Reynolds' measure, as one man. This class of memorialists had, more than others, *felt* the want of this expedition; and their ardor in its behalf was marked with energy. The memorial from the inhabitants of Nantucket was commended to Congress in the report of the Secretary of the Navy, who evidenced much laborious and extended research, and set forth the necessity of protection to our commerce in the Southern Ocean, with a zeal becoming its magnitude.

The session, however, was too near its close to pass a law on the subject, and, in lieu of a bill, the House voted a resolution, affirming the expediency of sending one of our small public vessels into the Pacific and South Seas, and requesting the President of the United States to allow such facilities to the Navy Department as would enable this exploration to be undertaken.

These resolutions reflected, at that moment, the sentiments of all our great commercial cities, the Legislatures of the States, comprising more than half the population of the Union, and represented on the floor of Congress, by one hundred and twenty-nine of its members.

SECTION V.

The Navy Department went about the work it was thus empowered to do, for there was neither time nor pretext for delay. The Peacock was repaired for the expedition—officers of approved skill were ordered to be in readiness—seamen were enlisted—books and mathematical instruments ordered—and the aid of scientific counsel sought by correspondence with men of science throughout the country.

Samuel L. Southard was then Secretary of the Navy, and, giving to the expedition the sanction of his highly cultivated mind, did all that prudent foresight could suggest to render it alike useful and honorable to the nation. The succeeding session of Congress, the reported bill of the preceding one passed the House of Representatives by a large majority. In the Senate, too, there was known to have been a decided majority in its favor. But the detail of the plan elicited a difference in opinion, and in the confusion incident to the close of the session, Congress finally adjourned before the bill, as modified, was reached by the Senate. This was the termination of President Adams' administration.

Under General Jackson, Governor Branch of North Carolina was placed over the Navy Department. He was opposed to the expedition, and the tone and feeling of the new administration corresponded with his view. "Retrenchment and economy" had been the party watchword, and, under its specious pretence, the expedition, so well-matured and auspicious of such salutary results to the country, was suspended!

It was then that Mr. Reynolds went abroad and gave *five years of his life* to the circumnavigation of the globe. He penetrated the South Seas, and sailed along the confines of the Antarctic circle. He confirmed, by personal investigation, all the information previously derived from others, and, with an abiding conviction that honor, interest, duty, and humanity, called for this national expedition, more than ever before, he returned to the United States, to that end, in 1834, and renewed his labors before Congress, which were most happily triumphant.

CHAPTER II.

Our whale ships, in their untried paths, had for years, been discovering new reefs, new islands, and new dangers; and these facts were always communicated to whatever vessels they might chance to meet. Instead of the beaten track, these American whalers, after doubling Cape Horn, made their voyages along the Spanish main. And, for more than thirty years, the European constructors of maps and charts appropriated this very information, *obtained through Americans*, to their own benefit, and without ever alluding to the name of the individuals from whom the information was derived.

The annals of no other nation furnish the same record of daring and successful enterprise that is presented by the silent and unobtrusive action of the American fishermen!

Mr. Reynolds ascertained, from this pure and original source, the topography of the whole range of seas from the Pacific to the Chinese and Indian oceans, and visited Newport, New Bedford, and Nantucket, in 1828, to consult the log of each of the sturdy mariners he might find in port, and to commune with them on the great commercial importance of the national enterprise.

So, of those engaged in the *seal* trade. The occupation of these men is still more adventurous and daring. In the smallest vessels they sweep the rocky shores of Patagonia, and the islands around Cape Horn, and the whole coast of South America. They skirt the eastern and western shores of Africa; they circle the islands of the Pacific; plunge into the Southern Ocean, and are often close to the limits of the Antarctic circle! When the Emperor Alexander of Russia sent out two ships for discovery, they became, on one occasion, involved in a thick fog between the South Shetland Islands and Palmer's Land; to their great astonishment, as it dissipated, they descried a small vessel, of fifty tons' burden, between their ships, with the American flag at the masthead! The Russian commander hoisted his colors, and sent an invitation to the American captain to visit his ship. After the customary interchanges, the commodore inquired of the captain as to their present locality, and was informed that they were in sight of the South Shetland Isles; "and if you wish to visit any of them in particular," added the American, "it will afford me pleasure to be your pilot." "We were felicitating ourselves," said the Russian, "that we had made a *discovery*, until the light showed us an American vessel alongside, which now offers to pilot me into port, where several of his own nation are at anchor! We must surrender the enterprise to you Americans, and be content to follow in your train. I behold, before me, a pattern for the oldest nation of Europe, since, instead of making discoveries, I find here the American flag, a small fleet, and a pilot."

Captain Palmer was the American, and the Russian commander, Stanjykowitsch, was so highly impressed, that he named the coast Palmer's Land, which name is still inscribe don Russian charts.

Mr. Reynolds afterwards visited the whole of the extensive group of islands north of Palmer's Land. In 1831, a British vessel touched at a single spot, and substituted an English for the American name!

SECTION I.

The memorial of the East India Marine Society, fully setting forth the enterprise of Americans in behalf of commerce, and urging the expedition, projected by Mr. Reynolds, slept in manuscript until 1835, when it was communicated to Congress by a call of the House.

The exposure of so many of our citizens to shipwreck on seas, on coasts, and among islands, without a chart to guide them, and often their massacre by savages, for lack of maritime power to enforce respect, had become alarming to that class of our countrymen engaged in maritime enterprise; for it was a well-known fact, that only a few years before, when the government sent the Potomac to avenge the savage slaughter of our citizens on the coast of Sumatra; on the news reaching here that the "Friendship" had been captured, the Department had not a single chart of that coast, against which it ordered a heavy armament! And the captain, having to rely on his *wits*, with such information as he could gather, ran the frigate on the shore of Sumatra before he knew he was in anchoring distance! At the beginning of the present century we had, at least, thirty vessels, in a single season, at the Island of Sumatra, on account of its trade in pepper. And the English and Dutch had almost allowed our sagacious merchants, by direct and indirect traffic, a monopoly of the commerce of the Sunda Isles. And yet, there we were, with no chart by which to sail a United States vessel! What a shame! There, too, were the Fejee, or Betee Islands. Captain Cook named, but did not visit them. They consisted of fifty or sixty, without any data by which their harbors or dangers could be made known.

We have seen how differently other nations have acted under like circumstances. England, ambitious to rule the waves, paid, before 1770, three millions in bounties, to compete with the Dutch whale fisheries, and, before 1786, had drawn six millions, and upwards, for the same end! The American whale fishermen never had a cent of bounty in all their lives!

These sailors, too, have been the best friends of the country; and the fisheries reach the interests of every class of our people. Oh, how many brave spirits have been the victims of mutiny and massacre, because the government remained so long indifferent to the fate of seamen, or the means to advance their welfare!

The capture of the ship Mentor, of New Bedford, December 6, 1831, illustrates our position. That vessel struck the rocks near the Pelew Islands, *not then mentioned on any chart*, and, after losing an officer and part of her crew among the breakers, the captain and remainder of the crew were made prisoners by the natives. The recital of the death of some of these, the barbarous treatment of others, and their escape, as well as the condition of those left as hostages in the hands of the Pelew chiefs, is enough to sicken the heart of the most obdurate.

SECTION II.

The question may now be asked, "Are the lives of our mariners less precious than those of foreigners?" We know that many ships, freighted with human souls, have sailed from our coasts, never to return. Other nations have not paused under like circumstances, to consider the expense. The French expedition to ascertain the fate of La Perouse, who commanded the Boussole, and Astrolabe, in 1791, was more creditable to that government than all its discoveries. The kings of Denmark bound themselves, by their coronation oaths, to protect their inhabitants when exposed to the Arctic regions. So, England no sooner knew that several of her whale ships were locked into the Arctic seas, than the Admiralty anticipated the government. The expedition was fitted out, and the distinguished Captain Ross tendered the command. And the French government, subsequently, on learning the loss of the Silloise, in the polar seas, offered one hundred thousand francs to any nation that might extricate the suffering crew.

Mr. Reynolds found the charts given of the Pacific *defective*, and islands, like the Gallapago group, without any chart indications whatever. The American whalers, therefore, were the constant prey of the natives. Our consul, at Oahu, wrote, at that time, to Commodore Downs, that often fifty or sixty Americans were confined in the fort, and not a single whaler entered without mutiny ensuing, and constant desertion thereby occurring. Similar reports were made from other consulates ; all going to prove that no commercial and free people should withhold their contributions, while a spot of ground remains on the whole earth unexplored!

Mr. Reynolds showed, by the most incontestable evidence, that the national dignity and honor called for the expedition he had matured for the United States; that our commanding position, as a commercial nation, required it, that nature and her laws must be better understood, in a country like ours, where so much *mind* is ready to act upon *matter*, in subserving the great purposes of life; and that the astonishing progress we had made, imposed the duty upon our statesmen of making surveys of new islands, remote seas, and unknown territory. He, therefore, conceived a plan for our first national exploration, which should be worthy of the magnitude of its importance; and proposed that an enlightened body of naval officers should be joined harmoniously with a corps of the most scientific men of the country.

Not only to attain to high southern latitudes, but to explore from the west coast of South America, running down the longitude among the islands, *on both sides of the equator*, especially south to the very shores of Asia, was the field to which Mr. Reynolds invited the attention of

Congress and the country. His views of the detail were in exact accordance with those expressed by Mr. Jefferson, in 1803, in instructions he gave to Merriwether Lewis, for the expedition across the continent. This letter settled the constitutional scruples of the strictest constructionists, and stands side by side with the Delaration of Independence by the same author!

SECTION III.

A religious not less than a commercial view called now for this enterprise. There is no other way to make known the "salvation of our God unto the ends of the earth" but in pursuing geography as a science. God, in His wise providence, left the figure and magnitude of the earth for man's investigation, and has stimulated this exertion by the "unsearchable riches of Christ!" The Bible and missions follow the moral and political movements of this nation, and are close to the American navigator who ploughs the ocean for new islands or continents!

And while patriotism, science, and commerce have interests, that of the Protestant faith has still more staked upon these results! In this connection with the utility of American researches, let us remember that those nations most proverbial for wealth have scarcely a name in history, while the hardship and adventure of others, even though they failed to be successful, have been entitled to admiration and respect.

It is well known that but two outlets exist to the Northern Polar Seas; these are Bhering's Straits and the Spitzbergen Seas. Mr. Reynolds clearly demonstrated *why* the British navigators had failed in finding a northwest passage, which resulted entirely from adhering pertinaciously to the injudicious instructions of the British Admiralty. He maintained that the existence of this passage was no longer a question of doubt, and could be attained by keeping mid-channel through Bhering's Straits and rounding the headland of our continent, thence into the Seas of Spitzbergen. He insisted, from the results of personal experience, that ice is never found in the main ocean, remote from the land—*not even at the Pole itself!* And all subsequent investigation has confirmed that assertion.

The entire surrounding coast of the North Polar Seas is inhabited. The Laplanders and Fins occupy the European part; the Samayedes and other rude tribes the Asiatic part, and they subsist on reindeer and fish—the Esquimaux race occupy the American part. Many large rivers of Asia send their sluggish currents of fresh water into the Polar Seas. This cause, on such an extent of coast, produces ice, which is drifted by northern currents, in the spring, between Greenland and Spitzbergen. It there collects, and is finally forced by pressure into the adjacent bays and islands. This was the route on which the British expedition was bound, and necessarily impeded it.

It was indeed remarkable that at the time Mr. Reynolds projected the first scientific expedition, there was more than one million and a half of square miles in the southern hemisphere that had never felt the footprint of man! Nor had the keel of a single navigator ever divided its waters! Who can tolerate such culpable national neglect? Some may inquire, were no efforts made before those of this American to explore the high southern latitudes? We answer that, in 1772, Captain Cook, accompanied by Lieutenant Freneau, made the first voyage in search of a southern continent. They got as far as sixty-eight degrees of south latitude, and there encountered ice of six or eight inches in thickness. It concentrated around the vessels, and, sooner than attempt to go around the ice—summer having almost closed—Captain Cook retrograded, and went in pursuit of other discoveries northward.

Had Cook possessed then the information Reynolds did, in 1834, he would have selected another meridian and pursued his journey south! For Reynolds proved that same ice to have come from large islands east from Palmer's Land.

SECTION IV.

In 1773, Captain Cook left New Zealand on his second search for southern lands. But again the ice arrested his progress; and he declared it his opinion that the mass of crystallization extended to the Pole, or joined to some land southward, which must be as frigid and sterile as the ice itself.

Weddell, who attained in his day to a higher parallel than had been reached by any other man, did not agree with Cook at all, as to the ice extending to the Pole. His views encouraged Mr. Reynolds, and confirmed his own experience, although he denied Weddell's assertion that cold was more intense in the distant Antarctic regions than in the Arctic. Briscol subsequently went out in the employ of Messrs. Enderby, of London, in a whale ship, in 1832, and the existence of southern land seemed to have had confirmation by him. But the mainland taken by him, in the name of his sovereign, had been visited by our own *sealers* fifteen years before, and furs were taken then, by our people, in the American name!

Mr. Reynolds had beheld, on board two vessels —one of one hundred and sixty, the other of eighty tons burden—the castellated region of the Antarctic, with its floating pyramids of ice; and he declared it as his opinion, that the ninetieth degree, or South Pole, could be reached by the navigator, and that the effort ought to be made by the country, in connection with other objects of the enterprise.

Without government patronage he had sought adventure, and satisfied himself; and he plead, earnestly, before the Congress of his country, that it might sanction his project, only to add new lustre to the annals of American philosophy, and add nautical glories to the imperishable honor which connects itself with that name. He appealed to his countrywomen, at the same time, and contended that "their views of public measures were the silken and golden threads in public opinion." And, when we consider that the jewels which Isabella suspended from her person, enriched the world with a continent, when monarchs hesitated, and ministers disputed, with vehemence and weak superlativeness, we shall not disclaim the fact, that it was woman, truly, who gave new hopes to liberty, when the race from whence it sprung was almost lost!

When our republic was in its infancy, the great Catharine, of Russia, sent to General Washington a request for the vocabularies of all the Indian tribes in our country. The result of this gave rise to a new science, which she instituted, and has modified the grammars and lexicons of every language in Europe, which this science of *philology* now pervades.

After Mr. Reynolds' admirable exposé of the nature and utility of the expedition to the South Seas, on the 3d of April, 1836, members of both Houses of Congress no longer doubted it was fully worthy of the patronage of the government. And, on the 14th of the succeeding month, they demonstrated that wise concurrence, by giving to it the sanction of law. It was clearly manifest that, by it, the capital of human knowledge would be extended, the boundaries of science enlarged, and a substantial fame would, thereby, be added to our great republic.

SECTION V.

Our statesmen were, then, convinced that it was the policy of the government to point out harbors for our seamen, and save them from captivity, shipwreck, and famine, on unknown coasts, rather than to keep a useless fleet up the Mediterranean, to contract the follies and vices of European aristocracies; they, therefore, rightly estimated the value of this American deed, by the moral sublimity of the motives which had incited it. Congratulatory letters from men, eminent for learning and science, came to Mr. Reynolds from all sections of the country; and a full interchange of their views as to the *personnel* of the expedition was thus elicited.

Hon. J. K. Paulding suggested the frigate "Macedonia" should be attached for the benefit of scientific pursuits and occupations; and that

Captain Catesby Jones should be appointed to the command. James E. De Kay thought the employment of scientific citizens of the country a *sine quâ non*, with such an harmonious arrangement as should impartially reward whoever might merit distinction. Professor Silliman, of Yale College, regarded the expedition so vital to national honor, whether as connected with science, navigation, commerce, or the humanity of the country, that he urged, with great pertinacity, the acquisition of the highest scientific talent it possessed, without regard to the expense; that meteorology, zoology, volcanoes, earthquakes, geology, mineralogy, magnetism, and electricity, osteology, entomology, ornithology, and natural history, generally, might each command its appropriate investigation.

Hon. Benjamin Rodman, of New Bedford, the home of the mariner, gave vent to his national and natural fervor at the same period, when addressing his American brother:

"I congratulate you on the success of your *darling* plan, and now there is a hope of a national duty being performed. I see no way that we can look for improvement, but by the means which, through your exertions, *more than those of any other man living*, are now appropriated for it; and may Heaven bless you and the enterprise."

Thus did Mr. Reynolds soon concentrate the wisdom and virtue of the people. The seamen felt a thrill of inward joy to find preparations for a more stable protection, and the merchant breathed more freely when he saw that the moral influence of the nation was about to be cast upon the side of commercial intelligence and enterprise. But such had been the advancement of the age, that geographical discoveries and an amended chart, would not alone satisfy the men or the wants of our country. Animate as well as inanimate creation needed, therefore, a critical examination. And commanders of liberal minds and expanded views became essentially necessary to the expedition. In this spirit, Hon. Jos. Delafield, President of the Lyceum of Natural History of New York, after thanking Mr. Reynolds for the fund of information he had been, through him, enabled to communicate to that Institution, said :

' Your [Reynolds'] efforts have been so far crowned with success. Your former services, present exertions, and the better part of a life devoted to the South Sea discoveries, have identified you with the expedition. We have long watched your untiring exertions in this matter, and trust the time has arrived when the wishes of your friends are to be gratified in learning that the superintendence or direction of the civil department is to be chiefly committed to you."

SECTION VI.

The time seemed now to have arrived when the gratification of discharging the debt for practical science and intelligence, too long due foreign nations, could be experienced. How? By taking our national stand on the same platform of practical intelligence. This was the *first* opportunity, and is it wonderful with what eagerness our wise and prudent men embraced it?

Winslow Lewis, Jr., of the Society of Natural History of Boston, in common with other friends, addressed the *Author* of the expedition:

> "I congratulate you on the successful termination of *your* application to Congress, in behalf of a South Sea Expedition. It was to your unmeasured zeal and untiring exertions that this great undertaking owes its existence; and I learn, with much satisfaction, that it still continues to have the advantage of your personal presence and experience."

And as science as well as commerce relied on this exploration to enlarge their boundaries, Mr. Lewis urged the propriety of a *practical* anatomist to accompany the expedition, with a special view to the advancement of natural history.

So desirable did it seem in all eyes that this, *the first* American voyage of discovery, should be worthy of the genius and enterprise of the nation, that the whole mercantile influence of the country looked upon it as eminently conducive to the commerce and navigation of the country, as well as to human prosperity and happiness.

Hon. H. D. Gilpin, of Philadelphia, in addressing Mr. Reynolds, dwelt upon the necessity of calling men of *real* science to its aid—men of the same courage, disinterestedness, and perseverance, as those who had distinguished expeditions of the kind in the Old World.

"But," said he, "to you who have studied the subject so fully, and devoted to it so much thought and experience, it is scarcely necessary to say anything as to the contemplated arrangement."

It was so manifest that Mr. Reynolds, in maturing his plan, had consulted all the great European voyagers of discovery, that there appeared an entire unanimity in the conclusion of the scientific corps of the country, as to the *solid* additions which would be added thereby to the treasures of knowledge. So we find Hon. Henry Junius Nott, suggesting the expediency of confining men to a *single* branch of science, if possible, and insisting on the importance of having an individual familiar with the languages and with philology.

"The commercial investigations," said Mr. Nott, to the author, "I presume *you* will take under your own charge. I am happy to learn the voyage to the South Pacific is resolved on, and one of your activity, perseverance, and practical good sense, is to be connected with it."

"I have often had this question put to me," writes Captain Thomas AP C. Jones, "as to '*what situation, if any, will Mr. Reynolds occupy in the expedition?*'

"The answer, I presume, is with yourself; for it cannot be denied that to you, and your unwearied exertions, is due the credit of so interesting the public on the subject, as to induce Congress to pass the law. Who, then, has a better claim to participate in its toils, and to share its honors, than he who may justly be called the *originator* of the voyage? Who can bring so much valuable knowledge, derived from various sources, *some of which you alone have been permitted to draw from, as you could?* I mean not to flatter, when I say, *not another citizen of the United States.*

"Then it cannot be doubted but that any commander, qualified to conduct the enterprise as the law contemplates, as well as the executive head under whose auspices it will be sent out, will gladly avail themselves of your services, to aid them in organizing the scientific department, and further identify you with the expedition, by assigning you some honorable station in it."

Captain Jones, in this same letter, showed, by luminous argument, why a frigate should be attached to the expedition; *why* able officers should be engaged for that particular service; *why* it should be both of a *military* and *scientific* character; and *why* Mr. J. N. Reynolds, the great projector, was entitled to paramount consideration in its connection.

The fact that the United States had, up to that moment, done nothing but abandon its own survey of the coast; that its books, maps, and charts, were but the imperfect productions of private individuals; that England, France, Russia, and even Spain, had acquired a more accurate knowledge of the Atlantic and Pacific seas, was continually humiliating Americans, and subjecting them to national and individual mortification abroad. In this view of the case, Hon. Caleb Cushing, present Attorney-General of the United States, then a member of Congress, thus addressed Mr. Reynolds:

"I think great credit is due to you for the *successful* exertions you have made to awaken the attention of the public, and of Congress, to this subject; and I hope that justice will be done to you in the arrangements to be made for the expedition."

When at Madrid, Don Martin Fernandez de Navarette, a distinguished author and, then, superviser of the government bureau of maps and charts, in showing Mr. Cushing the advances of science, in all other enlightened nations, referred to the total absence of any from the opulent nation of the United States. For, even at that time, Topino had reaped precious results in the Mediterranean for Spain, and she had not been idle in collecting charts of the East and West India seas.

CHAPTER III.

THERE was another problem which this expedition was well calculated to solve, and in which every American has the deepest interest; and this was the *source* of the aboriginal population of America. And strong hopes were now entertained that some *American* might by these means explain it. We had already taken the prize medal at the Royal Institute of Paris, for the best essay on the original languages of our country; Mr. Duponceau, our countryman, was the author. But the fault of our people has been to study *man* too little, and hence the neglect of his distinguishing characteristic, *speech.*

In order to disseminate the benefits of our well organized society, and to extend the blessings of our heaven ordained government, we are called, as a people, to place high before mankind our elevated system of morals, and our pure Protestant religion.

Who doubts that the science of philology, now eliciting the attention of the most remarkable talent of Europe, got its first impulse from a woman? We all know that, when Catharine the Great, of Russia, made her vocabulary of two hundred names, and sent it to President Washington, for specimens of the Indian languages of North America, which he furnished, that she no more penetrated the vastness of that effort to the world, than did Sir Humphrey Davy comprehend the brilliant results to chemical science, when he deduced observations from a frog, suspended on an iron hook! No more than Newton, as he watched the apple which fell from his tree, foresaw its effect on the laws of gravitation!

The *facts*, then, alone are needed, to bring to philology the prestige Cuvier has given to geology! These must be had by studying the *unwritten* languages of the earth. In no other way, can we reach the affinity one nation bears to another. This science already has dispelled much that was fabulous and superstitious. The gypsies, a remarkable race, dispersed over Europe, and occasionally migrating to our own country, are shown by their language to belong to *Hindostan*, and not Egypt, as was supposed. The Hungarian and Laplander, though geographically apart, are found to have a common origin. The Sandwich-Islander and the inhabitant of Otaheite, though twenty-five thousand miles distant, sprang from one family! Seeing, therefore, how great an addition might be made to this science, by the American exploration to the South Seas, Hon. John Pickering, of Massachusetts, offered Mr. Reynolds his suggestions on the great importance of employing a competent individual for this branch of knowledge, in which, so much of moment to the country might be attained.

SECTION I.

Nor were his thoughts on this matter peculiar, for we find similar suggestions, supported by argument and learning, from the pen of the distinguished Charles Anthon of New York. It has been a favorite theory with the learned professor, that the early races of the American continent were identical with those from whence the inhabitants of the South Sea Islands have descended. The mummies found in the caves of the West, with the accompanying fabrics, strongly resemble those of the Sandwich, and other islands of the

Pacific. The *language*, which would decide the question, *he thought*, the expedition would then test. All the knowledge of the Indo-Germanic languages was acquired by this science, and this might be the time to fill the gap in the early history of the American nation!

Mr. Reynolds, like his friend, had given much research to this subject, and they alike concluded, as we believe justly, that the North American Indians *never were the original settlers of American soil!*

As might have been expected, the joy of Professor Anthon was soon indicated to Mr. Reynolds, and supposing he had accepted the appointment of corresponding secretary, in the intended South Sea expedition, he referred to it as a just mark of executive favor; and adds:

"If I know you well (and our long acquaintance leads me to think I have some claim to that privilege), no one could have been selected at the head of the scientific corps, better calculated to bring all things into full operation, and to direct them in such a way, as must lead to ultimate success. A mere naval officer would not have answered for such a post. A mere civilian would have been equally unfit. An individual was required, who should be conversant with *both* elements, and in whom enlarged and liberal views should be found. Not the result of information obtained from others, *but the offspring of his own matured and manly intellect.* I am glad to find that our executive has had the good sense and discrimination to select such an individual. It would have been too bad for another to have reaped the harvest of praise, after your untiring exertions had fostered so goodly a crop. Let me congratulate you, and express the earnest hope of the final success, which awaits yourself, your companions, and our common country."

Professor Josiah F. Gibbs, of Yale College, soon seconded the motion of Professor Anthon, for an *anthropologist* and *philologist.* To the former, the physical conformations, features, complexions, habits, customs, political institutions, languages, traditions, literature, and, above all, the *moral* and *religious* impressions of the people, belonged for investigation. To the latter, the phonology, or sound of language, its radical words, its syntax, etc. Thus, the connection of the different tribes of men can be learned, and their common origin defined ; their progress and present location. This discovery in language is a new development of the human mind, and will become the best means of learning its operations.

Except the mountains of the Moon, in Central Africa, the South Sea explorations promised more new facts from an investigation of the animal and vegetable kingdoms, than any part of the known world. Professor Charles Gray, of the Lyceum of Natural History, New York, zealous in support of the expedition, communi-

3*

cated with Mr. Reynolds upon the necessity of a *practical botanist* to be connected with the expedition. We remember that the East India Company set an example, worthy of imitation, in the splendid botanical collections of her Wallich; and, in a commercial, as well as purely scientific view, it seemed impossible to compute the value of vegetable discoveries to the enterprise of the nation.

Zoology, too, came in for its proper and important share in Mr. Reynolds' programme of the South Sea expedition. He perceived that the original character of the inhabitants of the islands of the Pacific was rapidly changing; that the globe itself was occupied by a race of people, totally *unlike their early progenitors*, so that it was impossible for us to say from whence our own species sprang; and that very much may be gathered from the animals, which are found, in a newly discovered country, to give an idea of the character of its inhabitants. The *tortoise*, huge and helpless, for example, would not have been found at the Galapagos had it not been evidently useful to that people. With these ideas, Dr. Charles Pickering, of Philadelphia, pressed upon Mr. Reynolds the great propriety of giving to this branch of science the amplest scope for investigation.

SECTION II.

The patriotism which dictated Mr. Reynolds to collect all possible light, in aid of the expedition, was fully impressed, at this period, upon the intelligence of the country. The safety of our commerce, and our seamen, and the national honor, were all involved. The three great powers of Europe had concentrated all the knowledge of a maritime nature on the globe, and now, the first step to place us in their rank in maritime discoveries, was presented! Hon. A. Beaumont, of the House of Representatives, and Peter S. Duponceau, of Philadelphia, expressed similar views in their letters to the author of the expedition, at the same period.

When the bill, authorizing the exploration, was on its final passage in the House, a very large majority of the members voted for it, headed by the Hon. John Quincy Adams. It was then that the Hon. Mr. Hamer, of Ohio, the friend and neighbor of Mr. Reynolds, addressed that honorable body. Mr. H. said :—

"He had known Reynolds from his boyhood, and knew him

well. He came from his neighborhood, in Ohio, where he was educated, and studied law. He was a man of as pure principles and fair character, as any man on that floor. His efforts in this cause had been wholly free from any selfish considerations, and, in all he had done, in the last seven or eight years, to promote it, he had been actuated by those feelings of patriotism which should animate every *American* heart. He had no doubt, if the expedition was authorized, Mr. Reynolds would be employed to accompany it; for he possessed more information in regard to those seas, and was, every way, better calculated to make the expedition what it ought to be, than any man within the circle of his acquaintance. He was in possession of *all* the facts in reference to that portion of the globe which was to be examined and explored, and he possessed the entire confidence of all who knew him. His writings had attracted the attention of men of letters; and literary societies and institutions had conferred upon him some of the highest honors they had to bestow. Still, this gentleman, who was an honor to Ohio, and the whole country, might not accompany the expedition. But that fact would have no influence upon his course. Mr. H. was authorized to say that Mr. Reynolds' zeal for the success of the measure, and for the interest of the expedition, would continue unabated; and whatever he could do to ensure its prosperous termination would be cheerfully performed."

Public opinion, the great moral element of triumph, was now strongly on the side of this national enterprise. Members of eight different State Legislatures, viz.: New York, New Jersey, Rhode Island, Pennsylvania, Maryland, Virginia, North Carolina and Ohio, had recommended it to Congress.

The East India Marine Society of Massachusetts, whose members had doubled either Cape Horn or the Cape of Good Hope, pressed it with zeal and fervor. Two distinguished commanders in the American Navy, Commodore Downs and Captain Jones, defined its utility, and urged it as a *practical business affair*, and adopted every view expressed by Mr. Reynolds, in his able address before the Committee of Naval Affairs.

The subject of the expedition, be it remembered, had been for eight years before Congress, when it was finally authorized. It had been twice adopted by the House, and once by the Senate of the United States. The first of these resolutions passed in 1827, '28, the bill in 1828, '29, which was not acted upon by the Senate for want of time. The want of funds prevented the first action of Congress being made effective. No thoughts of disunion then entered into their calculations of this expedition. On the contrary, nothing seemed so well designed to render a people, one and indivisible.

It was in all respects such a one as Thomas Jefferson endorsed, when he sent Lewis and Clark to the Rocky Mountains, to open the resources of the country, commune with the nations, and add to the treasures of science and general national intelligence. It was but a counterpart of those instructions, given by Mr. Monroe in

1822, to Major Long, and those afterwards submitted to Mr. Featherstonhaugh, the geologist, when the government sent him to Arkansas.

Mr. Hassler made charts of materials he got within the very sight of our coast. Gedney had discovered a channel at the City of New York, two feet deeper than any known to the oldest inhabitant, or the most sagacious pilot. If such exhibitions of nautical science were to be made upon our constantly *travelled* waters, how much more did the people of the United States engaged in the commercial marine, need this survey in the South Seas? For as far North or South as our naval fleet had penetrated, it never lost view of our commercial marine. Commerce is to our country the very pulsation of life! Its mysterious channels make the revenues, and supply the means by which we exist as a nation! It is the duty of the supreme legislature, and the interest of the sovereign people, therefore, to give every facility to its advancement!

SECTION III.

Hon. Michael Hoffman, Chairman of the Committee of Naval Affairs in 1828, requested Mr.

Reynolds to furnish in writing, or otherwise, the advantages to commerce, by the exploring expedition to the South. So entirely satisfactory was Mr. Reynolds' response, so full of interesting detail, so familiar with the rank of every article of commercial benefit, that on the 14th of March, Mr. Ripley reported, that the information the committee had thus derived, was so entirely corroborated by that furnished through experienced naval officers, who had made reports by order of the Secretary of the Navy, on the subject, that they recommended the appropriation asked by Mr. Reynolds, and reported a bill for that purpose. Hon. Samuel L. Southard, then Secretary of the Navy, gave briefly, but cogently, his reasons for favoring the expedition Mr. Reynolds had projected.

In 1835, Mr. Reynolds' report of September 24th, 1828, was ordered by the House, and it was requested by Mr. Dickinson, then Secretary of the Navy, that it should be returned to the naval archives. This report was addressed to Hon. Samuel L. Southard, and furnishes a well digested mass of facts, in regard to the islands, reefs, commerce and hydrography of the Pacific and Indian Oceans; and which it is incredible almost to believe, could have been acquired by the researches of a single man, in the longest lifetime!

Mr. Reynolds in this document declared, "Power, judiciously exhibited, to be the great peace-maker of the world!" He maintained that it was for our interest and honor, to be acquainted with the *capacities* of the globe, and to know what resources can be drawn from the great *common* of nations, the *ocean*. That in South America, where new states and empires had arisen, our navy had enforced our greatness and our prosperity upon them. That we owed it to the merchant, who had put millions into the channel of trade, before one cent was ever given by the government for his protection, to send out this United States naval expedition, on his account. That whale ships could not become discoverers without detriment to their especial interest and business; that the Northwest coast trader had a more definite object and direct path than the whaler. That we could no more support our national importance without a navy, than our navy could be supported without commerce! That we had not sent forth a particle of our strength, or expended a dollar of our money, to add to the commercial and geographical information, except in partially exploring our own territory! That we actually conducted our *prizes* into port, by the maps and charts of the people we had vanquished! He appealed to the people of the United States, if it was honorable to repose on the knowledge furnished by other nations, and remain all the time idle?

Tyre, Greece, Carthage, Venice, and Florence, even after their opulence was gone, left the means of acquiring wealth and honor to succeeding ages. Their commercial and naval monuments were left standing! As the Argonautic expedition opened a new path to commerce, and aggrandized its own country, so have the adventures of every people on the face of the globe gratified the avarice or pride of their country, and been the theme of commemoration for future ages! Our commerce has been extending everywhere since we became a nation, and yet it had been protected nowhere!

The English, French, Spanish, Danish, Neapolitan, Norwegian, and Barbary powers, had cheated and insulted us. They laid out their milestones and guide-boards, and kept us in leading strings!

"The spirit of the nation," said Mr. Reynolds, "is aroused, and will never sleep again; honor, justice, feeling, conscious physical strength, all forbid it. We fear no storms, no icebergs, no monsters of the deep in any sea. We will conduct ourselves with prudence, discretion and judgment; and if we succeed, the glory and profit will be yours, citizens of the United States. If we perish in our attempts, we alone shall suffer, for the very inquiry after us will redound to your honor!"

SECTION IV.

The memorial of the people of Nantucket, stated that there were more than one hundred and fifty islands, reefs and shoals, known to our whalemen, not laid down on any chart; and around these, floated nearly forty thousand tons of our shipping! Think, oh think, of the amount of life and property of this nation, then at the mercy of concealed dangers!

Had not our country once been agitated from centre to extreme by the capture of a few American citizens by the powers of Barbary? Did not the people then spontaneously proffer to bear the expense of their liberation? And when the fate of enterprising navigators depended, probably, on some hidden reef or island, was it less a duty to respond to the wants of our suffering countrymen? The touching solicitude Mr. Reynolds felt on this point, is best expressed in his own terse and beautiful language:

"Everything conspires to urge us forward at this time. The advantage of commerce to science and national glory, seems now to be sealed and sanctified by the calls of humanity and an imperious duty. I wish not to be importunate, nor do I fear that I am, for the accumulated weight of circumstances is above all argument and entreaty, as it strikes the heart and the understanding at the same time.

"The future safety of our mariners demands this expedition; the advancement of commerce, and our navigating interests demand it; the people demand it; and our national honor cannot suffer this fact to go abroad, and not carry with it the probability of some effort for future information and security."

This appeal, so characteristic of the intellect and energy of the author, recalls the remarks of the gifted Irish orator, Burke, in his celebrated speech in the English Parliament, on American conciliation:

"As to the wealth which the Colonies have drawn from the sea by their fisheries, you had all that matter fully opened at your bar. You surely thought those acquisitions of value, for they seemed even to excite your envy; and yet the spirit by which that enterprising employment has been exercised, ought rather, in my opinion, to have raised your esteem and admiration. And pray, sir, what in the world is equal to it? Pass by the other parts, and look at the manner in which the people of New England have of late carried on the whale fisheries, whilst we follow them among the tumbling mountains of ice, and behold them penetrating into the deepest frozen recesses of Hudson's Bay, and Davis's Straits; whilst we are looking for them beneath the Arctic circle, we hear that they have pierced into the opposite region of polar cold; that they are at the antipodes, and engaged under the frozen Serpent of the South. Falkland Island, which seemed too remote and romantic an object for the grasp of national ambition, is but a stage and resting-place in the progress of their victorious industry.

"Nor is the equinoctial heat more discouraging to them than the accumulated winter of both the Poles. We know that whilst some of them draw the line, and strike the harpoon, on the coast of Africa, others run the longitude, and pursue their gigantic game along the coast of Brazil. No sea but what is vexed by their fisheries. No climate that is not witness to their toils. Neither the perseverance of Holland, nor the activity of France, nor the dexterous and firm sagacity of English enterprise, ever carried this most perilous mode of hard industry to the extent to which it has been pushed by this recent people; a people who are still, as it were, but in the gristle, and not yet hardened into the bone of manhood."

Mr. Reynolds presented to Congress a list of four hundred newly discovered islands, running through a series of consecutive years, and showed, thereby, that a thorough examination of these seas was needed, to encourage that class of our citizens who were absolutely engaged in the most dangerous service known to the country, as well as for the preservation of our commerce. The coast of California had been only imperfectly surveyed, Mr. Reynolds stated, at that period; Vancouver had only partially examined it, from Ceros Island, north; and many islands, bays, harbors, and reefs, on that portion of the Pacific coast, had not been mapped. That our cruisers had extended from the coasts of Peru and Chili to the northwest coast of New

Zealand, and the Isles of Japan; and several vessels had been wrecked on islands, and reefs, not laid down! He sustained himself by records which proved that there were, then, at least, one hundred and seventy thousand tons of shipping, twelve thousand men, and twelve millions of capital invested in the whaling and fur business, on our coasts, which derived from the government no more aid, as American interests, than those of Patagonia or New Zealand would have received!

This immense fleet of four hundred and sixty sail, from forty distinct ports, scattered along the seaboard of seven different States, made one tenth of all the tonnage of the United States! And the fisheries, *alone*, even at that time, contributed over six millions, annually, to the wealth of the country.

SECTION V.

And now, having given the origin of the *First* American Exploring Expedition, we shall proceed to show how far that expedition executed the intention of Congress, and the design of its distinguished projector, Hon. J. N. Reynolds.

In examining into the detail of the present executive action, and of the *cabal* who have sought to shear from the navy of our country so much of its glory, the author found, in the public archives, a case so remarkably illustrative of the same mysterious influence, so eminent for deep and base envy, and malignity towards elevated merit, which characterized this present action, that she at once seized upon the facts, in connection with the origin and history of the First American Exploring Expedition; and will show that, as incompetent officials who *occupied*, but did not *fill*, positions of authority, under the government, defeated the magnitude of the enterprise, as designed by its author, so has justice to the wronged covered with denunciation the men, upon whom rests the responsibility of having defeated the spirit and intent, nay, the very letter of the law, which authorized the late "Navy Retiring Board!"

A year after the law of Congress ordering the expedition, its departure seemed more and more doubtful in the public view. The people could not account for the delay, as the commissioners had reported to the President, in January, 1836, that the *Macedonia* could be ready for sea in ninety days. It was now 1837! Hon. Mahlon Dickerson was known to have opposed the enterprise in the preceding Congress, and urged members "to strike it out." But, as Secretary of the Navy, his obligations ought to have imposed obedience to the law's behests. While this delay continued, the French government, seeing the future glories arising from this expedition to our young nation, aroused her maritime powers, and actually sent, well-equipped, three expeditions to the South Seas, each with a frigate, and was preparing a *fourth* expedition, before the Secretary of the Navy had done any thing that looked like sincerity in the matter!

No one would have believed that we were the descendants of that energetic people who, in 1797, when the French Directory insulted them, felled the oak from the forest, and built and manned their sloops of war, and were pouring their hot shot into the French cruisers in the West India Islands, within one hundred days from the time the order was given to build the vessels! President Jackson, it was well-known, was fully resolved that the expedition should go out, wanting in nothing that could tend to promote its ultimate object, or complete its triumph.

He was of too lofty a spirit to comprehend the design of the petty action of this contemptible cabal, and, even in sickness, his heart was full of the greatness of the enterprise! In the meanwhile, there was a secret action designed, at last, to *strangle* it, of which the General's philosophy had not dreamed. In order to derange the whole plan, and render it inadequate to meet the expectations of the country, of the President, and of Congress, Mr. Dickerson, after devising other means for delay, called a committee, some thirteen months after the law passed, to assist him in adopting means requisite for the exploration.

Commodores Chauncey, Morris, Warrington, Patterson and Wadsworth, tried and trusty men, were assigned that unpleasant duty. For what could have been more so, than to be summoned to sit in judgment, upon the deliberate opinions of the people of the United States, in Congress assembled? What more so, than to review the action of the President of the country, who had most thoroughly examined, not after President Pierce's fashion, but in sincerity and honesty, the character, scope and design of the expedition. But President Jackson had now been succeeded by Martin Van Buren, or this board would never have been instituted. The high hopes and expec-tations of the nation, would not have been s slighted, and its aspirations for an enviable fame as well as for permanent benefit and distinction spurned!

The *instructions* given to this body, were, so far as a perversion of the law was concerned, sim-ilar to those given by Mr. Dobbin to his Counci of "Fifteen!" The major object of the expedi-tion was singularly omitted! The great commer-cial interests among the islands of the Pacific, and the many ways by which science might be ele-vated, and the interest of the country extended, were all passed over, without scarcely an allu-sion. The whole purpose and plan was misrepre-sented, when this board were told that "The expedition was to explore the Seas of the Northern Hemisphere, more particularly in high latitudes, and in regions *near the South Pole as could be approached without danger.*" etc.

SECTION VI.

Mr. Dickerson, then Secretary of the Navy, is now no more. And we shall therefore forbear to make any other comment on his action than the truth of history imperiously demands, when justice is vindicated. In all the private relations of life, that gentleman was amiable and courteous, and he lived and died above reproach. But he, most unfortunately, was surrounded by a clique of small officers and vicious men, who possessed neither heads nor hearts of sufficient capacity to grasp the objects contemplated by this expedition. Men, who could no more comprehend the value of national renown, than they could build a world! Men, who had no higher ideas of the navy, than to subserve their own interests, and overlooked the fact that it was made to give glory to the republic, and not to aggrandize themselves!

In a word, Mr. Dickerson was very much in the same category after the law of 1836, that Mr. Dobbin was after that of 1855! Both surrendered to weak and bad influences, and both proved, that any other place, than that of Secretary of the Navy, would have been better for themselves, better for their country! When men commit felony on their own reputations, public opinion rises above party, and fixes its imperishable seal of condemnation where it belongs! With this remark, we proceed to treat the conspirators to destroy the enterprise as the real perpetrators of the act designed to throw back, with contempt, a solemn law of Congress upon its members, and upon the country!

We say the instructions given the board, were a willful perversion of the object of the expedition. They knew very well that the memorials which came to Congress from that portion of our fellow citizens who had most interest in our commerce, elicited from the members the greatest consideration.

General Ripley's report in 1828, and Hon. Dutee J. Pearce's in 1835, were luminous and unanswerable arguments, in favor of protection to our fisheries in the North and South Pacific and Indian Oceans. These men had seen Commodore Downs' letter, too, after he had circumnavigated the globe in the Potomac, as well as the original report of Hon. J. N. Reynolds on "the islands, reefs, and shoals of the Pacific," in which there was irresistible evidence of the labor to be performed by the expedition, among the thousand islands laid down, through *error*, on the charts, as well as among those that had no place assigned them on these maps. In the very face of this knowledge, upon which such earnest comment had been made on the floor of Congress, this board were directed to look mainly to the means of getting to the South Pole, or near it, and to see if the present force be not too large, for that single object! We, see then, the mournful spectacle before us, of a high, but weak official, attempting to cut down the first national expedition undertaken by this great republic, and that, too, in the very face of a solemn law of the land! If this cabal had taken the trouble to have searched among the archives of the Navy Department, they would have seen enough to convince them of the effect of a large force, in accomplishing the purposes of the expedition as designed. In 1824, the British Government sent Lord Byron in the Frigate Blonde, to the Sandwich, and other islands. What was the effect? Why, these savages at once were impressed with the belief that no nation on earth could equal the greatness of the English! And the result upon the American residents and traders in that quarter was so unfortunate, in consequence, that they wrote to Commodore Hull, then in command of the Pacific Squadron, to send a frigate immediately to remove or modify the effect the Blonde had produced. Mr. Southard, then Secretary, sent the Frigate Potomac to Quallah-Battoo, to chastise the Malays, whose hands had been stained with the blood of our countrymen. And more real and lasting benefit ensued, than a dozen sloops of war could have accomplished.

CHAPTER IV.

When the French had not one-tenth of our interest afloat in the North and South Pacific oceans, they sent three frigates to these seas, to extend and protect their trade, and subserve the cause of science. Mr. Reynolds had taught the tricksters, but they forgot the lesson, that where our commerce was, there must be our navy to guard its interests! And every speech made upon the subject of the enterprise, which had been scattered over the nation, was a withering rebuke to the maladministration of the Navy Department, in convoking a naval board, to draw from it a report, to justify the reduction of the force the law authorized for the expedition. To show the miserable subterfuges of this cabal, it is only necessary to state, that, at one time they declared the idea of going to regions near the South Pole, was sheer nonsense! While at another, they made it the primary object of the enterprise, in their instructions to the board!

The truth about the matter was, that Mr. Dickerson was opposed so thoroughly to the expedition, that although Congress had passed a law authorizing, and made ample provision to carry it into effect, he could not, as the servant of the government, so far sink his own individual enmity, as to implicitly execute the act, as he was bound to have done, and therefore allowed these men to rule. President Jackson *overruled* them, as soon as he saw the delay, and the Globe, on the 13th July, 1836, announced his order to have the Macedonia, two brigs of two hundred tons each, one or more tenders, and a storeship, immediately fitted out; and, that Captain Thomas Ap C. Jones, had been appointed to the command, and officers for the other vessels were about being selected. As soon as this official notice appeared, the clique sent Mr. Dickerson to the President, to correct a misunderstanding in his mind, by arguing, that "protection of our commerce," "the impression of our force," "our character, policy, and power," could not belong to an expedition intended only for high latitudes! The next excuse made for the delay, was the *impossibility of procuring men.*

No conspirators ever labored so zealously to

defeat an enterprise as they did the First American Exploring Expedition! They held up the scientific corps as an encroachment on the rights of naval officers, and went so far as to say, that these officers should fix their salaries, or, at least, protest against this compensation exceeding a certain annual sum! Thus was jealousy fomented between officer and citizen! There is no title of which a son of our soil may feel more proud than that of *citizen*. And who but they make our navy, and support and judge its officers?

It was no reproach to the navy that the varied scientific knowledge a national expedition required, called for men in an entirely different line of action from that for which their duties unqualified them. It was a world wide fact that, while our national vessels had sailed round the globe, no record of a laborious scientific research existed! Instead of checking a disorganizing spirit, then, at its first inception, the Secretary actually encouraged it, as a means most fatal to the enterprise! He designated the scientific corps as mere oyster or clam catchers! And so determined was he to dispirit and annoy these men, that, although Congress made a specific appropriation for their compensation, from the 1st of January, 1837, their pay was withheld, and they were kept from active duty, until the 4th of July, of that year!

It was, really, a most humiliating position, under which we were thus placed before the enlightened nations of the world. That our country which, in the American Revolution, captured by her private armed ships, fifteen hundred sail from the enemy, broke the charm of British invincibility by sea, and humbled the spirited corsairs of the Mediterranean, should now, after marching into the front rank of nations, be thrown into derangement and excitement about manning a small squadron with a few hundred seamen! But such was actually the case! And, although the memorialists, committees, members of Congress, and the press, urged that a frigate and other vessels be at once fitted out for the expedition, it was, positively, *fourteen months* after the passage of the law, when the public were informed that "*the only insurmountable difficulty*" was finding the requisite men, "*in three or four months, without interfering with arrangements already made!*" Thus, did the cabal *expedite* that voyage of discovery! Congress went so far as to make a special grant for the increase of the seamen's wages, at the previous session, but every dollar of it was withheld from the poor sailors who were shipped for the expedition.

SECTION I.

Commodore Jones, too, was offered the "extraordinary facility" of detailing officers to visit New Bedford, New London, etc., for the purpose of procuring crews, but that inducement which is well known to be essential to cause men to ship, either in the merchant or naval service, was withheld, as no *money for advances* was allowed to these officers! And it was an undeniable fact that, after prime hands had consented, in New Bedford and other districts, and the commander of the squadron approved the requisition of an officer for one thousand dollars to pay the passage of these men to the naval rendezvous, the Secretary refused to cash the draft! On another occasion, fourteen sailors reported themselves ready for enlistment, at the office of an agent, in Alexandria, D. C. The agreement was about being consummated, when the officer repaired to Washington, to ascertain whether the thirty dollars, the usual advance, should be charged to the men, or whether, in compliance with the special provision of Congress, that sum should be allowed as bounty. Before he had time even to make the inquiry, he was ordered to return the money placed in his hands forthwith to the treasury, and tell the seamen to "go to Norfolk upon their own hook! and ship there." Of course, not one was so insane as to obey!

Such were the "extraordinary efforts," and such the "extraordinary success," in procuring men for the First Exploring Expedition of our country! The belief that the feeling of the Department was enlisted against the measure, now became general throughout the nation. The fact that the uncertainty about the sailing of the expedition had so long prevailed, and the non-allowance of the extra pay Congress had provided for the crew, soon had a chilling effect upon its ardent advocates. It was, evidently, the design of the Department to create the idea that great privation would follow this service, and all the wages of the crew would be expended in providing clothing for the icy latitudes near the South Pole! And the public mind was not long in comprehending the "facilities" which this great national enterprise received from the Navy Department. With ordinary effort, the whole complement of every vessel might have been shipped in sixty or ninety days after the passage of the law, and that, too, without interfering with the protection of our commerce, or with the regular action of the naval service. The men, as we have shown, stood ready to enlist for the cruise; men, who would have honored the expedition! The public records, also, show that when the Department reported to the President, and, through him, to Congress, that "*the frigate and storeship, which were on the stocks when this measure was authorized, have been finished and equipped, and are now receiving their crews*;" *that the ships were not finished, were not equipped, were not receiving their crews!* So far from it, *it was not until the next June, six months after this official statement, that the frigate was completed, and in a condition to receive her complement of men!* When that report was made of the frigate's readiness for the expedition, *she had not a single bulkhead up, or a yarn over the masthead!*

We find, in this most incongruous report, that, after the foregoing statement, the President was informed that the Department had not "yet attempted to organize the scientific corps," but would as soon as "the accommodations were ready for them in the vessels." The reader can make his own comments upon this singular consistency! Now, every man and woman of common sense would know that the organization of a corps of men for scientific purposes had nothing to do with their apartments on shipboard! No, no; that was all the merest skulking of the cabal. But, one day, in December, a distinguished member of Congress remarked to the President, that "no appointments for the expedition had been yet made for the civil department." General Jackson, surprised, rang his bell, and summoned the Secretary to attend at 12 o'clock! In three days from that time, the scientific corps were commissioned! And, to him, the *sole* credit is due for the able, efficient, and scientific board, which were attached to that exploration.

SECTION II.

Some may inquire, what reason was assigned to the President for not having made these appointments before? Why, that Mr. Secretary was waiting for a new appropriation by Congress! But the General very soon dismissed that excuse, by showing, from incontestable documentary evidence, that more than *one hundred thousand dollars* of the last year's appropriation, were at that very time unexpended.

When the bill was pending before Congress for this national expedition, these mutineers sought constantly to create opposition, by representing the immense draw it would make on the treasury. Mr. Dickerson then declared to members, that it was an extravagant enterprise, which *had nothing to do with the protection of our commerce, and was only to explore high latitudes South ! ! !* The object of this was apparent! It is known, that a portion of our public men entertain the opinion that the government of the United States has no authority under the constitution, to send out an expedition solely to promote science. Therefore, to have divested it of its relations to commercial protection and general utility to the country, would have been to destroy it! But, the clear-sighted Reynolds had made the measure impregnable, by the very defenses from which its enemies would gladly have separated it. Science was *not* the primary object of the expedition!

It was the cherished idea of Mr. Reynolds, in maturing this great American expedition, to have it, in all respects, a *national*, American matter. It was due to the country, and the just pride of her free-born sons! And American artists deserved to have their skill at least fairly tried, before any step was taken to provide the instruments abroad. But the conspirators did not think so. And instead of first appointing the corps for whose use they were intended, and obtaining the views of these scientific men as to the instruments needed, as well as the mode of providing them, he sends an agent, Lieutenant Wilkes, off to Europe, to procure books and instruments for many branches of science, of which he knew no more than the Secretary himself! And reader, what instruments do you suppose were thus obtained, that could not be had in these United States? The records tell us they consisted of two astronomical clocks, one journeyman's clock, two astronomical telescopes, and forty-one chronometers! Now, we find upon examination, that for several years previous to that period, astronomical clocks had been made by American workmen, not surpassed in accuracy and finish by those of any foreign workshop in the world! And Halcomb, the American constructor of telescopes, had won pæans of praise for the accuracy and portability of his instruments; while our American box-chronometers had received premium after premium from men *who kept up with the time of day!* Thus, among the heterogeneous mélange of scientific works provided by this agent of the Secretary, not over *ten*, with the exception of the voyages, were worth any more to the object than the *Arabian Nights!* There had evidently been no *naturalist* consulted; for not a *manual*, *model*, or *workbook* was in the lot! And such instruments as were really necessary to have been procured in Europe, were never mentioned! So it was, that after fifteen months had passed away, *proper books* were to be provided, *and instruments were still to be constructed.* All for the good faith of the government's official!

One thing ought not to be forgotten, that, after the studied attempt to excite enmity between the civilians and naval officers of the expedition, the Secretary was for taking the hydrographical and astronomical labors from them, to whose profession they belonged, and making these improper assignments to unprofessional men. But as yet, the integuments of these men's consciences had not been penetrated! The voice of public censure had reached them in vain!

The object of appointing the naval board, at this crisis, was clearly to defeat the law of Congress, by reducing the force of the expedition. For this reason, Commodore Jones had no place in it! He was known to have been too fully committed to its interests to see the nation sent back fifty years in intelligence by any act on his part! But, fortunately, the board bore no semblance to that subsequently selected by Mr. Dobbin! They were men who would not so far compromise themselves as to overlook the claims of patriotism and duty! And, looking to the law of Congress and the memorialists, they decided to advise no other course than that pointed out by the proper authority!

SECTION III.

In the meanwhile, the Department, expecting to be sustained by the board it created for the purpose, allowed Wilkes to take the instruments intended for the expedition, on board the Porpoise, in order to cause a new *difficulty* to its sailing! No men ever labored more zealously to defeat an object, than did that clique to destroy the expedition! They represented the duties of the civil corps as being degrading and irksome! although, at the same period, the French expeditions, incited by our own, had volunteers from the best citizens of the country, even to stand before the masts!

In the expeditions of Napoleon into Egypt, he wisely foresaw the advantage of a corps of *savans*, to the ising greatness of his country; and he knows little of history who has not seen that, while they took nothing from the glory of the military commanders, they made imperishable the benefits of their own scientific discoveries. This was the enterprise in which we were to make our *début* in the field of maritime enterprise and discovery, and the *projector* had labored long and earnestly to make it national in all respects. By it, the commercial interests of our country were to be protected—new regions explored—unfortunate seamen succored—charts of harbors made—dangerous passages surveyed—important islands penetrated—their population to be sought for conference—the lives of our mariners made more secure, and our trade increased!

More than one hundred mariners, American seamen, had been shipwrecked at the Feejee Islands, *alone*, and most of them cruelly murdered by the natives, while not a single effort had been made to awe those savages by our power, or conciliate them by our kindness. The effect of a national *frigate* at such a spot was apparent to the common sense of all. The mere *exhibition* of such a force as Congress designed, and Commodore Jones recommended, might have tended to the immediate rescue of our captive mariners.

Often a dozen vessels, from a single port in the United States, were engaged in traffic with these Feejee Islanders for the Chinese market. What was the result? These vessels returned to the United States, freighted with the rich goods of that country, the duties upon which had yearly added largely to the national treasure. It was a matter of ridicule to all geographers, when they found the instructions for the guidance of the expedition from the Navy Department named but *three* places on the whole globe, and they as well-known as the ports of New York or Portsmouth! The points for general rendezvous were luminously pointed out by the *only* individual competent to the undertaking, Mr. Reynolds, the originator and founder of the enterprise.

This energetic American showed that one of

the most populous group of islands in the Pacific, in the neighborhood of the Feejee and Society Islands, rich in all the productions of the tropics, and lying in the very track of our great whaling operations, was, at that time, for all minute and practical knowledge, an unknown land! When the intelligence of the country was awakened to the extent and variety of trade, and the consequent amount of revenue collected from these regions, it soon saw that it *owed* fifty times the amount that the expedition would cost, for the revenue that had already accrued, without any expense for protection. And, even if that had not been so, it was due to the unaided enterprise of her citizens, and the future interests which it would so well subserve.

SECTION IV.

The condition of the finances of our country in 1837, encouraged this cabal in the hope that it might now break up the entire expedition; and a new commission was instituted, to renew the effort to cut down its force.

Commodores Hull, Biddle, and Aulick composed its members, and without visiting the squadron, or informing themselves of the real objects of the enterprise, they reported favorably for the conspirators, and recommended the sloop-of-war Peacock, instead of the Macedonia, and a reduction of the minor vessels. The purpose to reduce the naval force of the expedition, soon excited the surprise of scientific observers in Europe, as well as this country. For even when France and England were taxed to their utmost capacity, by a long and expensive war, they both sent out splendid expeditions of discovery. But, we Americans were not born to be servile imitators of foreign powers! We, as a people, were the last to enter the Pacific Ocean, but we had moved with matchless celerity, and pushed ahead of every other nation in maritime and commercial enterprise on the globe! At home, we had turned the forest into the abode of civilization, and framed our institutions to meet the wants of our *own* people. And in steam navigation, ship building, and the use of mechanical agents, we then challenged the whole world to equal us!

By the most irrefragable arguments, Mr. Reynolds showed that there was no expedition of a like character ever sent from Europe, whose example should warrant the reduction of the American flotilla. Commodore Jones, enfeebled in health, and discouraged by the endless impediments and malignant action which thwarted his noble exertions, resigned his command on November 30th, 1838. It was then tendered to Shubrick, President of the late Council of "Fifteen." The vessels did not please him, and he declined. It was next offered to Captain Kearney.

In the meanwhile, the *misapplication of the funds, the changing of vessels, the effort to create discord, the delay of the reports, the withholding the specific information which was asked by Congress, the indecision and inconsistency, avoiding the friends,* especially, the PROJECTOR of the expedition, and rewarding those who created difficulties in the way of its progress, compelled the Executive to interfere, and take its final arrangement from the hands of the Secretary of the Navy! It was then transferred to Hon. Joel R. Poinsett, Secretary of War. The friends of the measure were now jubilant with joy, as the era of a new policy in the matter was *believed* to have been thus inaugurated! But alas, what a fatal mistake!

For soon it appeared that Poinsett had all along been the *secret* coadjutor of the Navy Junta, and whatever had been done by them, was with the full approval of that wonderful man, Poinsett! It then appeared, that he devised or abetted the scheme of appointing captains, all known enemies to the expedition, to withdraw the Macedonia from the squadron, that she might be sent immediately as the flag-ship to the West Indies, under command of his particular friend! We have said that Captain Kearney was invited to the command, but Poinsett interposed, and had that order withdrawn. Not only so, but similar conduct towards that officer in regard to other vessels, both by Poinsett and Dickerson, obliged Kearney reluctantly to retire from the expedition, in which he entered with so much zeal and professional ability.

Captain Gregory was then tendered the command: he stood at the head of master-commanders and, independent of the expedition, was entitled to the promotion to a post-captaincy. Now, instead of extending to this officer the deference due to his position, they refused to send his name to the Senate for his just promotion until after he should accept the command of the expedition. This the Captain refused, very properly, to do, although he was both promoted, and appointed to the command! But this manœuvre was for the settled purpose of defeating him, and so it proved. Poinsett and his coadjutors had, long before, made him a *marked* man! Why? because Gregory had not consented to take the responsibility of objecting to Mr. J. N. Reynolds and others, whom this lilliputian coterie, Poinsett & Co., had determined to sever from the expedition, but lacked the courage to avow their base design! Hence it was, that the rules of the service, and the rights of high-toned officers, were trampled down.

SECTION V.

Captain Kearney had agreed to take the squadron substantially as Commodore Jones left it. He refused to object to the scientific corps, and asked no change but the appointment of Lieutenant Gedney, as second in command; and, to it, Mr. Dickerson had consented, and ratified it. While Kearney, with his known promptness, had directed Lieutenant Gedney to prepare letters for Lieutenants Dorwin and Glynn, requesting them, in five days after their receipt, to proceed to Rio, and wait the arrival of Captain Kearney himself, in the flag-ship! Next morning, Captain Kearney and Lieut Gedney called at the Navy Department, to dispatch orders, and put the squadron in motion. When lo! the Macedonia was *withdrawn*, and the whole arrangement made by the Department the previous day, declared a nullity!

They, then, proposed to substitute a large merchant vessel for the scientific corps, as the flag ship, and offered that command to the Captain, who, being determined not to be driven from the expedition, accepted; but, finally, disgusted and disheartened, as we have stated, he withdrew. It was ascertained, beyond all question, that Joel R. Poinsett perpetrated all that mischief in twenty-four hours! After Gregory, Captain Joseph Smith, a gallant and distinguished officer, received as insincere a proffer of the command as that made to his brother officers, by whom he had been preceded in that honor! Captain Smith asked for Lieutenant Wilkes among the junior officers, to command one of the small vessels! a station, *altogether*, as high as his rank, standing, and qualifications, fitted him. And, for this situation (the command of a small vessel in the squadron), he had been named by the Secretary of the Navy to Commodore

Jones. So, to reconcile matters, Captain Smith thought fit to name Wilkes, once more, for as high a position as his ardent admirers had then presumed to claim for him! Imagine, therefore, with what startling effect came the absolute refusal of Wilkes to take a subordinate position in that expedition! He declared he would resign his commission in the navy sooner than do so; and that he would *take nothing short of the entire command!*

And, would you believe it, Americans, that but two days elapsed after this most insubordinate and disobedient action, on the part of Wilkes, before he was appointed to the entire command!

Nobody expects one of that cabal to turn state's evidence, and convict the culprits; but no one doubts the less, that Lieutenant Wilkes declined the station offered him by Captain Smith under the express authority of Joel R. Poinsett! Who believes, in or out of the service, that Wilkes would have *dared* to have committed an act that would have jeopardized his commission under different circumstances. Not one! not one! Hear these men! They told the public that Captain Smith would not go *with-*

out Wilkes! and that Commodore Jones would not go *with* him? There stood Captains Kearney, Smith, Gregory, Kennon, Aulick, and Armstrong, with a Lieutenant Commodore made over their heads! A Lieutenant, whom Gedney had taught the first rudiments of hydrography! Lieutenant Magruder had, also, been attached as first lieutenant of the Macedonia; and he, very properly, sent a remonstrance to the Department, against the injustice of superseding him; and it lies there yet among its archives. What did he say? Why, that he was of the same date as Wilkes, was examined by the same board, that he passed higher than Wilkes in mathematics and seamanship, ranked, consequently, *above* him, and had seen much more sea service since they had been commissioned lieutenants! Yet, there he was, supplanted by his inferior!

Reader, mark the parallel between the action of that cabal to break down the Navy in 1838, and that in 1855. In many cases, they, the parties, are identical, and in all cases, influenced by the same *animus furandi!* Look at Shubrick's action at that day, the same spirit of insubordination, which since has distinguished him. Yet he found favor with that same cabal, and recently sat in judgment upon his brothers in the service! Look at Wilkes, elevated there by the same influence that retains him now, while Lieutenant, now Captain Gedney, the accomplished hydrographer, is laid on the shelf. But as though it was not enough to elevate Wilkes over his superiors, it was alleged *that none of them had the requisite talents!* What rendered this the more insulting, was the fact, that Lieutenant Wilkes had never been recognized by the corps of scientific officers, as even being one of *their* number! He had aided Gedney and Blake in a survey of Narragansett Bay, some years before, and we believe had surveyed, subsequently, George's Bank! But he never had been ranked as a hydrographer with Lieutenants Gedney and Blake.

SECTION VI.

Captain James Armstrong, whose services were passed over, to give the command to a junior lieutenant, was another case, which called for public reprehension, similar to the instances in which distinguished seniors were set aside by the late Navy Retiring Board, to make places for aspiring juniors. Captain Armstrong was ordered to the command of the Macedonia in 1836 ; from then to 1839, he had been constantly with his vessel, amid delays and discouragements no language can describe. The records of the Department showed, that for thirty years he had borne himself with honor in the service. He was at New Orleans, on board the bomb-ketch Etna, and afterwards commanded a gun-boat, though a young midshipman ; and engaged in the fight which subdued the Barrataria pirates. He was in the brig Siren, in the sloop-of-war Fralies, in the frigate Congress, in the Washington, the Independence, the Columbus, the United States, commanded the Porpoise, and then was appointed to the command of the Macedonia, when she was designated for the expedition.

This captain, who had served his country with so much honor under Commodores Chauncey, Bainbridge, and Hull, and who had been for *two years attached to the expedition*, was, without even the courtesy of explanation, ruthlessly thrust aside by these naval bandits, to make room for an instrument who would enact their behests!

An officer like Captain Armstrong would have given prestige to the enterprise at home and abroad. He was able, skillful, prudent, with the capacity to manage the fleet, and take care of the crew committed to his charge, and was, in all respects, fitted to conduct the South Sea exploration. He was without the weakness or folly of Wilkes, and sought no acknowledgment for scientific attainments which he did not possess. But, like Commodores Jones, Kearney, Smith, and Gregory, he scorned the servility essential to propitiate the favor of these designing men!

It now became necessary to put forth some plea of justification for the outrage upon the usage of the service, and the injustice perpetrated on the public good, in the appointment of Lieutenant Wilkes to the command of the expedition!

"How can it be done?" became then a paramount question with the cabal! But, having accomplished their ends so far as to secure *their instrument*, there was not much apprehension but that, amidst so much versatility of talent and inventive genius, some plea might be made, which would justify the outrage! So the "Naval General Orders," of the 22d of June, 1838, appeared in the form of a proclamation, declaring the expedition purely *scientific*, thereby leaving the President power to depart from the usual custom of appointing from the senior ranks of the navy, and according to their respective grades!

Lieutenant Charles Wilkes was then announced as having received the appointment as first officer of the expedition, and Lieutenant William L. Hudson, as second officer, to command the sloop-of-war Peacock! Hudson, at that moment, stood above Wilkes on the Navy Register, yet the *junior* was put in the whole command! Now, be it remembered, that Mr. Poinsett had, just before, deemed it essential to have Captain Gregory promoted to the rank of post-captain, before he considered him elegible to the command! And yet, Gregory was at that time at the very head of the list of master-commanders in the service! It was also equally well known, that Captain Aulick had been invited to take the second position in the squadron; and that Lieutenant Tatnall had been offered, unofficially, the grade of commander, which he had in the same way accepted, only a few days before Wilkes' appointment; and when, as we have reason to believe, they were actually in treaty with Wilkes, as the *only proper* man for their purposes! We leave to some future Plutarch, the task of unveiling all the inconsistency the case could unfold! But the forbearance of Congress and the people seemed the more surprising, since this clique dared to assume, that in appointing a lieutenant to command the expedition, they had actually changed the character of the enterprise!

CHAPTER V.

In the celebrated report, in answer to a call of Congress, of March 19th, 1837, in reference to the two sloops of war, Pioneer and Consort, intended for the exploration, the same disregard to that supreme legislature was manifested ; when the important official documents were withheld from Congress, and trivial unimportant papers were sent in their places. Why? Because the documents proved the *fitness* of the vessels for the service which Poinsett & Co. had concealed. The Macedonian had been withdrawn, *covertly*, under the pretence that she was needed to protect our commerce in the Gulf of Mexico, while the Mexican ports were blocked by a French fleet, and the Macedonian left at her dock at Norfolk! Thus they delayed the enterprise ordered by Congress for more than *three years!* They abstracted two sloops of war, and a gun brig from the protection of commerce, in order to send them on the expedition, which they pretended *was not naval!* And when, for less than half the money it cost to fit these vessels for the survey, others, already, and far more appropriate for the service, were at hand!

In making the naval appropriation for the service, a discussion arose in the House of Representatives, the 11th of April, 1838, when the outrage committed upon professional feeling and pride, in the appointment of Wilkes, received its just comment. Hon. Mr. Wise, of the naval committee, now Governor of Virginia, expressed himself in his usual independent and significant manner. He said:

"That he had not accused Lieutenant Wilkes of purchasing his command at all; but he had been informed that intimations had been given to the officers of a higher grade, that it was expected, if appointed to the command, they would discharge certain individuals; and one of these men, like a true officer, had replied, that if such dismissals were to be made, the Department must take the responsibility of making them. Mr. W. did not believe that it was the painter that was to be discharged, but there was an *individual who had done more, in the first instance, to get up the expedition than any other man in the country, and who had expressed himself very freely in the public journals in regard to the Secretary, and whom it was the object of the Department to get clear of.*"* Mr. Wise said, farther, "that, if his information was correct, Lieutenant Wilkes had been selected, not on the ground of his peculiar scien-

* Governor Wise had reference, as the reader must know, to the Hon. J. N. Reynolds, of New York.

tific attainments, nor on that of the special character of the service, but for a reason entirely different." Mr. Wise said "he had his information from a respectable source, and such was the belief of some gentlemen in the navy."

Mr. Ingham, chairman of the naval committee, attempted the defense of the government officials, and contended under a misrepresentation made to him, and for which he was not responsible, that the force having been curtailed nearly one half, it was necessary that Wilkes should reduce the scientific corps in a corresponding proportion! Mr. Ingham, therefore, said, it was very singular, indeed, that when the expedition was to contain but one half the vessels, and the whole outfit cut down in the same proportion, that there should be no reduction of expense! Mr. Wise said that Commodore Jones had told him, only the previous day, that there would not be a dollar's reduction by the present plan! Here, we discover that, the public as well as members of Congress, were deceived, cheated, by the representations made from the Department, that the squadron prepared under the guidance of the *Lieutenant Commodore*, consisted of but *half the force* organized under Commodore Jones, and, under this deception, these official managers had, in a great degree, defended and justified their procedure before Congress and the country! So far did this clique go to fix this impression upon the public sentiment, that Governor Dickerson embraced an opportunity, after he closed his *four years' service* in the Navy Department, to congratulate the country that the *expedition had been reduced one half!*

Now, Americans, the truth about the matter was, that the naval force, then under the command of Lieutenant Wilkes, was *larger than the squadron which lay in the port of New York under Commodore Jones!*

Mark it, reader, that, after a three years' war against the magnitude of the expedition, by Joel R. Poinsett & Co., and a long and intensely active effort to strangle the enterprise, *on that very account*, they actually gave to their Lieutenant Commodore a *larger* naval force than that commanded by Commodore Jones! Will any dare to deny this? We invite them to the proof! The squadron under Lieutenant Wilkes consisted of—

1. The sloop-of-war, Vincennes, Lieutenant Charles Wilkes, Esq., Commander-in-chief, with twenty-two subordinate officers. This is a twenty gun ship; which cannot, *according to law, be commanded by an officer under the grade of master-commander.*

2. Sloop-of-war, Peacock, Lieutenant William L. Hudson, commander, with nineteen subordinate officers. This vessel, now second in the squadron, had recently been the flag-ship of a commodore in the East Indies.

3. Ship Relief, Lieutenant A. K. Long, commander, with nine subordinate officers.

4. Brig-of-war Porpoise, Lieutenant Cadwallader Ringgold, commander, with twelve subordinate officers.

5. Schooner Flying Fish, Passed Midshipman Samuel R. Knox, commander.

6. Schooner Sea Gull, Passed Midshipman James W. Reid, commander.

SECTION I.

We perceive, here, that the Macedonian, of *thirty-six guns, and three hundred men*, was withdrawn, and the Vincennes, Peacock, and Porpoise substituted therefor, consisting of *fifty-six guns, and four hundred and sixty men!* And we further discover not only that the aggregate tonnage and number of vessels in Wilkes' squadron were greater than that under Commodore Jones, but that the aggregate draught of water was greater; and that an *addition* of one schooner was made to the flotilla, which addition had been most pertinaciously *refused* to Commodore Jones! This is the manner the first American enterprise of discovery was made "altogether scientific," and its force reduced to "one half" of its original proportions! Another attempt of their miserable trickery was, the final sailing of the squadron without the full complement of men! mere illusion to deceive the people; because, as they knew, their number could be increased in a *foreign* port, as they pleased!

Having disposed of the silly plea, that the force of the squadron was reduced under Wilkes' command, and its naval character taken away, we will next see how they entrenched themselves behind *reduced expenses.*

Under Commodore Jones, the squadron consisted of the Macedonian, Pioneer, Consort, Relief, and Active, and the expenses did not exceed one farthing that of the new organization under Lieutenant Wilkes! While, for efficiency in navigating high latitudes, protecting commerce, surveying or scientific research among the islands of the Pacific, the comparison between the *good* and *bad* plan disgusted and disheartened every practical seaman in the nation! Was there ever a more flagrant violation of law, a more flagrant violation of the published regulations of the Navy Department, a more flagrant outrage upon the professional service, than was committed by men then invested with temporary authority? But the science and intelligence of the country had now passed judgment on them! and the secret springs of the contemptible action of Poinsett & Co. were manifested by the public records before the country, with which only we have now to do.

It was remarkable foreknowledge on the part of a low lieutenant that he should have *six months before* predicted the possibility of being called to command the expedition! But such was the fact, that he did. Congress was then *in session*, and every effort was made to hide their plans and intentions. The friends of the expedition were feared *in* and *out* of that body! Officers of the navy were now obliged to cease their complaining of the wrong done them, for the paramount rights of the commander were then settled, although the details of the arrangement were not to be fixed until *after the Senate adjourned!* Thus it was that these heads of Department dared to do what they could not find Congress so corrupt as to sanction.

Then it was that the new commander spoke freely of *his* plans as being endorsed by President Van Buren and Mr. Joel R. Poinsett! *He* declared his intention "to make the expedition naval in point of fact, but as he could not draught a scientific corps from the navy, a portion of the present members would be retained, the rest dismissed." Why? Because the squadron *was reduced!* Look at this inconsistency, reader, and repress your deepest indignation, if you can! That, while in the face of the truth, as furnished from prepared documents, these men had *added* to the naval force under Wilkes, he had the impudence to assert before the country that a *reduction of one half* had taken place! And this was all done to make it scientific, says Poinsett & Co.; but their protégé blundered so badly as to make discrepancy in their respective tales, for Wilkes said he meant to make it entirely *naval!* What a remarkable instance this of high moral and official integrity! And it did not await its reward for *post mortem* honors!

SECTION II.

The ground upon which the learned Mr. Wilkes was thrust into command, was that the enterprise was not to be naval but *scientific!* What did the commander then do for science? He summarily erased from the list the departments of anatomy and comparative philology; while *entomology* and *crustaceology* were pronounced useless, or only deserving the attention they might receive from the zoologists, who already had more than their proper duties assigned them! Well might it cause grief to every friend of science, to every one interested in the true glory of his country, when an incompetent lieutenant was allowed to lop off from the expedition these members, after they had made every preparation to join the expedition, and under the *plighted faith of the government*, by whom they were commissioned, and were ready to sail with it! Nor was this all; for the departments of natural philosophy and physical science, which a Humboldt or an Arago would have assumed with modest distrust, this little lieutenant-commodore took into his own keeping, in addition to all the other duties which devolved on him!! The assistant zoological draughtsmen and landscape and portrait painters, trifles in Wilkes' estimation and those who governed his acts, were also set aside! As to *Palæontology*, which educated people know to be a science that treats of fossil organic remains, vegetable and animal, and that it has done more to unfold and analyze the globe we inhabit than any other science, these men spurned with contempt! They declared it all "humbug," and the department as worthless, in connection with the expedition! How mortifying! how humiliating to national pride!

"The secrets of Nature," says the learned Buckland, "that are revealed to us from the history of fossil organic remains, form perhaps the most striking results at which we arrive from the study of geology. It must appear almost incredible to those who have not attended to natural phenomena, that the microscopic examination of a mass of rude and lifeless limestone should often disclose the curious fact that large portions of its substance have once formed parts of living bodies. It is surprising to consider that the walls of our houses are sometimes composed of little else than comminuted shells, that were once the domicils of other animals at the bottom of ancient seas and lakes.

"It is marvellous that mankind should have gone on for so many centuries in ignorance of the fact which is now so fully demonstrated, that no small part of the present surface of the earth is derived from the remains of animals that constituted the population of ancient seas. Many extensive plains and massive mountains form, as it were, the great charnel-house of preceding generations, in which the petrified exuviæ of extinct races of animals and vegetables are piled into stupendous monuments of the operations of life and death, during almost immeasurable periods of past time."

Cuvier said "*that the wreck of animal life formed almost the entire soil on which we tread.*" And from a sight so imposing, and so terrible, was our young and intelligent nation to be kept, because a naval cabal did not understand its meaning or its benefit? Cuvier's great works as a naturalist, arose from his examination of the fossil bones of the environs of Paris. Deshaye's fame, came from studying the fossil shells of the same region. Brogniart's celebrity rests on the same science. Desmarest got his honors in the same way. And Agassiz, in whom Americans have pride, owes his reputation for science, to his work on fossil fishes. Buckland wrote a work on the fossil bones in the caves of England and Wales. But, the Bridgewater Treatise, Lyell's, and other like works, were as impenetrable to the intellects of these managers of the expedition, as the component parts of an Egyptian mummy!

Before the vandal act of excluding palæontology had been committed, it would have been well to have consulted the archives of several of the states where, in connection with geological surveys, that department of science had been then created!

It is well to remember, that Wilkes only enacted the will of Poinsett & Co. They delayed the expedition, sowed discord among the officers, made jealousy between them and the scientific corps, by throwing out the idea that the latter would cheat them of their glory; refused to order any one to join the expedition; released those who did not wish to go; rewarded those who abused Commodore Jones, and J. N. Reynolds, its author; allowed Wilkes to keep the instruments in his possession, which he brought from Europe, when it was his duty to have handed them to Johnson, for whose department they were provided; corresponded secretly with officers under Commodore Jones, and ordered Jones to sail, while they kept out of his power the instruments he needed to do so; refused to allow the scientific corps to draw their pay, after President Jackson forced their appointment; and finally, did all they possibly could to disgust these gentlemen, and drive them to the necessity of resigning their commissions in the expedition.

SECTION III.

All this while, these men made General Jackson believe they favored the measure, because they were afraid of their places. But after getting their *favorite* in the command, these men saw they had done all necessary to monopolize the glory, and having raised the cry of *economy*, they pretended to reduce the naval force, and cut down the scientific to correspond! Was ever a greater amount of villainy practised than that in connection with this first American enterprise of exploration? We believe no records on earth, could show a more diabolical conspiracy!

In retrenching the scientific part of the expedition, the deepest malignancy and envy prevailed. Hale was retained from sheer timidity:—they feared the savans who pressed his claims. Dr. Reynell Coates was dismissed, because Wilkes thought the purser's steward could answer for the anatomist! Professor W. R. Johnson was also stricken from the list, because Wilkes professed to understand "Natural Philosophy," as well as he did, and there was no necessity for his services! It seemed that once this Mr. Johnson served on a committee with Professors Bache and Henry, to test some magnetical experiment of Wilkes, on "Smith's Compass Needle." These gentlemen pronounced Wilkes' deductions utterly absurd, and the very *reverse* of his *demonstration!* This was enough to settle the question with Johnson, although he had been endorsed for scientific capacity, by such eminent savans of the country, as Professors Farrar, Silliman, Henry, and Mitchell. It was absolutely necessary that the man who obtained the *bonâ fide* command of this national enterprise, should bind himself, soul and body, to do anything and everything the conspirators required should be done. They therefore gave to Wilkes more enlarged powers than were ever conceded to Commodore Jones! For Wilkes had the privilege of *choosing his own officers, which was refused Jones.* He had *increased pay* allowed both himself and officers; this also was refused Jones! Wilkes was given an additional schooner, which they had *denied,* likewise, to his superior. In short, these officials, whose whole influence rested upon the appendage of office, made their dictum overrule the authority of Congress, and the will of the American people! They reduced the *scientific* corps, and made it more *military* and *naval*; while throwing all possible mystery around their doings, they attempted to cheat the people, with the facts before their eyes!

Honorable Joel R. Poinsett, was the man who laid the last hostile hand upon the enterprise, which was designed to enrich and enlarge the boundaries of human knowledge, and bring upon the country high national renown! It was Poinsett, we remember, who took the squadron from the command of Captain Kearney, which would have placed it above the reach of the enemies of the enterprise, as he foresaw, and therefore prevented it *in a night!* Through him and his confederates, Smith, Gregory, Kennon, Aulick, and Tatnall, were all badly treated!

These conspirators degraded American genius by their stupidity, and caused the blush of shame to our learned societies, by their course towards the various departments of science. Entomology, for example, they utterly *rejected*, although it equals in extent, all the other sciences of the animal kingdom put together! The societies of London and Paris devoted to this subject, comprised hundreds of members, and their transactions at that day, were published throughout the civilized world! Moreover, they had agents and correspondents in our own country, as everywhere else. How must we have appeared to them, when, in the first great scientific voyage of discovery, a department of natural history, so essential to the study of geology, was declared nugatory!

The French government, at the same time, had engaged *twenty* naturalists to complete a work of sixty volumes, on that single subject! Cuvier's work, so classical and philosophical, as to rank him ever as the prince among naturalists, was on the shelves of every well selected library of our country, and had better have been examined by these wiseacres before they pronounced the science of entomology useless, and dismissed Mr. Randall thereby, with so much good will! Just as they did Dr. Reynell Coates, from the department of comparative anatomy, and Professor Johnson, from that of natural philosophy!

SECTION V.

But there was one other gentleman, against whom a greater degree of malevolence was concentrated, than was exhibited towards all besides. This was Hon. J. N. Reynolds, *originator* of the expedition! The fiat had long gone forth, that he must not accompany the enterprise, to share in its future glory. How to get rid of him was the trouble, but it had to be done, at any cost. The distinguished officers appointed to the command, would not, therefore, do! They knew and acknowledged the services of Mr. Reynolds, and all desired he should accompany the expedition.

But Wilkes said *he* would absolutely refuse to take him, and pretend that he did so for the sake of harmony; and that he would say further that he knew nothing of the powerful recommendations of all the West to the President for Mr. Reynolds' appointment to a position in the expedition. That moment the bargain was struck. He sold himself to his confederates, and he fully answered their purpose!

On the 30th of July, 1838, Mr. Reynolds, now a citizen of New York, addressed a letter to Poinsett, demanding to know why neither he nor his friends had received a reply to the communication of the Western delegation in Congress, addressed to the President *two months* previous, in reference to his appointment in the South Sea Expedition. He then stated that,

> "If it was determined he should hold no station, with or without defined duties and a salary attached, he wished to know if he could, as a *volunteer, without compensation and without duties defined, accompany said expedition, asking no other protection from the Department or commander than was guaranteed by the rules of the service to a sailor before the mast.*"

The immediate reply of Mr. Poinsett, on the 1st of August, 1838, shows the evident collusion between himself and President Van Buren and Commander Wilkes. He affirms that he never knew that such a letter existed! that he had a private one from a gentleman in Ohio, asking that Mr. Reynolds should go out as a commercial agent, and added,

"But I knew the President had decided that no such officer should be appointed, nor could I, with my views of the subject, recommend such a measure to his favorable consideration.

"Being about to take my departure from Washington, and expecting to be absent some weeks, I addressed a letter to the Secretary of the Navy, in which I expressed my opinion of the composition of the scientific corps, their number and description, but without designating the persons. I think he ought, and presume he will, *be governed in his choice by the wishes of the commander of the squadron, for it is essential to the success of the expedition that the utmost harmony should exist between the naval officers and the members of that corps.*

"Your desire to accompany the expedition is natural, and, under ordinary circumstances, your having, *in some measure*, originated the design, would give you a strong claim to be indulged in your wishes; but all subordinate considerations must yield to the paramount one of conducting the expedition to a successful issue.

"Your letter has been sent to the Navy Department."

Attend particularly to this letter, reader! He admits ignorance of what he *ought* to have known, and then confesses he had conferred with the President on the subject! Who can explain away the belief, that with a knowledge of Mr. Reynolds' efforts to procure the law authorizing the expedition, *and the independent manner in which he had denounced the official action of the government*, that Poinsett and Van Buren had not, when on the subject, made allusion to such a letter from a delegation in Congress? Who believes it? Who? With another remark on this singular *jesuitical* letter, we leave you, reader, to approve it, if you can! This innocent secretary thought the *wishes of the commander* should govern in the selection of individuals for the *sake of harmony*, &c. This exactly corresponds with what Wilkes had already agreed to say of Mr. Reynolds, viz., that *harmony* required he should *not* be in the expedition! What martyrs to truth, ye magnanimous men! The pretended reference, too, to the Navy Department was to implicate Hon. J. K. Paulding, then Secretary of that Department. But it was notorious that the whole matter was hurried through; proclamation of change in the organization made; Wilkes appointed, and all regulations perfected to *prevent* Mr. Paulding from having the power to interfere in their action! They knew he would not stoop to such a course, *but would arrest it*, and that he had already, in his letter to Mr. Reynolds, shown *his* views of what was proper to be done for advancing the expedition as originally designed.

SECTION V.

We cannot forbear now from giving the official confirmation of our own premises, which so completely identifies Mr. Reynolds with the first work of American exploration.

To his Excellency the President of the United States.

The undersigned, members of Congress from the State of Ohio, avail themselves of this occasion to express their gratification upon learning that the Exploring Expedition, authorized by a recent act of Congress, is about to be fitted out in a manner worthy of our great republic.

They feel it to be a duty which they owe, as well to their constituents the people of Ohio as to their common country, to remind the administration of the claims of J. N. Reynolds, Esq., to a prominent place in the proposed expedition. His long and ardent services in calling public attention to this question, and urging its adoption by Congress; his zeal and untiring industry in collecting information in reference to it; his intimate acquaintance with all the interests of the commercial community (between whom and himself there exists a long and intimate intercourse), whose interests are afloat in those seas; the kind relations subsisting between him and most of the scientific men and societies of our large cities, as well as his personal acquaintance with the South Seas, and his unusual mass of information in regard to their localities, eminently qualify him to be placed at the head of the *civil corps* which is to accompany the squadron.

The services and quailfications of Mr. Reynolds have been acknowledged by every committee who have reported upon the subject, and are appreciated by Congress and the whole country.

The undersigned believe that they express as well their own sentiments and those of their constituents, as of the friends of the expedition generally, in asking that Mr. Reynolds be placed at the head of the civil and scientific corps, having a general superintendence over, and that he be authorized to write the history of the expedition, having such rank, powers, and compensation, as the administration may think proper to bestow.

Respectfully, your obedient servants,

Benjamin Jones,	William Patterson,
William K. Bond,	David Spangler,
Thomas Corwin,	Elisha Whittlesey,
R. Storer,	I. Sloane,
Josh. H. Crane,	William Hermon,
Samuel F. Vinton,	J. M'Lene,
S. Mason,	John Thomson,
T. L. Hamer,	Taylor Webster,
Elias Howell,	Daniel Kilgore.
John Chaney,	

July 2d, 1836.

To his Excellency Andrew Jackson.

Sir:—In the Exploring Expedition which has been ordered out under the direction of the general government, we would respectfully recommend J. N. Reynolds, Esq., as the chief of the civil appointments.

The unremitting zeal of this gentleman in the cause of his country and of science, his former experience as a navigator, his scientific acquirements and capacity, would seem to us to point him out as the person most deserving the appointment.

J. Fry, Jun.,	Jos. Henderson,
J. B. Anthony,	J. Miller,
Edward B. Hull,	Henry A. Muhlenburg,
J. R. Ingersoll,	H. L. Pinckney,
A. Beaumont,	John Reynolds,
George Chambers,	R. Johnson,
E. Darlington,	A. Huntsman,
David Potts, Jun.,	Francis Thomas,
J. B. Sutherland,	Dutee J. Pearce,
Isaac M'Kim,	William Sprague,
John M'Keon,	A. Vanderpool,
G. W. Owens,	William L. May,
Ely Moore,	Z. Carey,
Samuel Barton,	George L. Kinnard,
R. H. Gillet,	A. Lane,
J. Y. Mason,	John Cramer,
James Harper,	C. C. Cambreleng,
John Reed,	J. Toucey,
Benjamim C. Howard,	R. Boon.
A. Ward,	

To the President of the United States.

HOUSE OF REPRESENTATIVES, 2*d July*, 1836.

SIR:—I have learned with pleasure that the Expedition to the South Seas will be dispatched in due time, and that you have directed it to be fitted out as becomes the interest and character of the country over which you preside. Yes, I rejoice that you have done so, for I sincerely believe that no act of Congress for years has been so honorable to our national character, none that will reflect more credit on your administration; as the undertaking will attract the eyes of the whole civilized world, and its results become matters of interest and of record in every part of Christendom.

To be appointed at once, with a liberal allowance, to the first place in the civil department of this expedition, I beg leave strongly to recommend my friend J. N. Reynolds, Esq.

In reference to this gentleman I must be permitted to speak with freedom, for I have known him long and intimately. His labors in this cause, so perseveringly continued, are well known to the whole country; in an especial manner are they known and appreciated by the whole of that portion of our fellow-citizens interested in the commerce of the Pacific, and who have expressed so much interest in having this expedition fitted out.

I was in Providence in October, 1834, when Mr. Reynolds made an address before that body, for the purpose of getting an expression of the Legislature of my State in its favor; which was readily given, as the people of Rhode Island take a lively interest in the undertaking.

From that period to the present session and final action of Congress on this subject, I have held with Mr. Reynolds a constant correspondence, and Mr. R. has at all times consulted with me as to the steps necessary to be taken to effect the object for which he has labored so long.

At the last session I made a report in favor of the expedition from the committee on commerce, which was not acted on by the House for want of time.

At the present session Mr. Reynolds again conferred with me, procured a recommendation from the Legislature of New Jersey, and, when he arrived in this city, I agreed with him that it was the best plan to commence in the Senate, which was accordingly done. The result, since that time, is known to you. *The measure passed by an overwhelming vote of both houses, and has been much approved in all sections of the country.* These are some of the circumstances which enable me to speak so strongly in favor of *Mr. Reynolds, whose labors and sacrifices in this cause have made him well known to the members of this House. I do not hesitate to say that to his efforts, more than any man living, is the country indebted for the successful prosecution of the measure before Congress.*

These facts made known to you, it will, I am sure, no longer be a question as to the part which shall be assigned to him. The organization of the scientific corps could not be committed to better hands; and especially do I wish that *to him may be assigned the duty of writing the official account of the cruise.*

With great consideration and respect,
I am your friend,
DUTEE J. PEARCE.

To the President of the United States.

HOUSE OF REPRESENTATIVES, 2*d July*, 1836.

SIR:--I beg leave respectfully to recommend J. N. Reynolds, Esq., for the chief of the civil appointments connected with the Exploring Expedition to be sent out to the South Seas. In this I am governed by a desire to see merit adequately rewarded in the appointment of *a gentleman whose past services and scientific nautical researches appear to point him out as one who has earned the place and is eminently qualified to fill it.*

The friends of Mr. Reynolds, particularly in the western country where he was raised, have long admired the ability and utility which have attended his devotion; and, I may add, they would be much gratified if *this meritorious son of the West* could be placed in a situation where he might earn still higher distinction for himself, and, at the same time, confer greater advantages upon his country.

With sentiments of the highest esteem,
Your friend and most obedient servant,
GEORGE L. KINNARD.

To the President.

SENATE CHAMBER, WASHINGTON, 2*d July*, 1836.

SIR:—I would inform the President that many of my constituents feel a deep interest in the Exploring Expedition authorized during the present session, and which I understood the executive has decided to fit out the present season; and that, having a high opinion of the character and qualifications of J. N. Reynolds, Esq., and of his capabilities to be useful in said expedition, I respectfully recommend him to the President for the *highest civil appointment connected with the expedition;* and will add, that his appointment will afford me personally much gratification.

I have the honor to be,
Respectfully, your obedient servant,
JOHN M. NILES.

WASHINGTON, 5*th July*, 1836.

DEAR SIR:—I enclose you several papers in relation to the appointment of J. N. Reynolds, Esq., as chief of the civil and scientific corps which goes out with the exploring squadron to the South Seas.

No. 1 is the *unanimous recommendation* of the representatives from Ohio (without distinction of party) that he be thus appointed.

No. 2 is the recommendation of some *forty or fifty Members of Congress from other States*, asking for him the same station. This paper was got up without the knowledge of Mr. Reynolds or any of the Ohio delegation, and *I have no doubt a hundred additional names could have been obtained, if any one had taken the trouble to circulate it through the House. It was not deemed necessary, and was not therefore done.*

It contains the names of a majority of representatives from Indiana, of Illinois, and Rhode Island; of a great portion of Pennsylvania; and of gentlemen of distinction from a majority of the other States of the Union.

No. 3 consists of letters from gentlemen of respectability and science, from various quarters of the country, to the same effect. They *all speak the same language and breathe the same spirit.*

These documents, taken together, leave no doubt of the state of public opinion upon this question. All who have reflected much upon the subject feel the necessity of an *efficient organization, with a responsible chief*, to produce unity and harmony of action. All who are aware of the large space which Mr. Reynolds fills in the public eye, in connection with the great enterprise, at once point to him as *the most suitable person to fill this station;* that he ought to obtain it (in the character of commercial agent, or such other as may be thought advisable), and be allowed to write the history of the expediton, I have never doubted for a moment.

Few persons seem to be aware of the immense importance of this expedition to our national character. It will rivet the attention of every intelligent man in Christendom for years to come, and it will be looked upon hereafter as an epoch in our history. It will surprise the elder nations of Europe to see that a new people like us have undertaken this voyage. But how much will their wonder be increased to perceive that we have organized it upon a plan which, for enlargement of conception, liberality of sentiment, and efficiency of action, renders it decidedly superior to anything of the kind which they have attempted.

That this great undertaking may redound to the honor of your administration, and to the glory, happiness, and prosperity of our beloved country, is the ardent prayer of

Your excellency's obliged friend
And obedient servant,
T. L. Hamer.

To his Excellency Andrew Jackson.

To his Excellency, Martin Van Buren, President of the United States.

The undersigned, members of Congress from the *West*, beg leave, once more, very respectfully, though earnestly, to call the attention of the administration to the claims of J. N. Reynolds, Esq., to a prominent place in the Exploring Expedition. This measure was early and warmly supported by the West. It was originated and first called to the attention of Congress by one of her sons. She still continues to feel an interest, and still indulges the hope that it may be so equipped as not to disappoint the just expectations of the country; she still hopes to see it depart in skillful and experienced hands, unshorn of its naval or scientific strength. Congress has made repeated appropriations, which leave no doubt of the hold of the expedition upon science, the intelligence, and pride of the nation.

The whole Ohio delegation, as well as many other members of the House, immediately after the passage of the law authorizing the measure, addressed communications to the late executive. After congratulating him on account of the interest he took in directing the expedition to be fitted out in a manner worthy "our great republic," they proceeded to call his attention to the claims of *one* who had done so much in calling public attention to the importance of the enterprise, and in urging its adoption by Congress. The friends of the measure knew the important part Mr. Reynolds had acted, and they were influenced not more by a sense of justice than a desire for the success of the enterprise, in asking for Mr. Reynolds a prominent portion in it. The commercial interests of the United States in the seas to be visited are well-known to the executive; they are immense, and still susceptible of great extension. In asking that Mr. Reynolds be placed at the head of the civil department attached to the expedition, was only asking, in other words, that he should receive the appointment of commercial agent. Until recently, many of us supposed that station had been assigned to him; that he ought to have it, and be authorized to write the official account of the expedition, we have never doubted. That he is eminently qualified to perform these duties, under the sanction and regulations of the department, cannot be doubted; *that he has abundantly earned the distinction* which they would confer upon him will admit of as little question.

Mr. Reynolds has uttered no complaints to his friends, and it has not been until since the passage of the last bill of appropriation that they became aware of the actual position the Secretary of the Navy had assigned him; and not even then, till the discussions in the House seemed to leave some doubt whether he was to accompany the expedition, in any capacity, had led to direct inquiries upon the subject. Any officer, conversant with the history of this expedition, and knowing the relation Mr. Reynolds has maintained to it, both in and out of Congress, and should object to his participating largely in its labors, would, *from that fact, in the opinion of the undersigned, be himself unfit to command;* and the interests of the expedition, and the honor of the country would, in all probability, be best consulted by his dismissal, and the supplying of his place by one of more just, liberal, and enlarged views.

The undersigned have learned, with deep regret, that to Mr. Reynolds, *the originator, the indomitable advocate,* who has, for so long a time, persevered against every discouragement, whose knowledge upon the subject has been so fully appreciated by committees and members of Congress, and has enlisted so large a share of public feeling throughout the country, has received from the Department the meagre, unmeaning appointment of "*corresponding secretary to the commander,*" to perform such duty on the expedition as the justice or caprice of a commander might direct; while the names and duties of all others composing the scientific corps, as well as juniors in command, were conspicuously named in the general instructions for the guidance of the expedition, were thus recognized by the Department in a document to be preserved in all coming time; but in that list, and in that document, *the name of J. N. Reynolds, we learn, is nowhere to be found;* that no duties were assigned him by the Secretary; in a word, that the action of the Department, whether intended or not, would go to show that Mr. Reynolds was not recognized by government, or known in the enterprise, except only so far as he had an order in the form of an appointment from the Secretary, directing him to report to the commander for duty.

The undersigned forbear further comment on this subject, and content themselves with protesting, in the name of their constituents, *the people of the West,* as well as in their own names, against the continuance of such obvious injustice to their fellow-citizen, who has, in their opinion, earned far different treatment at the hands of government. *They are aware that many difficulties have thus far attended the fitting out of the expedition: upon these difficulties they feel no disposition to dwell. It is enough for them to call the attention of the President to the subject, in a spirit of frankness and kindness,* feeling assured that their communication will be received in the same spirit, and that the President will, at once, give such directions as will be satisfactory to all the parties concerned. Very respectfully, &c.,

THOMAS CORWIN, Ohio.	THOMAS L. HAMER, Ohio.
JAMES ALEXANER, Jr., Ohio.	J. RIDGEWAY, Ohio.
ALEXANDER HARPER, Ohio.	WM. KEY BOND, Ohio.
DANIEL KILGORE, Ohio.	CALVARY MORRIS, Ohio.
J. W. ALLEN, Ohio.	D. P. LEADBETTER, Ohio.
WM. H. HUNTER, Ohio.	P. G. GOODE, Ohio.
CHS. D. COFFIN, Ohio.	S. MASON, Ohio.
A. W. SNYDER, Illinois.	THOMAS MORRIS, Ohio.
WILLIAM ALLEN, Ohio.	O. H. SMITH, Indiana.
JOHN TIPTON, Indiana.	LUCIUS LYON, Michigan.
JAMES RARIDEN, Indiana.	WILLIAM HEROD, Indiana.
WILLIAM GRAHAM, Indiana.	R. BOON, Indiana.
GEORGE H. DUNN, Indiana.	ALBERT S. WHITE, Indiana.
WILLIAM L. MAY, Illinois.	ZADOK CASEY, Illinois.
JOHN CHANEY, Ohio.	J. WEBSTER, Ohio.
E. WHITTLESEY, Ohio.	

WASHINGTON, *May 1st*, 1838.

To J. N. Reynolds, Esq.

NEW YORK, *Nov. 12th*, 1837.

DEAR SIR:—The members of the scientific corps, attached to the Southern Exploring Expedition, have, with deep regret, understood that you entertain some idea of resigning the commission by which you are, at present, associated with us.

Without pausing to inquire whether the position in which you are placed by that document, is such a one as, in justice to your unwearied exertions for the success of this great national enterprise, should have been assigned to you, we would earnestly request you to reflect farther upon the subject before making a final decision.

That you would, of *necessity*, occupy a prominent station in the expedition, has so long been considered by us, in common with the whole country, as a point beyond all question, the present contingency takes us wholly by surprise; and we have heard, with not less astonishment than grief, that, in the official list of the civilians connected with this undertaking, *the name of J. N. Reynolds is nowhere to be found.* Upon the manifest injustice of this omission no comments are requisite. *We believe that, through the length and breadth of our land, wherever the name of the Exploring Expedition has been mentioned, every voice will be lifted up against it.* Neither is it required that we should enter into a detail of the many reasons for which we consider your accompanying it to be of the *utmost importance to the harmony and eventual success of the expedition.* Permit us, however, to assure you that such is our conviction, and to express our sincere hope that the knowledge of this fact may induce you to sacrifice your present views and feelings in this matter to the wishes of the corps, and to consent to retain a position which, however it may fall short of what in justice should be yours, will secure to us your co-operation in carrying out, successfully, the great objects of the voyage. *Our country, never forgetful of the claims of her children, will, we cannot doubt, in the end, award you all that is so justly your due, however it may be attempted to deprive you of it at present.* Trusting that our appeal, therefore, may produce the desired effect, we remain, dear sir, with the highest respect and esteem, Your sincere friends,

Alfred T. Agate,	James Eights,
Joseph P. Couthouy,	Horatio Hale,
Reynell Coates,	Raphael Hoyle,
James D. Dana,	W. R. Johnson,
Asa Gray,	Charles Pickering,
J. W. Randall,	J. Drayton.

The *Cincinnati Republican* at that day, made these just reflections on the outrage :

This appeal or remonstrance, for it is a little of both, was sent to the President early in May last; but its publication has been withheld until the present moment, in the hope that justice would have been done Mr. Reynolds. But we learn that it is determined that Mr. Reynolds shall not accompany the expedition, and the communication, though signed by a majority of the delegates in Congress from the West, who are friendly to the administration, has not received the courtesy of a notice from the President.

When we take into consideration the uniform support the expedition has always received from the West, and especially from the Ohio delegation, who took an interest in the enterprise from the fact that it had *been originated and successfully prosecuted by a native of Ohio,* the conduct of the executive seems almost unaccountable. Here are the wishes of the almost entire delegation of the northwestern states strongly and manfully expressed. On what ground of petty jealousy are the demands of this letter denied?

Was it to gratify a secretary notoriously opposed to the expedition from the moment it was projected, and whose ground *of hostility to Mr. Reynolds was mainly owing to the fact that he had again and again defeated him before Congress?* We assign no other reason for the conduct of the President in this case.

Of the arrangements which have given dissatisfaction, the appointment of Lieutenant Wilkes to the command, over the heads of his seniors and superiors in every respect, is not the least reprehensible. Why was he selected? Was it because he was ready to do the bidding of an incompetent secretary? *This is no party measure. Strong men on both sides have been and are its supporters.* The country at large bears the expense, and has a right to ask why matters have been thus managed. The people of Ohio have a voice in the matter, and a right to inquire if injustice has been done to one of her citizens—*the author of the measure—who has, by his researches and publications, fixed milestones and guide-boards for those to carry on the expedition who have now got possession of it, without the magnanimity to do justice to its projector.* The conduct of the managers of this affair towards Mr. Reynolds will find no response from honorable men. They may do him wrong, but cannot put him down; *for, going or staying,* HIS TRIUMPH HAS BEEN COMPLETE. *The spirit which his labors has awakened will not sleep; for, whatever is done in this expedition, or by others which may and no doubt will follow, for the extension and security of commerce and the acquisition of scientific knowledge, the country will not forget to whom it has been mainly owing.*

Was it wonderful that this bigoted ignorance should manifest its persecuting spirit towards the individual whom it could not equal in intellect, in philanthropy, or moral courage? Was it singular that the true significance of liberty was unknown to them? Was it strange, that an intelligence so far in advance of them should have been misunderstood, and misrepresented? He who is the mouthpiece of the time, generally obtains greater concessions from the obtuse and narrow-minded ; because they honor that heroism which compliments themselves !

Mr. Reynolds was the great oracle of the *future!* And it needed moral heroism to place himself in the advance guard of a great national enterprise, in accordance with his convictions of patriotism and duty ! Every great event is the beginning of a new epoch in the history of humanity, and he, who by his devotion to justice and truth, makes his country wiser, happier, or better, places that country under a debt of gratitude to him ! We say, therefore, that were the magnitude of that effort on the part of this American, fully weighed in all its intellectual, moral, social, and political bearings, on the *future of this nation*, the name and praise of its author would echo not only from every city, but from every hill and through every plain in our country ! For what but this feeling warms our hearts towards the heroes of our liberties, who sacrificed their reputations, their treasure, and their blood, to serve the cause which so preëminently blesses us ? And what nobler deed can man perform for his country and his race, than to inspire a more exalted intelligence, and develop a nobler progressive thought ?

The author, as we have seen, was not permitted to accompany his own expedition, but his triumph was not the less *complete!* Because he shed an unfailing lustre on his country, and became thereby, the *beacon light* which has illumined the dark and intricate pathways of science ever since, and elevated our state of national progress and intelligence!

All subsequent expeditions and voyages of discovery in this country owe their origin to him who made their "milestones and guide-boards!" To the men of science who accompanied that great enterprise, honor and praise are both due; and despite the difficulties and embarrassing surroundings, they made an imperishable record of their fidelity to their high trusts!

Lynch's exploration of the Dead Sea, testifies the value of the First American Exploring Expedition! Fremont's courage and noble daring in California, testify it; the Arctic Expedition of Doctor Kane, testifies it; and the American people, by one consent, ratify and endorse its utility and greatness to our common country; while the limit of its results no human wisdom or foresight can compute!

Engraved by J. C. Buttre

Geo. D. Prentice

OF KENTUCKY

THE PACIFIC RAILROAD.

CHAPTER I.

The invention of printing, in 1436, prepared the way for the discovery of America in the same age, and made it a necessity. Why? Because it civilized and enlightened men; and when this was done they wanted more room; their commerce wanted more field; their kingdoms wanted more latitude; their navigation more scope; in fine, every faculty of man expanded, and with a double energy the great work of revolution had begun.

To obtain control over the commerce of the East has been the prize for which the ambition of nations had contended for ages; and to find an easier and more direct route to India was the cause which moved Columbus to set out on the discovery of a western continent. The commerce of the East controlled the world. Its riches, transported over deserts by the Arab, furnished London, Lisbon, Amsterdam, &c., with their opulence and grandeur. When the Turks held power on the Bosphorus, this wealth went to Europe and Asia through the Black Sea. When the Venetians wrested that power from the Turks, the Mediterranean became the channel of this Eastern commerce. The attractions of the gold mines of Peru and Mexico, the wars of the Dutch, French, and Danes, did not divert public desire for a direct route from Europe to Asia, until England conquered and established her empire in India over one hundred and fifty millions of people. The French explorers sought this line in vain; and Lewis and Clark, under President Jefferson, of our own country, met with no better success. At last, however, the difficulty is solved! A railroad through this continent is the power which is to control the commerce of the world; and the United States alone affords such a route. The Pacific Ocean is then to be the centre of commerce for the world, and our country thus becomes the centre of civilization.

The moment this road is built, Asia, with its five hundred millions; Europe, with its two hundred and fifty millions; Africa, and all the islands of the ocean on either side, will seek this transit for their commerce. To go to India now, from the United States, is an undertaking which involves the risk of health and life, a voyage of five months, and of twice crossing the equator. With the railroad, twenty days would be the maximum time for penetrating the heart of India from the city of New York. There, we then shall exchange our products and spend our surplus in the riches of the East.

The trade of the East with Europe now is annually near four hundred millions, requiring three thousand vessels. With our railroad, the cost and time would be so reduced that it is fair to believe this commerce would be increased to seven or eight hundred millions. American vessels and American seamen will then go into the ports of Japan, now opened to us, and return freighted with the products of China and India.

With Asia on one side and Europe on the othe and our steam and sailing vessels at command, there can never be any competition while the nation endures.

The energy of the Anglo-Saxon has already

demonstrated a power which challenges the admiration of mankind. It has been by the Anglo-American that the oceanic currents have been defined, and the Gulf-Stream pointed out to navigators all over the world. It was by the Anglo-American that the Dead Sea was explored. The Anglo-American opened by treaty the ports of Japan, after being so long closed to all but the Dutch and Chinese. Americans have proved the existence of an open Polar Sea, and braved the perils of the Arctic Ocean for Sir John Franklin. What have they done within their own borders? They have taken the Mississippi valley, a wilderness thirty-five years ago, and settled it with upwards of twelve millions of souls. Twenty years ago, where not seven thousand people dwelt, north and north-west of Chicago, they have put upwards of a million The queen city of the West, Cincinnati, which contains one hundred and sixty thousand people, only dug its cellars a few years ago.

In 1820, the first line of packet-ships sailed from the United States to Liverpool, and prudent men predicted them a failure. In 1835, the learned Dr. Lardner declared the navigation of the ocean by steam to to be impracticable. Three years after which, the Great Western and Sirius steamers came into the port of New York.

The first proposal for a railroad from Boston to Hudson was made thirty years ago, and pronounced an absurdity. Now we have, at least, *twenty thousand* miles of railway constructed in the United States, involving a capital of more than *five hundred millions* of dollars. In 1808, the general government refused assistance to the Hudson and Erie Canal, after New York had appropriated six hundred dollars for a survey. Mr. Jefferson, then president, said, it "might be feasible one hundred years to come"!

The first American who is known to have conceived the idea of railroads by steam was Oliver Evans, of Pennsylvania, who made known his plan in 1781 and 1789, after the adoption of the constitution.

Joel Barlow, in his "Visions of Columbus," in 1787, predicted the Erie Canal in New York, thirty years before it was begun, under De Witt Clinton, in 1817. At that time, political parties took ground against it; but the energies of Gov. Clinton prosecuted it to success. In ten years it had paid the cost of completion, while its present annual receipts are half its original cost. Towns and villages immediately rose up by the Wabash and Erie Canal in like manner, and as railroads got on the line the banks of every navigable stream were covered by a population devoted to commercial enterprise.

The inhabitants of Portland, Maine, have embarked in the enterprise of building a railroad from there to Nova Scotia, which is now completed, and reduces the voyage of Europe to America two thousand miles. It is three thousand from New York to Liverpool. This effort found favor with European as well as American capitalists, and will tend rapidly to commercial prosperity

When we consider that England, to save a distance of only twelve miles between London and Dublin, built a bridge across the Straits of Menai at a cost of twelve millions of money, we can better understand the economy of expending money to shorten our route eleven thousand miles to Europe.

Everything, therefore, demands, on the same principle, that the Pacific Railroad should be made to shorten and cheapen the transit route for the commerce of Europe and Asia, which we shall certainly command. Consider, Americans, how in a few years we have spread from a fragment to a continent! We have only one sixth less of territory than the fifty-nine states of Europe put together. We are ten times larger than Great Britain and France. We are one and a half times larger than Russia in Europe. And, when the Atlantic and Pacific states shall be united by the railroad, it is impossible to realize how vast and how grand the results will be to us.

In a philanthropic view, it is incomparable with any war, or revolution, or discovery, save that of our beloved country, and the national freedom secured by our Republican institutions. The railroad will at once become the strongest fortification for the country, and moving batteries of men would be its defence in time of war. The passive intellects of the East will soon feel the attrition of American energy and enterprise; the population that flows in from the Old World will thus be Americanized; and Protestant education, which is as the brain to the body of our institutions, will build up the American systems of free schools, which are the essential element of our liberties.

Liberty has expanded our resources on the

Atlantic, and will, in the same way, advance them on the Pacific, until the islands of the ocean, and the shores of Asia, shall feel the benign influence of American commerce and American laws. The West, then, demands the Pacific Railroad, to add to the prosperity of the country, to open new outlets for the distribution of commerce, and new sources for our national wealth and enterprise. Americans, it is the navigable rivers on the Atlantic which have populated your states. This made it easy to receive and send off the products of the land, and sent settlers first upon the water-courses. As these became populous, the settlers on them drove back into the interior the succeeding emigrants. The valley of the Mississippi was thus peopled. So the borders of the Hudson, Connecticut, and Penobscot Rivers, and Narragansett Bay. At the beginning there were no interior communications to protect the settlements on the rivers, and hence they were not populated so rapidly as the Mississippi valley. Steamers were coëval with that settlement, and this has caused its rapid increase of population.

During the early peopling of the country, and before the introduction of steam navigation, pack-horses were used to carry goods; but the danger and expense rendered this mode of trade exceedingly limited. The usual time, then, was six months to make a journey from New Orleans to St. Louis by water, which is now performed in eight or twelve days. It was the steamboat, and that alone, which opened the commerce of the Mississippi valley. Corn, wheat, iron, hemp, coal, would all have been comparatively useless without this mode of transportation.

You see now, Americans, how and why the valleys and rivers of the Mississippi were penetrated. On the coast of the Pacific the case is altogether different. The states and territories we own there never can be settled as the Atlantic states have been. Why? Because neither steamers nor sail-boats can penetrate them. A land route is the only way this ever can be accomplished. But will an ordinary road do it? No, it could never be made to pay expenses of transportation. People would therefore refuse to dwell there, while they could seek the water-courses of the Atlantic and Pacific for settlement. The cause why individual enterprise entered into our favorite valleys, and occupied them, and grew wealthy, was owing to their access to the sea, and other navigable waters, which penetrated the interior country.

Now, what has been done for the Atlantic states by steamboats must be done for the Pacific states by railroad. And let us be assured of one thing, that, with a railroad across the continent, the value of the whole country would be increased incalculably beyond what all our rivers have done, or possibly can do. No other inducement ever will carry settlers to the interior countries of the Pacific states. But, with a railroad, they would soon convert that whole country to a flower-garden. The entire year, at all seasons, would be open to the markets. The energy and enterprise of the settlers would increase with the means of transit at hand. The ice in the Atlantic states, in the cold season, has always been a bar to industry; but this would no longer interfere with progress.

The Pacific Railroad will, of necessity, do all the business of the waters in those territories; the Hudson, the Ohio, and Mississippi, would pour their commerce into that railroad passage. Thus this thoroughfare will extend our commerce and spread our population on the Pacific, as the steamboat navigation has spread the plains of the Mississippi and Missouri Rivers.

Look at California and Oregon, how within three years and a half they have gathered a population of at least a half a million! What has done this? The gold mines alone. If, then, with a land journey of three or four months, and a costly sea voyage of thirty or forty days, population has thus accumulated, what may be expected when the railroad shall have reduced the distance from San Francisco to Washington city to seven days, and the telegraph has brought us into communication in one single day? For such will actually be the case.

CHAPTER II.

AMERICANS, what has been the consequence of legislating for the states of the Pacific already, which cannot be reached under a six weeks' travel? Let the Indian massacres, and those of Panama, the dangers and sufferings of immigrants, the black catalogue of crime which has made almost a Sodom of California, the utter perversion of the rights of suffrage by the ballot-box, answer. The disorders which have been created there, the villanous practices of stuffing the ballot-box, the elevation of the scum of society and traitors to office, — all these, and other shocking spectacles, which, as a necessity, caused the Vigilance Committee to be appointed by the people for their own protection and safety against these ruffians and murderers, are greatly owing to their isolated condition.

For these causes, a separate republic on the Pacific must ever suffer the most serious dangers, and especially if there should be cause for foreign invasion. Nothing will remedy these evils in due season but the establishment of a railroad to the Pacific. This would at once rectify all the present difficulties, and regenerate the condition of the people.

The idea of a Southern republic may at first seem absurd. But would the united interest of Lower California, the western coast of Mexico, a part of the British possessions opposite Vancouver's and Charlotte's Island, and removed from the evils of a French population, be of no account, joined to California? Would not the commerce and the gold, and its free soil, interfere with the harmony of the Southern States of this Union? Most undoubtedly. Why not, then, settle the question, not for a time, but forever, by putting a railway, that shall bind with a cord of iron the states of the Pacific and Atlantic?

Independent of the trade of the United States and Canada, this road would be the great forwarder of the staples of China and the East Indies. The reason is, that it would be the shortest, quickest, and least expensive route. The passage by this land route can be effected from three to five miles per hour quicker than by any sea or water route that could possibly be devised.

No one can compute the extent of trade from a railroad across the continent, connecting the Columbia and San Francisco Rivers with New York, China, Japan, Oregon, Australia, the Sandwich Islands, California, the seaports of Europe, United States, and Canada. Americans, these would all commercially centre on this road. The distance from New York to California is thirty-two hundred miles. Allowing the usual rates of railroad travel, with time to eat and to rest on the journey, it will require seven days. If in an emergency, and the usual delays were abandoned, the travel could be made with ease in four and a half days, at thirty miles an hour!

Until gold settled California, the merchants of our country had but a limited knowledge of the trade on the western coast of the Pacific, to China, Japan, and India. Consequently, it was the local traffic of California, Oregon, and Australia, that opened to view the fact that the commercial capabilities of the Pacific are really greater than the Atlantic. The tea trade and sperm whale are confined to the Pacific; while the great staples, sugar, tobacco, wheat, and corn, grow as well on the Pacific as on the Atlantic.

The Sandwich, Society, New Hebrides, Friendly, New Britain, Philippine, and Ladrone Islands, are all accessible, by steamboats, from California; and all their products, therefore, would be turned to use, if the railroad were there. China will unlock her doors as never before when this temptation to extend her commerce is presented. Australia will reap the benefit; while California, the great outpost of the Pacific, will not pause in the opportunity to show the world, and especially this beloved people, what industry will accomplish, in connection with gold, in which resource she is now only second to Great Britain.

How has England obtained ascendency over the commerce of the world? By making it *free.* England, Holland, and the United States, which compose three fourths of the foreign commerce, acknowledge entire freedom in every commercial pursuit; and, now that we have entered the Pacific by right and title, with our steamships and our experience, what shall prevent us from acquiring a commercial ascendency over England, Holland, and the world? We ask you, Americans, if anything shall do it? You say, No. Then get about your railroad, and you may say this in earnest.

By the improvement in steam and ship-building, our mariners perform the same voyage to-day in half the time they did fifty years ago. We have already made railroads on the two continents, and we are altogether a changed people since 1800. For twenty-five years after that, our commerce had no facility from steamboats or railways; and it has been but twenty years since we began to realize their full value. All the sources of commerce then were those tributary to the seaboard, while the wealth of the country was kept, from want of communication, beyond their reach. We had not then, either, the men of method and mind equal to the emergencies of trade, as we have now. We had not a monied capital then, as now, opened to all. When we compare ourselves with the past, and see what new facilities of greatness the nation has found out, we should be grateful, elated with our destiny, and ready for action.

And if, with our small means, we have attained such development on our Atlantic borders, what, with our ships, our steamboats, our capital, our experience, and our railroad, are we not destined to accomplish on the Pacific shores? The railroad will open new strength, and new channels of thought, as well as action. It will make our country the agent and carrier of the commerce of the world; and it becomes all classes of our country — all who regard its prosperity, all who regard the benefit to their children and their children's children — to rally to the railroad as the great highway of our national prosperity and greatness.

While men are quibbling and blundering about the best route, Nicaragua might make a canal or railroad, and establish trading settlements, which would materially interfere with our prospects. Every day gives greater importance to the political, commercial, geographical, moral, and social reasons which show that we are risking much, losing much, by the delay.

The Atlantic was always more formidable to explorers than the Pacific; consequently the East, in the early ages, was more rapidly populated than the West. The oceans, we must remember, were as much ours by right, before we had a sail or harbor on our coast, as now. The Pacific territory was acquired by us through the Mexican war. It was purchased then by the sweat and blood of American men. It has been the means of increasing our commercial wealth and greatness. To occupy and enjoy this, the railroad has been projected by the wisdom of men who, from the beginning, have seen that this territory, obtained at so dear a cost to the United States, must either be made subservient to the interests of the whole country, or be wrested from us for a new republic.

It cost just twenty thousand dollars to discover America ; and for this small sum the Queen of Spain had to pledge her jewels, so great were the financial embarrassments of the government from the Moorish wars. It is true, Columbus never saw the United States in its present limits ; but he was at Cuba, five degrees from Florida. Henry of England took six years to determine the proposal which Columbus made him for aid in this same discovery.

How incapable was the human mind at that period to comprehend the advantage of spending twenty thousand dollars, to see if there was any such place at all as this New World of ours ! Just as incredulous are many to the prospective results of the Pacific Railroad. Yes, with all the light and knowledge, and the mathematical demonstrations of its effects upon our national destiny, the timid and circumscribed intellect is as hard to convince as the child is that there is not a man in the moon.

When America was discovered, England had not a greater population than we had when we declared independence. Printing had been but twenty-one years in use; the English language had not been spoken a century; there were but four merchant ships belonging to London, and the people were opposed to trade. Two centuries elapsed, after that, before England had dug a canal. Manufactures were almost unknown; and it was upwards of a century after the discovery of America before England built her first stage-coach.

And now, with a railroad access to the entire continent, the blessing of our unequalled government and wise and wholesome laws will make us felt and propitiated by the entire world. What makes England the first commercial power in the world, but the control she has over the markets of Asia and the continent of Europe? The possession of California has now added to the national wealth of America, by opening to us the same commerce of Asia.

Central as the United States are between the two continents of Europe and Asia, and producing the two great staples of tobacco and cotton, we need but a highway of steam from the Atlantic to the Pacific, and mail steamers from California to China, to overstep England, and claim supremacy in commerce to her. Why has England, thus far, made us dependent upon her for commercial news? Because she has an overland route, which secures her mail facilities. The mails are taken from London to Canton, and *vice versa*, in sixty-five days; to us, in seventy-seven days. If we construct a railroad, now, to the Pacific, and connect California with China by mail steamers, the whole distance from New York to China will be accomplished in the incredibly short time of twenty-four days. England then would become dependent upon the United States, not only for mail facilities, but for the products of Asia, which would be made available through us.

England, by her Cape of Good Hope and overland routes, has obtained a monopoly over the East India trade and that of China. The government of the East Indies forces *opium* to be introduced, which is the important drug for the Chinese markets. The sale of opium amounts to thirty millions annually. Besides, the cotton and other fabrics which England sends to China bring back to Great Britain annually twenty millions of dollars. Nothing but the American trade has saved China from being exhausted in money. We deal with China to about half the amount of England; for which we send specie, or bills drawn to our account, payable in London. Now, it needs but for us to establish more rapid communications, to enjoy all the advantages England now possesses. Our central position gives this natural facility. We have but to use the appliances of science and art which God has given us the intelligence to appreciate, to take the commercial balance into our own hands.

It is now reduced to a moral certainty that *cotton* cannot be grown to any extent in any soil yet found out but that of the United States. It is, therefore, the first staple of our trade. Tobacco is next in importance, as such. Its use is now becoming general throughout Europe and in some parts of Asia. It is only kept from China by England, who forces opium upon her people, and makes the difficulty of obtaining tobacco from us. We alone might substitute tobacco for opium, and thus rescue a people perishing so rapidly from the use of that poisonous drug; the Chinese greatly preferring tobacco, but the English, jealous of our staple, take care to throw every obstacle in the way of its introduction, well knowing that it would entirely supersede the use of the deadly narcotic in which they are so deeply interested. We might receive, in return for our tobacco and cotton, the amount in tea and silk, for which we now pay twenty-five millions annually.

Look at the true state of the case. England has to buy of us the *raw* material, out of which she fabricates the basis of her foreign trade. She gets our wool and cotton, and makes muslins, cottons, calicoes, handkerchiefs, and cotton yarn, of *our cotton*, and broadcloth, cassimeres, blankets, camlets, of *our wool*. We also make the same articles. Both export to China; yet we find, by a comparison of one year, that ours reach scarcely *one twentieth* part of England's, for the reason given, — that she commands the market by her mail facilities of communication.

Take the trade in *tea*, and compare our commerce and England's with China, in the sixty years from the time we began to trade with China in that article, and look at it. The first voyage of commerce from the United States to China was in 1785; but the trade was not really opened until 1792. It has so increased that now our importation of *tea* amounts to sixteen millions of dollars annually. From the beginning of our trade with China, we have imported from that country to the value of upwards of two hundred and fifty-eight millions of dollars, while our exports have amounted to only a little over eighty-six millions. Thus we have paid China in precious metals upwards of one hundred and seventy-two millions of dollars!

From 1792, when our trade began with China, to 1827, silver to the amount of eighty-eight millions and upwards had been shipped direct from the United States to China. In 1827, China, owing to the opium trade, had become indebted to England very largely, and American bills, payable in England, began to be used in lieu of coin; and from 1834, these American bills on Chinese accounts amounted to about sixteen and a half millions, while the specie in that time sent from England was only between seven and eight millions!

So, since 1834, England has been steadily draining our coin to the amount of seventy-five millions seven hundred and fifty-seven thousand seven hundred and ninety-seven dollars, and settling with China by bills of credit, for which we have to pay specie to her.

CHAPTER III.

Now, this drain of England upon us is preposterous. Our own products are sufficient to pay for all we get from China ; and it is *our* products which pay a premium to the labor of England, and cause a loss to our manufacturers and mechanics. It is the increase of *our* products by the art and value of British labor which actually pays for nearly the whole of the teas and raw silk England imports from China.

There are other advantages connected with the steamers to transpose the mart from China to the Pacific, meeting the railroad at that terminus. These steamers can be so constructed as to supersede the government force needed there, and save the treasury annually one million and a quarter of dollars. The extensive and unprotected coasts of California and Oregon render them liable to foreign aggression, and demand, in this point of view, the serious consideration of the people. Before the acquisition of California we had two hundred vessels employed in trade in the Pacific. Since then, there are, at least, six hundred and fifty American trading vessels. The amount of our property exposed there on the coast is nearly seventy millions. The whaling business alone is valued at thirty millions, with an employed force of eighteen thousand men in the North Pacific; and our annual revenue is estimated at ten millions.

Our acquisition on the Pacific at once inaugurated a new era in the industry, energy, and enterprise, of the American people. It was their voluntary labor which levelled mountains, felled forests, and swept the plains with a torrent of emigration, in the valley of the St. Lawrence, and the basin of our lakes. And when the facilities of moving whole bodies of men are given to the people by the railroad, and time and space at once annihilated, the pulpit, the press, and institutions for education, will multiply, and thus expand and strengthen the bonds of our liberties.

The geographical, physical, and moral power of the United States constitute the basis of their greatness. Great Britain has thirty-four thousand square miles; Austria, Hungary, and Italy, three hundred thousand ; France, less than two hundred thousand ; we, Americans, over three and a half millions ! Geographically, Russia compares as one to one hundred and twenty ; Austria, as one to nine ; France, as one to five and a half ; United States, as one to ninety-six ! While we have therefore a field to display our enterprise, all we want is avenues to exert it in its full vigor.

This railway will save ten or twelve days over the Panama route. It will transfer the capital of Europe to us, which is now used in monopolizing the trade of Asia. It will give to Americans the key of the West, and fix forever the channel of Asiatic commerce (which for centuries has been oscillating) upon the best, safest, and quickest route of transit through the heart of this nation. Safety, security, protection, advancement, all require the construction of this Pacific Railroad. The gold of California has now become the essential stimulant to all the industrial pursuits of the country. The destruction of the monthly shipment to New York would send a shiver through all the commerce, finance, and industry, of this country, that would be incredibly severe, in a single week.

Now, consider how easy foreign cruisers and

privateers could cut us off from this receipt of the essential element of our national vitality! The gold now comes to us over foreign seas, through foreign territory, and over a circuit of six thousand miles. In the event of war, whole fleets would interpose to take from us this arm of our strength. Ships, and troops, and missions, are now necessary to protect our national interest, and protect our commerce on the Pacific; the railway would then protect us, and save all our commerce and territory from foreign aggression.

Throughout the world's history, nations have been elevated or depressed as they advanced or lost commerce; and the changes for three thousand years in Asiatic commerce have settled the question, that the ocean is the obstacle to foreign trade. Land now has been found the facility, and the steam-car the only sure means to keep up distant communications. The United States have consequently the advantage over Europe. We have half the road to India on our own land, the rest on a peaceable sea which washes our shores, and with an impenetrable bar to Europe of the whole diameter of the earth.

This railroad, then, will exalt us to be mistress

of the commerce of the wide world. It will be at the same time the impregnable fortification to save us from the assault of vast armies, or from fierce and bloody battles within our own borders. Who would stop to count the cost of the mere construction, when every interest dear to the hope of citizen and Christian is staked upon the result?

Aside from the commercial and political necessity, the economy and convenience of the nation, the interests of all the people, demand this road now. Americans, take the whole history of the roads in this country in the past twenty-five years, and you will find every dollar invested in them has been worth ten to you.

The vast increase of the West in population and lands is only to be ascribed to its roads. In five years Illinois has doubled her population, and increased her lands five-fold. In these five years ten or twelve hundred miles of railway have been built.

In a moral and educational view, this road must have an immense value. The tendency of population is all west; the field for the growth and prosperity of the people is there. In a few years it will decide all our national measures in Congress;

it will control our national revenues; and, as the agent for transportation of newspapers, cheap books, and all those methods which tend to enlighten and strengthen the Protestant power of our country, the value of the road cannot be computed. The loss to the country by omitting to build this road has been more already than would have supported the entire annual expenses of the government.

The American people now almost unanimously demand this railroad as the great necessity of our times, and they require it to be built in whatever latitude the great mass of the population mostly move; — on whatever line is shortest, most expeditious in travel, and most convenient to the thirty millions of people who inhabit our thirty-one states and territories.

Three routes out of the eight surveyed at government expense have been pronounced feasible by the Secretary of War in his report to Congress. These are the northern, the central, and the southern lines. By all of them the harbor of San Francisco is acknowledged to be the essential terminus of the road on the west, as it is now the centre of all our commerce on the Pacific coast. The question, then, is, what point on the east as a terminus will correspond with San Francisco, as the centre of the greatest amount of population and commercial enterprise on the west?

The distance on the southern line from San Francisco to New York is three thousand six hundred and forty-seven miles; on the northern line, including distance yet unsurveyed, three thousand six hundred and thirty-four; on the central line, three thousand two hundred and forty miles. This would give a distance of four hundred miles shorter to the central route. Texas has granted to any company that constructs the railroad on the southern route ten thousand two hundred and forty acres of land for every mile of road built. Now, these lands of Texas are the only unimproved lands on this continent where cotton can be cultivated. Cotton is the staple of our commerce; the rest of the world is depending on us for its growth, and we do not own now a single acre of government land favorable to its production. In this point of view, the grants of land Texas offers become incalculably valuable to our whole country.

The charge for transporting goods across the Panama Railroad is a tenth less than before its construction. Four or five hours now serve to carry passengers and freight across the isthmus, which formerly occupied three days of dangerous travel. Freight is now reduced to one hundred and twenty-five dollars the ton. But a railroad from the coast of Texas would not only save time, but reduce the tonnage to one half the amount it now costs from New York to California. The saving of freight, the saving of time, would at once induce every prudent and sagacious merchant to adopt the railroad across the continent, and thus gain thirty or forty days.

The central route starts from New York to the Pacific, and has already been completed to Iowa City. From New York city it followes the Hudson River, the Erie Canal, the great lakes, from Buffalo to Chicago, to Rock Island. The easy passage for a bridge which is placed across the Mississippi at Rock Island seems to have been marked out by Providence as the means to facilitate commerce across the river, and renders the route to San Francisco the most direct and advantageous in the judgment of many eminent men. Next year the route will have reached Council Bluff. All this by individual enterprise, without government aid ; and which will make the next census count in Iowa over a million of inhabitants.

All that this route needs from the government to complete the road to San Francisco from Iowa City or Council Bluff is a grant of land, taking nothing from the treasury, but augmenting its revenues by bringing the lands into the market. This route is in the centre of about one half of the population of the whole country; and it is fair to presume, from what has been achieved by the industry and enterprise of the West, that the road will be built on this route, whether favored by the general government or not.

It was the Erie Canal of New York that made the first great revolution in the trade of the country, and exalted that state in wealth and grandeur. Ohio succeeded with her canals between the lakes and the valley, and western trade at once went into New York.

The canals of Maryland and Pennsylvania had no *water communications* from the Atlantic to the Ohio, and failed for that reason; while New York had a monopoly for thirty years, or until the railroad penetrated the entire West to the banks of the Mississippi. *Steam* conquers all other motors. The incredible revenues from the central road of Pennsylvania, and the Baltimore and Ohio road, for the present year, show this result.

It is steam which has given England her power over the continent, by facilitating the transportation of her coal, iron, salt, and other bulky articles. Why do the inhabitants of cities and towns enjoy greater advantages than those who are settled over a sparse country? Because there is an ampler field for purchase, a greater variety of employments for industry to suit the ability and capacity of the laborer, and greater quickness in finishing work. Where population is collected the competition is greater.

Now, the Pacific Railroad will do for the people of our vast country just what the city or town now does. It will concentrate numbers from small and distant places in an incredibly short time. This will at once lead to prosperity. Greece arose to commercial greatness in this way. Towns in Holland, Zealand, and Flanders, for centuries prospered by these means. Switzerland thus holds intercourse by the Rhine with Holland. While those countries without roads, or canals, or other water facilities, have never risen intellectually or commercially.

We have already witnessed the effect of the railroad upon our vast West, which has conduced to individual comfort and prosperity wherever it has penetrated. There is yet another advantage to be attained by the road across the continent, not to be overlooked by Americans, and that is, its effect upon the diffusion of Protestant principles over our land.

CHAPTER IV.

The endless holidays of the Catholic church have always checked industry; and it is a fact to be remembered, that, although the nominal Roman Catholics (but greater proportion infidels) are more numerous than Protestants in Europe, a much larger share of Europe's exports comes from the skill and ingenuity of Protestants than Catholics. In Ireland, linen-weaving, the only great branch of manufacture, is almost wholly in the hands of Protestants. In the vast margin of the West yet to be filled, it becomes a question of the first moment to the nation that it be occupied by Protestants, whose education tends to strengthen our liberties, while that of Romanism is designed to subvert them. The West will soon hold the balance in our national exchequer, and elect our chief ruler; and it is impossible to be too vigilant in promoting and spreading Protestant education over all that portion of our people. The railroad, more than soil, more than mines, will tend to this result, by bringing all sections of the Union together, and advancing knowledge to the remotest limits.

The revenue of our country arises chiefly by consumption; and the wealth and power of our whole country would be increased and secured by the increase of a Protestant American population. The individual income of such a people would also be increased. Why? Because the reward of labor in all the manufacturing and mechanic arts would induce the individual to adopt a uniform pursuit; while the father of a family would not be compelled, as now, often to sacrifice education and personal comfort for the mere sake of living.

Thus, Americans, as the commerce of the country expanded, so would all the arts and pursuits of industry expand, as it grew great and powerful. The Pacific Railroad must increase the medium which circulates and regulates commerce; it must enlighten and expand the energies of men; it must spread the influence of American institutions over mankind, and dissipate that very darkness, under which men have been deluded, and their means squandered, to grow rich without labor, or wise without learning. Foreign force and do mestic treachery have struck at the foundation of our political edifice. We need at once to balance the public mind by free Protestant culture, so that our people shall reason before they act.

Before the discovery of the mines of California and Australia, the coin came from Mexico and South America. Since the discovery of these, a new era has been inaugurated in our commerce with the world. In 1849 and '50, the first flood of gold came into the country; and in the three following years, '51, '52, and '53, the enormous sum of one hundred and sixty-six millions had been added to the circulation, including about thirty millions in the hands of individuals. This caused a change in the condition of the people, who, seeing the steady increase in three years, predicted a rise which would, at last, amount to one hundred millions annually. Then everything in speculation, expense, and importation, increased. Banks sprang up, and paper was used as gold; wages and work increased; railroad bonds were issued by the million; life and fire insurance companies multiplied. But on what was all this based? Was it upon the gold and silver in the bank vaults of the country? Not at all; but upon the *fiction* which men without reasoning adopted, and the delusion under which they acted.

By the returns of the first six years subsequent to the discovery of gold in California, two hundred millions of that metal had been added to the circulation of the world. Australia, though not so long known, brought fifty millions more ; making two hundred and fifty millions more money in use than before the discovery of these mines.

By the official banking returns of the United States and Europe for that period, we find that there was no more money on hand then than before the discovery. Where, then, did this metallic currency go? Why, it went directly into the hands of the people. It, therefore, was not the instrument of the credit structure, which is the proper and only means for making paper the representative of gold and silver; so that, while this increase of gold gave fancied security to the credit it induced, it had not really anything to do with it.

The mining districts, including all the valuable metals found on the Pacific, will, in themselves, make the railroad eminently desirable for the transportation of these metals. Consider, Americans, that, after eight years of constant mining, and *four hundred millions of dollars obtained*, they are still as luxurious as ever. Gold is seen embedded in every stream, mountain, and vale. The copper mines of Lake Superior and Eastern Tennessee have not made even the demand for this metal less profitable. Now, that obtained from the new copper mines of Ajo is wagoned all the way to San Diego, and thence to San Francisco; and still, with all that cost, a large profit is left to the transporter. The richest silver mines ever discovered are in Sonora, in Mexico, which now belong to us. Silver, perfectly pure, has been clipped by the sword of an officer, as a specimen. The Indians have deterred explorers, hitherto, from penetrating these mines; but, now that they have become American property, we shall find American enterprise entering them.

Americans, you perceive these rich mines of gold, iron, silver, and copper, will at once be made accessible by the railroad. Thus it will add to the capital of our country vastly more than it can possibly cost. This Pacific railway will be the harbinger of the future glory and aggrandizement of American institutions. In twenty days we shall be in the most populous cities of Europe and Asia We have already consummated treaties which secure commerce and trade to Americans, and protect their lives, property, and religious liberty, in Siam and Japan, so long closed against the trade of the world ; and then we will command the accumulated wealth of seven hundred millions of people, and which has enriched every nation that has had any kind of control over it.

England, to maintain her ascendency over this trade, has already three over-land mail routes, and is now engaged in devising three more, to carry this Eastern commerce to the British empire. But a railroad, to do this for England, would have to extend six thousand five hundred miles, and would take fourteen years to build it. Now, by the compromise of 1850, which Millard Fillmore signed, as President of the United States, we secured the ten leagues of country on the Pacific coast, which included California, and planted our flag there. And, by this means, — made our blessing, under God, — we can make our national road, which will convey us across the continent to the Bay of San Francisco in seven days ; and ten or twelve days from there, by steam, will land Americans in the populous countries of Eastern and Western Asia and Western Europe. It will give them a hold on the wealth of China, which has been increasing for six thousand years, and bring them in contact with her seven hundred millions of inhabitants in twenty days from the day they leave New York.

This railroad, then, will put sectional agitation among our people at rest, and set them about these new channels of trade and commerce. We have now control of the *cotton* market of the world, and the certain prospect of having the same power over *wool*. Iron, also, in every state but one, is abundant enough to supply the whole American continent; and, in a few years, we shall likewise control the market of this great item in trade. Gold, too, will then be more rapidly diffused over the civilized world, and this will facilitate the activity of our commerce. A greater amount of labor will then be made available, to work the mines of California and Australia, than ever before.

The effect of the discovery of the precious metals in California has been to stimulate the latent energies of men to an extent never witnessed before, and has been the means of forcing the necessity of a railway upon the common sense of the American people. The poor man will be more benefited than the rich by this road; and the labor employed in the development of our new territory, and the exploration of its mines, will prevent any superabundance of laborers in the most thickly-settled parts of the country, and stop the poor man from working for the pittance he now does.

The manufacturer, also, by the increased freedom to commerce which the constant and rapid transportation of gold from California and Australia will then command, will find himself better able to cope with the manufacturers of Europe.

According to Professor Blake, the great gold field in California, notwithstanding the large increase to the circulation of the precious metals, has not yet been fully explored. There is a field seven hundred miles in length, and about fifty in breadth, containing thirty-five thousand square miles, eleven thousand of which are rich in gold, sometimes extending to the depth of six feet in the sands of the coast. This is repeatedly washed out of the black sand by the tides. The number of square miles worked, but imperfectly, we are assured by Dr. Trask, in his work on geology, never exceeds four hundred at a time; and fewer persons were engaged in mining in 1854 than in 1852, although the product of gold was in '52 forty-five millions of dollars, and in '54 sixty-one millions. This was owing to the increased advantages of working the mines by proper machinery.

Now, by the highest authorities we find that the amount of gold in the whole world, in 1848, was two billions nine hundred millions of dollars, or six hundred millions of pounds; while, by the increase from the mines of California and Australia since that time, at least four billions of dollars have been added to that amount, which would make now, in the whole world, six billions nine hundred millions of dollars of gold, beside what is worked into jewelry and plate. And, Americans, does it not cause a thrill of triumph in your hearts to know that, of this increase to the precious metals, your own State of California has contributed three hundred and thirteen millions two hundred and eighty-five thousand five hundred and two dollars and seventy-seven cents; and other parts of America, seventeen million seven hundred and sixty-six thousand seven hundred and sixty-eight dollars and fifty-seven cents?

CHAPTER V.

M. Tegoborski, Counsel of the Empire of Russia, in writing of the influence of the gold fields of California and Australia, estimates that by them the amount of gold and silver in use in Europe will be doubled in thirteen years, and throughout the whole world in twenty-four years.

Beside, what is the effect of the discovery of the mines of California in Europe? Why, it has raised real estate four per cent. per annum, and advanced all kinds of produce in like manner. It has also advanced the wages of labor in like ratio. How? Because the poor working-man, before dependent on the employer for the mere sustenance of life, is now driven to another field of operation, and incited by the desire to accumulate, and thus changing often the state of things by making the rich man dependent on the laborer.

So those who remained as well as those who went to California were benefited. If that was so in Europe, let us turn to our own country, — we, the possessors of California. We see how our commerce is extended; we see, day by day, how eagerly the accumulations of gold and silver in our bank-vaults are taken and transported into other countries, to bring back their merchandise to us. Why? Because its shipment to England, France, and Germany, equalizes the value of gold, and prevents the dangers to trade which result from keeping it under bars and bolts. The railroad to the Pacific has now become a necessity to the American people, that they may enjoy the free heritage God has given them, opening all the avenues to wealth and industry, and making their voice heard on the hills, in the valleys, the cities, and the plains, of the whole earth. This, Americans, will be the great triumph of the American States over commerce, mechanics, and manufactures, which nothing can impede beneath the stars.

The railway and the canal will be the true conquerors of the world. Around them will centre the industry and energy of the Anglo-Saxon race There the Protestant emigrant will seek his new home. They will become the majority of the population, and the consequent possessors of most of the property of the country.

The telegraph will then become the electric medium of exchange, which, without a visible chain, will link the American Union to the world. "Lo, what hath God wrought!" were the memorable words which passed over the wires of the first telegraph ever made in the United States, a few years since, between Baltimore and Washington, a distance of but forty miles. Now, Americans, we not only find it in the full exercise of its magic power in all the states of this mighty Union, but actually preparing to bring us in speaking distance of the other continent.

You all know that the Island of St. John's, Newfoundland, is the most eastern point of North America, and Valencia is the most western harbor of the British Isles. The waters of the St. Lawrence have long since cut Newfoundland from the continent. Now a submarine telegraph has been laid, which brings Newfoundland and the main land again in contact; and the distance from St. John's to New York, of one thousand seven hundred and eighty miles, can be reached by direct communication. But still the ocean was to be crossed to reach Europe, and the question arose how this could best be done. Some proposed extending the line to Labrador, Greenland, Iceland, and the Faroe Islands; but to this there were insurmountable objections, and, after the investigation of scientific men, it was decided that the line must also start from Newfoundland to Europe, a distance of nineteen hundred miles, on account of the depth of the water, essential to the success of the enterprise.

The plan devised, and about to be executed, is this: A line of wire three thousand miles long will be placed on two war-ships in mid-ocean, one belonging to the United States, the other to England. These will each take half the wire. The wire will be covered with gutta percha coatings, and will be made of the best conducting material, accompanied by a machine, invented for the express purpose, by Dr. Whitehouse, of England, in order to ascertain when the wire is broken or damaged, and the exact point of interruption.

Thus, Americans, by your inventive genius, you are with one grapple about to join Europe to this country by a telegraph, which will start at Newfoundland, and end at Valencia, in Ireland, with one thousand nine hundred miles of cable resting in the Atlantic Ocean! This is not an ideal sketch, but a living reality, that in 1857, next year, the British Isles and the United States, though divided by a stormy ocean of three thousand miles, will by science and machinery *hold conversational intercourse* with each other; and, at the same time, the distance by railway between Nova Scotia and Portland, Maine, will have diminished our travelling distance from Europe eleven hundred miles!

These mighty works show the mutual benefit England and the United States are each to the other, while they continue as they are. While the energy of this great American people, too rapid for carrier pigeons, and even steam, and eager to extend and profit by every advantage in commerce, invention, finance, science, and arts, and to move in the rapid march of civilization over the whole globe, has already forged the chain which is to bind us to the three ancient continents of the Eastern world.

Well might Mr. Dallas, the American minister, declare that the great telegraph, now making, would afford Americans the opportunity soon to respond to the toast given to Americans in London before the dinner ended. "When famine distressed other lands, in the land of Egypt there was bread." So with our beloved country: from the diversity of its soil and climate, its power in raising subsistence will so increase as the humbler condition of society advances by intelligence, that it would be physically impossible to arrest the march of the American people in commerce, wealth, or mental activity.

Now we come to the great question, who is to make the road to the Pacific, — Congress, that is, the general government, or the people?

We say it cannot be built without the coöperation of the government, because there are fifteen hundred miles between Missouri and California, over which Congress alone has power to legislate. The constitution, which gives Congress the right to regulate commerce, allows the general government to build the road to California from New York, for a mail route, if it so decided. Congress can give or sell the public lands, as it pleases. Congress can appropriate money, if it pleases, to build a road or roads through the landed estate of the government for mail transportation, or military purposes. We do not advocate the especial claims of either of the three routes surveyed. Each has its advantages;

and all may be laterally connected, or ultimately and separately constructed. But, we say, had the present administration done its duty, and favored the building of the road to the Pacific three years ago, — instead of burning Greytown, making Ostend conferences to seize Cuba by "divine" right, and repealing the Missouri Compromise, which has brought upon us intestine war, — our country, instead of being divided, distracted, and agitated, would have been running a new race in dignity, and political and commercial greatness.

The administration, on the contrary, early receded from this national measure. The leading presses, which sustained it, followed in elaborate articles against the road. Senators of the same political school declared the measure would be worse than the alien and sedition laws of John Adams. They saw no power in the constitution, while grant after grant, in the last seven years, has been made by Congress to the Southern and Western States. The people saw nothing to prevent it, and with more energy than ever before renewed that demand.

Engraved by J. C. Buttre from a Daguerreotype

James P. Gerry
Commander
U. S. N.

THE LOSS OF THE

SLOOP-OF-WAR "ALBANY,"

COMMANDER GERRY, OFFICERS, AND CREW.

CHAPTER I.

THE Author in a previous work, "The American Battle," was induced, by the misrepresentations of officers, to make some statements which she afterwards learned, from an examination of the documents, to have been *untrue*, and which she therefore corrected in the previous editions of the present volume. The statements were then made, as she was assured, upon the most reliable authority, the verity of which she believed therefore rested upon the most credible testimony, rather than upon the zealous enthusiasm of the informers. As she cannot, and *will not*, to support any cause, or subserve any party or creed, allow a statement to bear the sanction of her name that is not supported by evidence of its *authenticity*, she has requested her publishers to withdraw that chapter from the future editions of "The American Battle" solely because it contains certain errors, caused by misrepresentations made to her. It was from a knowledge of this fact, brought to her notice by the examination of the official documents, and the pain she experienced in having innocently, but most unjustly, committed, through others, a wrong upon the gallant dead, and by her own high sense of right, that she was at once prompted to make a public exposition of the character and services of Commander Gerry, who must be regarded, by all who are correctly informed of his private and public history, as one of the brightest ornaments of the Navy, and possessed of every virtue that gives claim to the confidence and respect of his country and of humanity

The misrepresentation in the case of the late distinguished Commander Gerry, of the United States Navy, is first in importance, as it reflected upon one who is not here to vindicate his own claim to justice. But data, which none can deny, are at hand, as effectually to refute the charge as though he were personally present. The official documents, which the author has read, make no mention of any application from a subordinate to place a Bible and religious library in the cabin of the Albany, under command of Captain Gerry. There is not one word to be read in connection with this matter, from beginning to end, in these documents.

The history of no misfortune that nas ever befallen the Navy caused deeper affliction or more lasting sorrow than that of the loss of the sloop-of-war Albany.

Captain Gerry was her noble commander, aided by many of the most gallant and valuable officers in the naval service, when she met that mysterious fate which none survived to reveal. The last official intelligence of this ship was dated on the 28th of September, 1854, announcing that she would sail next day from Aspinwall for New York, and subsequent information leads us to believe Captain Gerry intended to return by way of the Mona passage. A terrific hurricane occurred in that latitude on the 21st of October, which it is supposed the Albany must have encountered, and there met her lamentable fate. After waiting long in expectation of her arrival, the most painful anxiety was awakened on account of these brave men, and the Princeton, under the command of Captain Eagle, an accomplished and skillful officer in the service, was sent to discover some tidings of their fate ; which, after a thorough search, he was unable to do.

The United States steamer Fulton, Lieutenant John K. Mitchell commanding, which sailed from Aspinwall, New Granada, March 2, also made a thorough search among the Bahama and Windward Islands and the Spanish Main ; but without any more successful result.

On the 18th of April, 1855, within seven months from the sailing of the Albany from Aspinwall, the department announced the names of the promoted officers by this melancholy event, and thus settled the conviction upon the public mind, that all hopes of the survival of Captain Gerry and his associates had vanished forever !

The department, in making this annunciation, made honorable mention of the distinguished services of Captain Gerry, "who, in pursuance of the orders of the commodore, had been actively cruising during the entire year, as commander of the Albany, and had visited, among other ports, those of Samana, Sisal, St. Thomas, Port Royal, and St. Jago de Cuba." And the Secretary of the

Navy further remarked, that "this ship had done good service, and Commander Gerry and his officers merit the approbation of the department, as I have reason to know that the appearance of our flag at these ports, and the bearing of the officers, contributed much to the encouragement and protection of our citizens engaged in commercial transactions in these regions."

Commander Gerry, was the youngest son of the late Elbridge Gerry, who died in the discharge of his duties, as Vice-President of the United States, to which office he was elected by the unanimous vote of the "Republican" party, in 1812.

In separating the British Government from the Colony of Massachusetts, and forming one to suit the people's choice ; in the foreign and domestic concerns of the country, while the war of the revolution was in progress ; in arranging for the cessation of hostilities, and the treaty of peace, Mr. Gerry bore a prominent and distinguished part.

He was in the front ranks of the Convention which formed the Constitution. He was a member of the House of Representatives in Congress, at the organization of the Federal Government. He was an ambassador to France, to negotiate our difficulties, and terminate our treaties with that power.

He was Governor of Massachusetts at the beginning of our second war with England, which he fearlessly advocated, and afterwards presided over the councils of the nation, during the continuance of that war, as Vice-President of the United States.

There is too, one remarkable fact to be remembered, that but *seven* of those who signed the Declaration of Independence, participated in the formation of the Constitution. Of these, Mr. Gerry was one.

And in the first and second Congress after the organization of the government, while many were found who had been distinguished, *either* in the military or civil service of the country, during the Revolutionary War, it was rare then, to find one who had taken an active part, both in the Revolution and the adoption of the Constitution, as Mr. Gerry had done. And when presiding over the Senate of the United States, in 1813, he was believed to be the only individual in either branch of Congress, who had served in the "*immortal Congress*" of 1776!

It may not be improper here to remind the

reader, that of those who signed the great charter of our independence, all were never present at any one time. Many who had no voice in making or originating it, who neither voted for the resolutions, nor for their publication, afterwards became members of Congress, and signed the Declaration of Independence.

This, they were instructed by their respective State Legislatures to do, and which was done from time to time, throughout the year 1776! Mr. Gerry was not one of the latter class. Though all who signed that sacred instrument, deserve the imperishable glory which will ever belong to their venerated names! But two of his colleagues of the Revolution ever attained an elevation beyond that of Elbridge Gerry. These were Adams and Jefferson, who, after assisting in inaugurating the independence of the nation, and sacrificing for its perpetuity, were summoned on its fiftieth anniversary to the judgment of immortality on the same day. And in consideration of the fact, that Mr. Gerry entered the service of his country when subject to England; that he signed the Declaration, and aided in making the Constitution; that he was a party to the first organization of the government, and presided over the destinies of his native State, when measures were being taken for a second war with England, which really gave us *nationality*, and when we remember that he afterwards was transferred as presiding officer over the councils of the nation, and with such entire acceptance to all sections, when the War of 1812 was raging with England, and the permanence and fidelity of our people to free institutions was being tested, we cannot but regard this series of patriotic services furnished by Elbridge Gerry, as connecting themselves with the history of no other man in the nation, of whom we have knowledge.

We may add that, as an appreciation of all this, Congress in 1823, passed a law, and made an appropriation to erect a monument over the tomb of Elbridge Gerry, in the Congressional Cemetery, at Washington City.

This is the first, and only instance, in which the nation has ever erected a monument to a *native* citizen at its own cost!

Capt. James Thompson Gerry, in consequence of his father's decease in 1814, withdrew from Harvard College, which he entered the previous year, and received a warrant as cadet at West Point, and after remaining there one year, he entered the Navy, December 20, 1815. He was made a Lieutenant, April 28th, 1826, and promoted to the rank of Commander, April 17th, 1842. He passed much of his naval life at sea, and with such scrupulous fidelity to duty as to have merited the highest encomiums in every grade of the service, and from all with whom he was officially associated. His mental strength, decision and energy of purpose, bore a striking resemblance to those traits in his father's character, whose virtues he emulated, and whom personally he strongly resembled. Like his father, too, he met death when in the actual service of his country.

Capt. Gerry, in early life, had performed much creditable service in the squadron of the Mediterranean and China Seas, and elsewhere. And had served also in the Home Squadron, with credit to himself, in the years from 1839 to the summer of 1843, in the sloop-of-war Warren, as lieutenant; and when promoted in 1842, he had command of the brig-of-war Somers, which vessel was upset and lost in a squall off Vera Cruz, after he had been relieved from the command. The squadron was ordered north in the summer months, and remained off the Navy Yard, Charlestown.

The Somers, in the subsequent summer, when

under Capt. Gerry's command, was ordered to the Philadelphia Navy Yard, and sailed again in November for St. Domingo, the Secretary of the Navy, *then* not deeming it advisable to detain United States vessels of war in the Caribbean Sea during the hurricane and sickly season. Capt. Gerry was an experienced officer in navigating these waters, and was on much important duty in the Somers, which was a dispatch vessel. He knew the necessity of our squadron on the Home Station being ordered North at the season of the year, in southern latitudes, so dangerous to life and property, by yellow fever, in the one case, and hurricanes, in the other. Capt. Gerry concentrated in his character those rare and prominent elements which at once inspired confidence in the stranger, and won for him the universal esteem and respect of every community with which he was associated.

The Albany sailed from Charlestown Navy Yard, Massachusetts, Nov. 29th, 1852, under his command, and with as efficient, gallant, and respectable an association of officers and crew as ever sailed in the service of the United States. We place on honorable record their distinguished names, while their memories are embalmed in the hearts of their many thousand friends and fellow-countrymen :

Commander James T. Gerry.
Nicholas Fish Morris, Private Secretary to Commander.
William W. Bleecker, First Lieutenant.
Montgomery Hunt, Second Lieutenant.
John Quincy Adams, Third Lieutenant.
Henry Rogers, Fourth Lieutenant.
Robert Marr, Acting Master.
Stephen M'Creary, Surgeon.
Richard D. Conman, Assistant Surgeon.
Nixon White, Purser.
Bennet J. Riley, Midshipman.
William Jones, Boatswain.
William Craig, Gunner.
James Frazer, Sail-Maker.
Rowland Leach, Carpenter.
Belliger Scott, Master's Mate.
William J. Bond, do. do.
Dexter Brigham, do. do.

Being— 18 Officers,
23 Marines,
156 Seamen.

Total . . . 197 as by the return to the Navy Department.

The officers were connected with the most respectable and distinguished families in our country. Bleecker, the first-lieutenant, was from the old Bleecker family after whom a well known street in New York is called. Adams was the nephew of the last President of the United States of that name. Rodgers, son of Commodore John Rodgers, of the War of 1812. Hunt, a highly respectable family in the State of New York. Marr was a son-in-law of Commodore Lavallette. Riley, son of General Riley, also of the State of New York. The other three wardroom officers were equally respectable, and we believe from the South. The rest of the officers above named were considered equal to any of their grade in the service.

Lieut. Reed Werden, now attached to the National Observatory at Washington, D. C., also belonged to the Albany on her cruise to the Fishing Banks and back to New York; and in the subsequent cruise, until about the 6th of April, 1854, when, on account of ill health, he was detached from the ship at Havana. The elevated character he sustains, as an efficient officer, in connection with his great moral worth, is well known to the service and the country.

CHAPTER II.

WHEN last seen at Aspinwall, September 28th, 1854, the Albany was bound for New York, after being on active duty for twenty-two months, and having sailed, during this period, nearly forty thousand miles, believed to be the greatest amount of service ever performed, in so short a time, by any United States vessel, on record. The crew were in fine health, the discipline of the ship was perfect, and the yellow fever, then an epidemic abroad, had not, because of this, invaded the vessel in its whole term of service. Commodore Gregory supervised the fitting of the Albany in 1852 in a proper and satisfactory manner, and she needed but slight repairs until her return from the Fishing Banks on November 7th, 1853, where, in a cruise of thirty-four days from the time of leaving New York, the Albany had experienced a continued series of gales and hurricanes, to which she proved equal. She had then been at sea six months and a half of the eleven and a half months since leaving Charlestown. She next left New York, December 12th, 1853, for the Island of St. Thomas and the Caribbean Sea, and sailed last from Pensacola June 29th, 1854, having gone there for repairs. When the Albany left Pensacola, she had sailed thirty-four thousand miles. Her officers were considered, in all respects, among the highest in the service, and her crew equally so, in their vocation, being mostly young Americans. Such was the received opinion, to the last tidings of that ill-fated vessel. At Carthagena, this admiration of officers and crew was reported by distinguished persons, who saw them there in 1854. At Pensacola, on the arrival of the Albany, seventy-five men were sent on shore, at liberty, by Commander Gerry, for forty-eight hours. The Mayor and President of Board of Aldermen returned a complimentary notice of their conduct to the captain, when the other half were permitted, in like manner, to go ashore, thus manifesting the admirable discipline of the ship.

"The New York Herald" published notices from the merchants of San Juan and Greytown, commending the conduct of Captain Gerry, in business negotiations between them and our government. Similar ones were published at Aspinwall, and expressed at Turk's Island. And, at Laguria, not only did the merchants signify their approval of Captain Gerry's business arrangements, but the Secretary of the Navy addressed him a letter, February 2d, 1854, especially approving his action on that island.

At Havana, St. Thomas, and, indeed, *all* the ports entered by the Albany, marked attention was shown to Captain Gerry. The fact that he was a son of the illustrious Elbridge Gerry, with whose history the civilized world are familiar, at once gave prestige to his position, added to his own personal merit as an officer and a gentleman.

The following anecdote is related by an officer who was present at an interview which occurred between Sir Charles Edward Grey, late Governor-General of Jamaica, and Commander Gerry, on board the steamer Isabel, destined for Charleston. Having been informed, when on board the vessel, that Captain Gerry was a son of the immortal Elbridge Gerry, he immediately apologized for having, in a letter to him, written his name "*Geary*." "It was the fault," said the Governor-General, "of the English consul; for the character and services of your father to the whole human family are as well-known and appreciated in England as in the United States; and I am proud to find you, sir, his son, a credit to his great name!"

The Albany was the dispatch-ship of the Home Squadron, and was sent by Commander Newton to perform nearly all the business between our government and the ports she was ordered to visit. This was creditable to Gerry as an officer and negotiator.

The official documents at the Navy Department show an extraordinary amount of important duty performed by Captain Gerry, as commander of the Albany. And, in July, 1853, in a continuous cruise of seventy-four days, exposed to every peril, but seven had been spent in port! When in a sickly port, Captain Gerry usually went ashore *alone*, sending the boats back to the ship; and, by this prudence, prevented disease among officers and crew. During the whole term that the Albany was under command of Captain Gerry, there was no case of epidemic or yellow fever on board, while abroad, though much exposed to the latter disease in warm latitudes. Many of the officers and crew were often much worn down from too constant sea service.

The utmost deference was paid to religious duties on board, and, in the absence of a chaplain, Captain Gerry had service performed on the Sabbath, in the usual form of the Protestant Episcopal Church, in which he was a consistent and most exemplary communicant, when called to sunder the ties of earth to join the upper service of his Heavenly Master. It would be impracticable, in a work like this, to give that elaborate history of Captain James Thompson Gerry, that his character and services eminently deserve. But we are free to say, in brief, that no officer in the service ever bore a more irreproachable reputation for efficiency and devotion to duty, and for that high mental and moral culture which gives value to the officer, and dignity and worth to the man.

But one son of Elbridge Gerry now survives, and he his eldest, who bears his father's name.

Mr. Gerry is now a resident of New York city. His numerous friends bear testimony to his integrity and elevated moral worth, and to his honorable bearing as a gentleman ; and that he has, also, emulated the virtues of his father through life. And, if these give a claim to respect, he is not less entitled to it than the distinguished relatives who have preceded him.

The first-lieutenant of the Albany, William N. Bleecker, son of the late Alexander Bleecker, of New York city, was an officer eminently deserving of praise. His life had been one of danger and vicissitude. From his first cruise, in the "Delaware," under Commodore Downs, in 1828, to his last service in the Albany, under Commander Gerry, in 1854, he visited every part of the known world. He was active on Mediterranean, Pacific, Brazilian, African, and East India stations. He visited China, in the Brandywine, and, during the Mexican war, he participated in the capture of Alvarado, Tuspan, Tobasco, and other Mexican ports, in the flotilla commanded by Commodore Perry. He had been, also, the first officer of the United States steamer "Michigan," under command of Captain Oscar Bullus, whose daughter he left a widow in charge of his orphan child.

It is a singular fact that this prompt and efficient officer, who had spent the greater part of his naval service of twenty-seven years, upon arduous duty afloat, had made two previous cruises to the West Indies in the same ship in which he met his untimely end.

The last letters of Lieutenant Bleecker clearly forebode his fears, that the Albany could never survive the terrific gales, so frequent at that season, in the Caribbean Sea.

The letter of Lieutenant Adams, published in the newspapers, at the time her loss was surmised, expressed similar apprehensions, should they encounter a hurricane.

The faithful duties of Bleecker, in his country's service, will ever be cherished in the memory of those who survive him.

In that priceless cargo consigned to the ill-fated Albany, there was another brave though youthful spirit, who deserves more than an ordinary tribute from the author.

It was Nicholas Fish Morris, son of Richard Lewis Morris, M.D., of New York. His mother, a daughter of Colonel Nicholas Fish, an officer of the Revolution and aid-de-camp to Washington. Young Morris (whose portrait appears in this volume) was also a grandson of James Morris, of Morrisania, and great grandson of General Lewis Morris, of Morrisania, likewise of revolutionary celebrity, and one of the immortal signers of the Declaration of Independence; while, on his mother's side, he was a lineal descendant of Governor Petreus Stuyvesant, last of the illustrious line of Dutch Governors of New York.

With an ancestry so intimately interwoven with the history of their country, and bearing the name of a grandfather so distinguished in the American Revolution, it was not at all surprising that young Morris should evince an early aspiration for a military life. As his education progressed, a preference, however, was given for the Navy over the Army, and an application for admission into the Naval School at Annapolis was made in the summer of 1853. It resulted in success, and the papers were being executed when it was found he exceeded by a few months the requisite age, and this ardent and impulsive youth was obliged to relinquish the cherished idea of his mind.

Just about this period, the Albany returned from a cruise, under the command of Capt. Gerry, who tendered to young Morris the position of "Private Secretary to the Commander," which, in view of his recent disappointment as well as the prospective advantages it presented, was at once accepted.

In October 1853, the Albany sailed for the

Fishing Banks, and returned in five weeks, by which time the character and bearing of Morris had won for him the confidence and admiration, not only of Capt. Gerry, to whom he was a companion and friend, but of all the gallant officers of the ship and the entire crew.

There was a candor and frankness, a freedom from all compromise of principle, united with a manliness of deportment and a noble daring in action, which gave singular worth to this remarkable youth. Nicholas Fish Morris was indeed a model, which may with great propriety be presented, not only to the youth of America, but to the fathers and mothers of the nation! Does the reader ask why? We answer, because it was to the *united* action of his parents, their precepts and their example, that made deep, unchanging, and imperishable, the love of *right*, which his life so beautifully illustrated. How often does it occur, and how sincerely is it to be deplored, that the mother's influence is counteracted, negatived, by the example of the father! How many of the most promising geniuses of the land have thus dated their fatal mistakes! It was otherwise with Morris. And thus was he early led to bow before the altar of his God, and trust to the all-sufficiency of that Saviour his parents loved.

His correspondence bears testimony to his faithful and uninterrupted continuance in the discharge of his private as well as official duties abroad. And friends yet survive who saw him in strange lands, engaged in that greatest and most honorable of all services, doing reverence to his Heavenly Master, upon his bended knees.

An inherited love of country made this generous, disinterested, and ingenuous young American anxious to defend and vindicate our nationality abroad; and, in 1854, when the invasion of Cuba upon the rights of American citizens, imminently threatened war, as the only means of redress, this true and youthful patriot thus gave expression to his natural and national fervor: "I most heartily wish there may be war, that I may have a chance of dying with honor, perhaps, great honor, in my young days, for the glory of my country and the rights of her citizens!"

In making these few remarks of young Morris, we could wish that every youth in our country, who aspires to an honorable and virtuous fame, was familiar with his brief but beautiful career.

Engraved by J. C. Buttre from a Daguerreotype

Nicholas F. Morris.

THE CULPABILITY INVOLVED

IN THE

LOSS OF THE ALBANY.

CHAPTER I.

THE next question which presents itself, is, by whom or under what circumstances, did it become necessary to expose the Albany, with her precious cargo of upwards of two hundred souls, to those perilous seas, in which she was engulfed? In this question, not only are the relatives and friends of the worthy deceased interested, but the whole country, nay, humanity itself! The author feels, therefore, called in this connection, to enlighten the country upon the subject, and to expose the shameful, reckless manner in which these matters are managed by the department, placing the lives of the best citizens at the mercy and caprice of ignorant chief clerks, and weak officials.

And after a thorough and careful examination of all the documents and evidence the case furnishes, the author unhesitatingly declares it to be her conviction, that the blood of these unfortunate victims, the odium of their cruel fate, rests upon the heads of John C. Dobbin, Secretary of the Navy, and John Thomas Newton, who commanded the Home Squadron, as she will show.

In the fall of 1853, while the Albany was in the port of New York, public notice was given to officers and crew, by the Secretary of the Navy, through Commodore Newton, that the ship would return to New York early in the summer of the ensuing year. And it was under the supposed good faith of this official assurance, that no further duty would be imposed, to exceed the time specified by the Secretary of the Navy, through Newton, that these gallant and true men bade adieu to their cherished homes, their sorrowing families and friends, to engage in the honorable service to which they were called by their country.

In May, 1854, the main-mast of the Albany was condemned at the navy yard, Warrington, Florida, and the Secretary of the Navy was immediately apprised of the fact, by Commander

Gerry, pending a critical illness of Commodore Tatnall of that station. The Secretary ordered the repair to be made. But, after finding the lower masts of a first-class sloop, as ordered, altogether too small, it was done by taking the foremast of a second-class frigate! And hence, after mending and patching, one was found to answer the Albany's purpose, "at small expense!" After this patch on the Albany had caused about *seven* official letters, it was formally approved at the Department!

It is perfectly well known, that there were not mechanics enough in the navy yard at Warrington, to put extensive repairs on any ship, during the time the "Albany" was there.

On June 10th, 1854, the Secretary addressed Commodore Newton, and required him "*to direct the movements of the Albany and Columbia.*" And on the 17th of June, 1854, Mr. Dobbin tells Newton, by official letter, that one of the vessels of the Home Squadron, meaning his vessel, or that in command of Captain Gerry, must go to Turk's Island on public business. Then Newton, instead of going himself, exercised the very discretionary power vested in him by Secretary Dobbin, and immediately issued orders to Captain Gerry, to proceed there with the Albany!

Capt. Gerry then left Pensacola, fulfilled to the letter the instructions of Newton, and after dispatching the business for which he went to Turk's Island, joined Newton, as directed, at St. Domingo, under the confident expectation of proceeding at once to New York! But Newton had other service than that for these gallant officers and men, and to their great surprise, and in violation of all faith between the government and these two hundred American citizens, and in the very teeth of the department's assurance to these officers and crew before they sailed out of the port of New York, that they should return early in the summer of 1855, we find near its close, an official letter from Newton to Captain Gerry, dated at the Gulf of Samana, the 11th of August, 1855, ordering the Albany "to proceed direct to Laguira, thence to the Island of Curacoa, to Carthagena, and to Aspinwall." And "to take care of our flag upon the whole coast of Central America!" In this letter to Commander Gerry, Newton adds, and *mark it*, Americans, that "*as you have represented to me* that the 'Albany' IS

DEFECTIVE IN MANY PARTS, *and that* EXTENSIVE REPAIRS *will be required upon her before she can with safety take another cruise, you will return, after having performed the duty assigned you in this communication*, to the harbor of New York, and on your arrival there, report to the Department."

It was, at the time this order was given, too late for the Albany to have been in those seas. To this letter, we find a supplementary one from Newton to Capt Gerry, bearing same date (fearing he had not, we suppose, sufficiently endangered this rotten, unseaworthy vessel), in which the Albany is directed to *touch* at the island of St. Thomas, and hunt up some suspicious vessel, seen to be hovering near the island of Porto Rico, merely on the *supposition* that it was a piratical craft.

To these instructions of Newton to Captain Gerry, Secretary Dobbin responds, and declares to Newton, they "are approved!"

Yes, Americans, without the slightest regard to the *integrity* of their minds, these two men trifled with the lives of upwards of two hundred human souls, embracing much of the high-toned chivalry of the country, and by the most arbitrary and despotic action on their part, forced a vessel, *they knew* to be *defective*, in many parts, into tempestuous seas and hurricanes, by which she was destroyed, or perchance to engage in battle with a powerful adversary!

The order from the Navy Department for that cruise which has called the nation to mourn the loss of the Albany, was a perfect outrage, a scandalous duty to have imposed upon the Home Squadron, under any circumstances, at a season of the year when sickness prevailed in those ports, and where the gales and hurricanes endangered the most substantial frigate, much more a rotten, patched-up sloop-of-war, with twenty-two heavy guns on her decks!

So thought Newton, and therefore chose to sacrifice the "Albany," all crippled, as he acknowledged her to be, rather than take the risk in the Frigate Columbia, which was in fine order (needing no repairs), as it was his duty to have done, and as the orders from the Department required him to do. By the showing of the documents, Newton was ordered on this cruise, but he did not choose so to expose himself to danger! And, with the fact of the "Albany's" sad condition, he sent her whence she could never return!

What excuse does Newton offer, for his violation of duty? We answer, one as specious as it is most untrue! "I had intended," says this *Commodore*, "to go myself, but could not on account of shortness of provisions."

Reader, note this, that Newton had in his ship, the same relative quantity of provisions as was at that time in the Albany! And he ordered the Albany to proceed to St. Thomas for bread and provisions, which were obtained there without difficulty. Now, why did Newton take advantage of this miserable subterfuge in order to shirk danger and return home? Why not have gone himself for this bread and provision, and thus have removed the *only* excuse he pretended to offer?

One of the very first duties of a commodore is to know where provisions and supplies can be had, at every point of his station, and their cost. And as the town of Aspinwall was one to which a *mail* was sent twice a month, he could not have been ignorant of the fact, which Commander Gerry reported when he reached there, that provisions of all kinds were in abundance, at ordinary prices.

No provisions! mark this! every pound of food in the whole squadron was Newton's. And by sending his boats to the "Albany," he could have taken all her provisions had he chosen, and sent her to St. Thomas to be replenished, which was within three day's sail, and then sent her home to New York in good season. This it was Newton's duty to have done, as the crippled condition of the Albany rendered every precaution essential to save her from the hurricane season.

But some may ask, "Had not Dobbin and Newton the *right* to exercise this imperious authority over the Albany?" They would have had, under a different state of facts, if they had not *both* known of the Albany's unfitness for sea in hurricane season, as there is the most *unquestioned proof that they did!* Captain Gerry thought the ship safe for the summer weather, and expecting to return to New York from Turk's Island, he informed Newton, before sailing from Pensacola, that the ship was ready for sea, in all respects. But, when he got the order of August 11th, to extend his cruise from two and a half months to three months *longer*, thus carrying him into the hurricane season, and the tempestuous weather on the Atlantic coast, he deemed it his duty to represent to Newton that the ship was, in many parts, *defective*, and not safe, therefore, to be sent on such a cruise as Newton communicates in his dispatches. This warning Newton *entirely disregarded*, and sent the ship, notwithstanding this representation from Captain Gerry!

Like a gallant and disciplined officer, Gerry *obeyed* that fatal order! At this time, the ship had sailed about thirty-seven thousand miles, without going into dry dock for repairs! But, as though the above order might not, even then, detain the Albany long enough, we find *another* and a *subsequent* one, dated September 2d, 1854, from the Department to Newton, directing him, if practicable, to instruct Commander Gerry, after he completed the cruise along the coast of Central America, as just indicated, to enter the port of Portsmouth, N. H., unless the cruise was protracted beyond the last of October! All this, bear in memory, was with Dobbin's full knowledge, that the ship was not safe, on account of being "defective in many parts." This order, had it been carried into effect, might have subjected the ship to the boisterous weather of November, that any well-informed landsman would know, must endanger a vessel, however staunch, to severe trial on our coast. All this should teach the American people how important it is to select men of *fitness* for the high and responsible duties of administering our national government; not men devoid of all qualifications, save that of being party politicians; while the nation mourns for the want of practical, efficient men; men, who are capable of investigating for themselves the business of their respective departments, instead of confiding it to the chief clerks who are, *de facto*, the administrators of our national affairs.

CHAPTER II.

WHEN the Albany left Pensacola, Commodore Tatnall, at that station, placed a valuable service of silver on board of her, from the generally received understanding that the ship was bound to New York, after having dispatched official business at Turk's Island; and to arrive in the following July or August, which he believed would be earlier than he could carry it himself. During the whole period the Albany was attached to the Home Squadron, she must have sailed about forty thousand miles, while the Columbia could not have exceeded ten or twelve thousand miles! The rest of the time Newton was in *port!*

When it is remembered that Elbridge Gerry was the first American who suggested a navy for this country, and, in the Legislature of Massachusetts, proposed that letters of *marque* should be issued by our government to the merchant vessels for their protection, it does seem deplorable that his own son should have lost his life while in the active discharge of his duties to that service, by the mal-administration of an incompetent Secretary and Commodore! A Secretary who left the valuable lives of officers and crew, who looked to him for protection in the discretion of his orders, to the dictation of an irresponsible chief clerk in the department. This clerk calls on the Secretary to sign *his* orders!

While Mr. Jefferson was most zealously opposing the institution of our navy, it is well known that Mr. Gerry was strenuously engaged in advocating its formation.

In 1854, Newton, when at Pensacola, was ordered to sail to San Juan in the Columbia, when he wrote to the Department that it was as much as the lives of officers and crew were worth to go there, as it was so sickly. He was, for this evidence of timidity in the performance of the duty assigned him, about to be detached from command of the squadron, when he was, most fortunately for himself, taken ill with some dangerous disease, at Pensacola, a casualty he so much feared might befall him if he proceeded to San Juan. Thus sick, he was brought home to New York, in the Albany, under command of Captain Gerry, and, thereby, his life was saved! Was it for this act of kindness towards Newton that Gerry afterwards was made a victim to his unscrupulous selfishness? Was the obligation, imposed by kindness, of such a nature as to become an offense which Newton could not forgive?

In 1854, Newton had over seventy cases of yellow fever aboard the Columbia, and in the succeeding year '55, when he returned from another visit to Saint Thomas, which port he was obliged to leave in consequence of the yellow fever being on board again, he had sixty cases of this malignant disease on arriving at Norfolk, where he was relieved from his command. And in this the whole country may rejoice that the further loss of human life under his instrumentality has, for a time, been arrested.

The *antecedents* of Newton may now, with much propriety, be investigated, inasmuch as, with all his long and black catalogue of misdemeanors, he has been one of the favored of the Secretary of the Navy and that official's "navy retiring board." About the year 1820, Newton was sent to Norfolk in a chartered vessel, with a draft of men under his charge. The vessel got aground at the mouth of the Potomac, in the Chesapeake Bay, and a gale coming on, he ordered a boat, under the plea of obtaining *assistance*, to set him on shore. He proceeded to New York directly, and the vessel and all on board were left to their fate and perished!

Between the years 1825 and 1830 Newton was in command of a small brig, and while cruising off the Havana, with an open barge in company, commanded by a son of the present venerable Consul of the United States at Jamaica, West Indies, a sudden norther arose about nightfall. Instead of taking the officers and men on board his own vessel, and abandoning this miserable craft, he cut the ropes by which she was in tow, and all hands in her that fearful night went to the bottom! Thus, either from entire nautical ignorance, or from a reckless disregard for the fate of others, fifteen or twenty lives were destroyed at a blow!

We are not informed that any investigation of the circumstances of this case ever took place.

Subsequently, about 1830, John Thomas Newton became a commander or master commandant. He was put in command of the United States steamer Fulton, being the *first* United States steamer built by that name.

She was employed as a receiving vessel at the United States Navy Yard, New York. Either by accident, caused by drunkenness of the gunner, or by some negligence, her magazine was fired, and the ship blown up. Many officers and men perished by the explosion ; at least seventy lives were reported to have been lost!

Among these there was a promising officer by the name of Breckenridge. Lieut. Platt nearly lost his sight. And a number of the survivors were maimed for life.

But amidst this frightful havoc Newton survived, and we next find him in command of a sloop-of-war! And in 1840 he was put upon duty in the steamer Fulton, the second of that name! And soon she became notorious by the bursting of a gun on board, which killed and maimed several men! He next commanded the steam frigate Missouri, the finest ship, at that time, in the Navy, being entirely new and well fitted for sea. Before leaving the waters of the East River, a man was lost from her deck by allowing the cable to slip through the stoppers, as he was in the act of hooking the "cat-block." The anchor went down, of course, and carried this victim with it! A few days after this the Missouri, in ascending the Potomac, was run ashore; and in taking out her anchor, for the purpose of hauling her off, by some mismanagement, it slipped, and carried both boats in which the anchor was placed, with their crews, to the bottom. In this disaster a lieutenant and seventeen men perished!

Following the brief career of this ill-fated vessel, under Newton's command, we find her again ashore on the south Nantucket shoal! Shortly after these three serious and fatal troubles of the Missouri, Newton left the United States with her for Alexandria, in Egypt, for the purpose of landing Mr. Cushing, who was on his way, as commissioner, to China. And, to close Newton's brilliant command in this ship, she took fire while at Gibraltar, and so rapid was her destruction, that she soon disappeared in a blaze!

For *this* act of carelessness Newton was convicted, and a nominal punishment passed upon him; but even a portion of that was said afterwards to have been remitted.

From the data we have given, it is not an over-estimate to say that Newton, by his recklessness, has caused the loss of about three hundred and twenty lives in the navy—equal to all the "killed" in action on the American side, in the naval war with Great Britain!—while, in a pecuniary view, he has occasioned destruction of property to the government of the United States of between one and two millions of dollars!

We wish particularly now to direct the reader's attention to the conduct of Mr. Dobbin, the present Secretary of the Navy, in connection with Newton's conduct subsequent to the loss of the Albany.

It did not seem to have occurred to the *sympathising* Secretary to institute a public scrutiny into Newton's action in directing the fatal cruise of that ship; nor even a private one, that we have heard, until, for some reason that does not manifest itself, the Department drew forth the following letter from Newton, dated June 20th, 1855, long after the publication of the documents which were elicited by a call from the U. S. Senate.

The Secretary, on the 4th of June, 1855, made inquiry of Newton for "a copy of the communication written to him, Newton, by Commander Gerry." That was eight months after the ship was missing. Mr. Dobbin, it appears, was under the impression that no written "communication" was made; but it really had not been of sufficient consequence in his mind to make this investigation before.

To this letter Newton said in reply: "I have to state, the communication referred to was made to me during a *conversation* with that officer, on board the Columbia, while at Samana Bay, in August last. He observed to me that he thought the "Albany" would require extensive repairs before she returned from the North again to rejoin her station in the West Indies for another cruise."

Americans, which statement will you take from Newton as correct—that written at Samana, the 11th of August, the day he gave the order, or that written from Staten Island, New York, ten months later, giving an entirely different version of the matter? At Samana he stated to the department that the "'Albany' was defective in many parts, and required extensive repairs, and was not safe to take another cruise." In the face of this report he orders her on a voyage that might detain her from three to four months. But when she was lost, that statement did not answer the desperate state of the Commodore's position. Hence we see the Staten Island letter to be a flat denial of the Samana letter.

We know that Captain Gerry did remonstrate against taking that extended cruise around Central America. It was then that he urged the necessity of proceeding direct to New York; and the very remark Newton ascribes to Gerry, in his Staten Island letter, proves that he did.

The attempt to circulate the idea which is believed to have been started from the Department, that Gerry could wish under any such circumstances to have extended his cruise, is now refuted by Newton's own language.

But suppose, for the sake of argument, that Captain Gerry did request the Secretary of the Navy to keep the ship out through the whole year, had the Secretary and Newton the *right* to risk the lives of those on board, and jeopardize the public property, merely to oblige Captain Gerry? It is too absurd a proposition to be entertained for a moment.

In concluding this very remarkable Staten Island letter, Newton says: "I enclose herewith a copy of a letter from Commander Gerry, dated Pensacola, June 15th, 1854, which the Department may wish to have. It will be recollected that the Albany underwent repairs at that station, and Commander Gerry reports her being in all respects ready for sea, and provisioned for three months and a half."

This was stated by Newton on this occasion, to leave the impression upon the public mind that she was safe for any voyage, however long. Now it is well known that in the usual manner of issuing an order to proceed on *any* cruise, these words are usually employed: "When you are in all respects ready for sea, etc., you will proceed to execute, etc." It matters not what may be the condition of the ship, the response is given as we quote above, in all cases, and did not apply to the condition of the Albany, as ready for a cruise of any indefinite length. Beside, this was written two months before the order was given at Samana, and the Albany could not then have had but six weeks' provisions—the same relative quantity Newton had, by his own showing!

CHAPTER III.

NEWTON wrote to the department, that "the Albany was, in many respects, defective," on the same day and in the same letter that informed the Department he had ordered her on this unjustifiable cruise!

The letter of Gerry, in the official documents from Pensacola, to which we have alluded, does not express what Newton attempts to convey by it; for these same documents report that *both* masts were then defective, but only one was taken out and the other left in. Why? Because it was supposed that she would return in smooth summer weather to New York, as formal notice to that effect had been given by the department. It was Newton's duty at Samana to have had the ship at once surveyed after the information communicated by Gerry, before sending her on a dangerous survey.

This is a significant fact, which shows again that the nation needs men who practically do their duty in office. Mr. Dobbin, on being shown the official document which stated the Albany was defective, and not fit for the cruise, acknowledged to a *Senator** that *he had not noticed it before, although, be it remembered, he had already officially approved the very order!* When the senator apprised him, he expressed great astonishment, and declared he never knew the fact before, alleging in extenuation that the papers were rarely seen, as they were, when received, filed away in the office. And the subsequent order, dated in September, was given to keep the ship out still longer, by ordering her to Portsmouth, New Hampshire. The truth is, Mr. Dobbin had his line of action in this matter overruled by the same influence that selected and controlled the "Navy Retiring Board." To these conspirators Newton seemed in all respects a marvellously proper man; so the Secretary must, of course, favor him in his unofficerlike and inhuman conduct towards the Albany, and not only accepted his flimsy and self-contradictory letter of explanation, but allowed his retention on the *active* list of the Navy by that Board, who disrated or

---

* Hon. Hamilton Fish, of New York, is the senator to whom we refer.

dropped from it men of the highest efficiency to duty, and against whom no charges are to be found in the Department. The conduct of Mr. Dobbin is even more reprehensible in the case of Newton than in that of Stribling, whose total neglect of his duties on board the San Jacinto was not only overlooked, but actually rewarded by a seat in the "Navy Retiring Board." And Newton was appointed to the command of a naval station soon after he was relieved from the Columbia—thus rewarding him in a similar manner to Stribling.

THE AMERICAN NAVY.

CHAPTER I.

THE honor of the country is borne by its good men;—they who dishonor these dishonor their country.

The Navy of the United States, as a question of international policy, was never so important to the American people as now; and it is lamentable to have seen the President of the United States strike a blow at this great arm of the public service, and, so far as he could, destroy the interest, the glory, and the moral strength, of the United States, in every ocean and clime.

For years, foreign governments have been steadily increasing their navies, and menacing Americans who have sought to maintain the dignity of their nation abroad. Nothing but this superior naval strength induced England to defy the proclamation of the Monroe doctrine by this government, and establish the colony of the Bay Islands, which has since involved the United States in troublesome negotiations. But for this, Spain would never have attempted her outrages upon American steamers, nor France have treated our protest against her occupancy of Sonora with contempt.

Our territory on the Pacific has since made the navy still more important to our commerce, in order to protect the shipping of our enterprising men, and give a new impulse to trade upon that coast. In the event of war, it is upon the navy alone we could rely to scour our seas, and prevent a foreign fleet from penetrating the rivers and harbors on our coast.

The law which passed at the end of the session of Congress in 1855, in reference to the navy, was not only ex post facto, but a fraud upon legislation and the American policy. Senators have admitted that they knew nothing about it. If a few days had been given to its proper consideration, the navy would not now be bereft of its chivalry and honor, the families of gallant men would not now be reduced to penury, while the government would have been saved the thousands of dollars expended in the discussion of the outrage, and devising methods of reparation. More money will be thus expended, before this evil is rectified, than would have paid the pitiful stipend of these two hundred and one officers the next twenty years.

The law which passed Congress, Americans, to reörganize the navy, on the 28th of February, 1855, had no more to do with our constitution than it had with the articles of our old Confederation. Does the sacred bond and covenant of our freedom allow a man to be punished prospectively for his inefficiency in times past? Can it prevent a man from pursuing any honest calling, by cutting down his present means of support, and yet holding on to the right of his personal services? It cannot. But, in the very face of this, this act, which the imbecility of the President and Secretary of the Navy has executed, does render an officer *furloughed* liable, at any moment, to be summoned on government duty, and oblige him to forfeit any other interest or engagement, by which he may be maintaining a helpless family.

The law is also unjust in not extending to the

board of fifteen, the *surgeons*, *pursers*, and *chaplains*, the same provisions it applies to other officers. Why were these classes privileged, and exempted from the same rigor as others? — these men, who even at sea lead a life of ease and idleness, while those who are subjected to all the peril of active sea service are made to forfeit their places?

Americans, if you wish to know the iniquity of this law, turn to the Navy Register! You will there find pursers credited with but seven years and nine months' sea service, who have been forty-one years and nine months in the navy, and receiving all the time their eighteen hundred dollars from the government. Is this right, is it honest, Americans?

There are surgeons, too, who have been but three years and six months in the service, out of a period of forty-six years and eight months, receiving their eighteen hundred dollars! Chaplains, waiting orders, who have performed religious services at sea but two years and four months, and been receiving from the government a thousand dollars, annually, for twenty-six years and three months!

The law, too, set out to reform the navy;— now

look at its execution in that view! It has made ninety-nine captains, one hundred and thirty commanders, and three hundred and ninety lieutenants! And, out of this number, the government had sent to sea on the first of the present year but fourteen captains (including commanders), nineteen commanders, and one hundred and fifteen lieutenants! All this is the result of having an incompetent Secretary of the Navy, who allowed the board of "fifteen" all the latitude they wanted. They dictated to him, and he, Mr. Dobbin, dictated to the President, who issued his rescript confirming their corrupt action towards American men. Our foreign stations are now all disgraced by the want of an efficient navy to represent our nationality abroad, while the expenses of the nation are increased to support a pack of idlers.

There was no need of any more legislation whatever, for what this law of February 28th, 1855, meant ostensibly to do. The Secretary of the Navy had the power *before* to *furlough;* and there are, at least, three instances on the register, to show that right had been exercised, and these men thus put out of the pale of promotion. The President, too, if he chose, could then have renominated those officers for promotion, or continued to discredit them, as he pleased. And the whole proceeding in reference to the late Navy Retiring Board has been a sham affair, from beginning to end; the product of base personal malignity, on the part of certain officers of the navy, aided by the efforts of weak but high government officials. The facts, in this connection, have the authenticity of the records from the navy department of the government, and are submitted to the consideration of the American people, who are eminently able to make their own comments.

In the first place, the Secretary of the Navy knew that the names of the victims were marked upon the register, in his office, before those who constituted that board were known to the people; and he informed Capt. Smith, one of the "retired," that he knew the reason why every man was dishonored. Weeks before the board assembled, Commodore Skinner found a register with similar marks in his office; they were seen in other places where these clubs to dishonor American officers congregated.

Dupont, Shubrick, Magruder, Pendergrast,

Jenkins, and others, were the leading actors in this business. Mr. Mallory, the bill-framer, in consultation with Dupont, had designated one hundred officers on the register for this fate, *before the passage of the law*, ninety-nine of whom are now victims. Fifty-seven of the officers thus dismissed from the service of their country were afloat upon duty at the time, by order of the Secretary of the Navy; some of whom were, at the very moment, in the performance of deeds of bravery under the American flag, which have added new lustre to our national glory. Lieut Rolando here furnishes a distinguished illustration. He volunteered to rescue the perishing crew of a Chinese junk, when all others feared to offer assistance; and not only saved five hundred and thirty out of six hundred from instant death, but, in the two successive piratical fights, won, for his courage and noble daring, such admiration from European governments as should send a thrill of pleasure through the heart of every true American.

The prohibition of the increase in the navy, by this law, shows clearly that neither the author nor the executioners knew what they were about. Congress never intended to interfere with the rights nor to injure the reputations of upwards of two hundred American citizens, no more than it meant to make three hundred promotions in the service, which has actually been done. Of the thirty-five new captains made by this board, three only are at sea, and but six on shore duty; leaving the balance to enjoy their new dignity in idleness. There is, then, but one more captain at sea to-day than there was a year ago; while there are three commanders less than there were at that time; so that thirty-six of this grade are also idle.

In the selection made by the Secretary of the Navy, of captains for important posts, he has, in every instance of which we have heard, passed over the absolute claims of the *efficient* captains, and named, for important sea and shore duties, the *new* captains or commanders made by the board, whose commissions as such were not then even confirmed.

The withdrawal of so many gallant officers from the active service, to promote young and inexperienced men, has left the navy, at this moment, with but sixteen midshipmen in all parts of the world. There are, therefore, twenty-six American ships now commissioned in the service, without a single officer of this rank upon their decks; and, while the law authorizes sixty masters in the navy, there are but eighteen of these, because none can be made so until after they have become passed midshipmen.

President Pierce and Mr. Secretary Dobbin thought the appointment of upwards of two hundred new midshipmen was at stake when the inquisition was engaged in the decapitation of officers; but a clause, in defiance of the common treachery, was discovered in the bill, which, to the eternal honor and wise forethought of the author, prevented the fruit, which they all thought so ripe, from being plucked, even to save the nomination, or preserve the succession.

We see now that by the act of the administration they have absolutely left the navy without a captain whom *they* deem qualified for the head of a bureau. In this dilemma, Ingraham, of Koszta memory, was brought on to the seat of government for that purpose, when the Senate refused to appoint a man to a captain's place who had never been commissioned. But, in spite of the Senate "tabling" him, he was kept there *by the Secretary*, while Capt. Smith, a "retired" officer, was of necessity at the head of two bureaus at the time.

Thus we discover that the navy has been so bereft of its original strength as to be without a qualified captain to fill the post, not excepting the notable Shubrick, respecting whom, as president of the immortal "Council of Fifteen," it is proper, Americans, you should know more.

He, with McCauley, also a member of the board, was declared guilty of insubordination by the officers of the Mediterranean squadron, in 1817, who memorialized Commodore Chauncey to cause their removal from the service. Commanders Crane, Creighton, Rogers, Gamble, and Nicholson, signed this memorial; and it stands without mutilation still upon the records of the department. They state that Shubrick and McCauley had incited contempt for the service and discipline of the navy, its reputation, order, and good government; that they held secret meetings to create disaffection, and went so far as to *threaten* Congress that if their imaginary grievances were not redressed by that tribunal, they would resort to *arms* for their own protection! — that no reliance, for these reasons, could be placed upon the fidelity of Shubrick and McCauley, in the service of their country, while they had forfeited all claim to their confidence, and endangered, by their example, the vessels intrusted to their charge.

After the war closed with England, in 1814, it was decided to place an American squadron in the sight of Europe. This squadron was sent, properly equipped, to the Mediterranean, under the command of Commodore Chauncey, eminent as a disciplinarian. Shubrick and McCauley were then attached to the ship of Capt. Oliver Perry, of that squadron; who, ambitious of having it perfect in all its appointments, exercised also increased discipline among the lieutenants and other subordinates. Heath, a man belonging to the marine corps, was among these; and, in a braggadocio spirit, showed resentment for himself and associates, by disrespectful and insubordinate language to Capt. Perry, in his cabin, who, high-toned and high-spirited, knocked the marine officer down, and afterwards confined him. He soon saw, however, that he had committed a military offence, and magnanimously offered, through a friend, to make reparation by an apology to Heath.

The terms proposed in this apology by Heath and his comrades were not honorable; and Capt. Perry, waiving his rank, consented to receive his proposition to fight him. Heath backed out. Shubrick and McCauley were the instigators of Heath.

When the squadron returned to the United States, Capt. Perry stated all the circumstances to the President, Secretary of the Navy, and Commodores Rogers, Decatur, and Porter, and offered to submit to trial, or any other punishment they might see fit to inflict. The President and Secretary submitted the matter to Commodore Porter, who, in view of Capt. Perry's honorable action in the premises, decided it settled, and advised that Shubrick, McCauley, and other officers of the squadron, who were guilty of this insubordination, be reprimanded; which was done, by Commodore Chauncey.

Hence we see the provocation for the insubordinate conduct of Shubrick and McCauley, and which was so outrageous as to oblige the distinguished officers of the squadron to ask for their dismissal from the service. This board have dropped from the navy Capt. John Chauncey, the son of the commodore, and laid aside the sons of Commodores Perry and Porter, — a singular coincidence, and worthy of comment.

But this is not the only instance in which Shubrick has shown that no cheerful submission engaged his affections to the government. In 1847, he betrayed the same spirit at the expense of his patriotism. He was ordered to the Pacific squadron by the Secretary of the Navy, to be under the command of Biddle, on joining him at that station. Two months after reaching Mexico, he asked leave to return to the United States, before Biddle had even received the information from the department. This was at an important crisis in the war, and we needed more material and power to meet the enemy than could then be concentrated ; yet he not only insisted that the Columbus was not needed, but actually directed all his influence to prevent the Saratoga from uniting with the squadron ; and in sight of the enemy, in time of war, commanding a gallant and well-manned squadron, was anxious to desert the national flag and return home, at a moment of doubt and peril in his country's history. This was not enough. He demanded that a frigate of the squadron should have the distinguished honor of shipping him back to the United States. The reason was, as he confessed, that the Secretary of the Navy had damped his ardor by disappointment, and had acted in an uncandid manner. Hence, to gratify his personal revenge, he was ready to sacrifice his country's glory.

Was this the conduct for a military man? Was this the conduct of a servant of that government which had constituted the Secretary his superior in authority? In the Brazilian squadron, 28th Oct., 1846, Shubrick also acted in violation of the Secretary's orders, by writing a jesuitical letter to the commander of that station, which induced him to send the Saratoga, bound to the Pacific under government orders, back to Norfolk for repairs, although officers stood ready to take her to that destination.

He is afterwards found claiming fresh laurels on the Pacific, in the taking of Mazatlan and Guaymas. The latter was taken by Capt. Lavalette, and not even by orders of Shubrick; while he represented Mazatlan as taken by superior force. Now, it is well known, that Lieut. Halleck and two American men took it without resistance, and raised our stars and stripes; and when ninety men did attempt, under Lieut. Selden, to march into the interior, the most of Shubrick's men ran at the first fire of the enemy, except one who was shot. Selden was wounded, and seventeen men killed, before the forces from Shubrick's ship, the Independence, were rallied by their officers, and came back. Selden is now a victim of the board. Heywood distinguished himself, with his gallant band of modern *Sanduskys*, at San José, and won a niche in the temple of fame equal to Croghan and Stevens, who, when all others had fallen by his side, stood firm to the guns. He is broken by this hero of peace, Shubrick, and his brothers, Stanley, Lewis, &c. &c., share no better fate. Why? Because they fought the enemy, in spite of Shubrick's non-resistance!

CHAPTER II.

Now, remembering that Shubrick is the man who has spent thirty-two years of his life in land activity, we proceed to his confederate in the board, Stribling. He has written a letter recently in laudation of himself, in which he has committed robbery upon the dead. He stated that he commanded the barges "Mosquito" and "Gallinipper," in the West Indies, in 1823; that he attacked and captured the "Catalina," under command of the famous Diaboleto, whom he killed with his own hand, thereby ending the piratical war.

Now, Stribling had no more to do with that engagement than he had with the discovery of America. It was the brave achievement of Lieut. Wm. H. Watson, who, with but twenty-six men, effected almost the total destruction of a crew of seventy or eighty, without the loss of a single American. This gallant act is modestly set forth in his despatches to Commodore Porter, who commends them to the department, and asks for Watson's promotion in the service.

Stribling, in the previous April, did take a small schooner Pilot, in which his official report stated that one man was *found* dead, and that several were supposed to be wounded; but he did not think it prudent to pursue them. He had, too, double their number of men; but he spoke with some horror of their amount of deadly weapons, especially of a "double fortified six-pounder,"— quite an anomaly in modern warfare.

And now, when Watson's nephew writes to Capt. Stribling, in defence of his uncle's reputation, Stribling replies that he only wrote from memory. A remarkably defective organ, surely, and should not, therefore, have been relied upon for data; particularly when it could have been so easily refreshed by the records at hand. It will take more credulity than Americans possess to convince them that memory had anything to do with the matter.

This is the same gentleman who, instead of having the San Jacinto in readiness to repel the enemy in the West India seas, in 1855, when she was sent to Cuba to protect the American flag, brought her back to New York in a worse condition than any ship ever before in the service of the government.

Dupont, like Stribling and Shubrick, has also elaborated his glory on paper. He states that he killed many hardy Mexicans in California, in the battle of San José, the only *warlike* engagement in which he ever participated in his life! But Lieut. Heywood, who came to his assistance and rescued him, says not one was killed. Lieut. Heywood was left in Southern California by Shubrick, with but eighteen or twenty men, without the means of subsistence, and surrounded by the enemy, without the possibility of succor within a hundred miles. But for a whaling-ship, he and his brave comrade Stevens would have perished from famine. Stevens, whose gallant conduct has had so much eulogy, has been dropped from the service.

Dupont, Godon, Pendegrast and Missroon, were the four of the board who had been long styled "mutineers" in the navy. When the Secretary of the Navy sent them back to the Mediterranean squadron, and Commodore Hull had, by his orders, reprimanded them for their bad conduct, he was afterwards obliged to write to Dupont and his confederates, Godon, Pendegrast, and Missroon, that one of three things he should do: either to dismantle the ship and shut her up in a Spanish port until lieutenants could be procured from the United States fit to restore her to her position; to take them to sea, with all their disrespect, discontent, and disaffection, and trust to better things; or, to make then such changes as his means would allow. "Who can go into battle," said he, "with confidence, surrounded by disaffected officers? Who, of those ordered to the ship as her sea-lieutenants, can I confide in?"

On the 21st of March, 1841, Commodore Hu wrote to the Secretary of the Navy that "Dupont was the leader of the difficulty on the Ohio; and that the pernicious influence he exercised had effected more serious injury to the service than he could ever repair." Commodore Hull specified acts, made definite charges of the official misconduct of these four men; and, to the close of his life, he expressed regret that they were ever returned to the Mediterranean, when they merited the severest punishment known to the service.

Dupont was the author of that remarkable article which appeared in the *National Intelligencer* on the 21st of May, 1855, and foreshadowed the action of himself and comrades, in the following June. Mr. Seaton, the respected editor, is sufficient authority for this fact. Commodore Skinner, on ascertaining from him that Dupont had asked its publication, carried it to the office, and was responsible for its sentiments, informed the Secretary of the Navy, without delay; and told him that in that article Dupont had insulted every captain in the navy. The Secretary, instead of doing his duty, as an upright officer would have done, and keeping Dupont out of the board, to which place he had already assigned him, kept him in it, with this evidence, in all its baseness, right before him. There is every reason to believe, as we do, that the Secretary had seen the article before it was printed.

Dupont acted, in defiance of authority, under Captain, now Commodore Smith, of the navy; and, according to the Secretary, was one of the "cabal" in this ship, to create disaffection and dissatisfaction at the accommodations assigned him by orders of the department. And *he* indignantly rejected other apartments when tendered to him through Capt. Smith, who says, in his official letter to

Hull, "the true military course for me would have been to have *compelled* him," &c.

From the time of the difficulty in the Mediterranean squadron, under Hull, Dupont and his associates have zealously labored for the passage of just such a law by Congress as was obtained at the last session.

No one of the four mutineers, Godon, Dupont, Missroon, or Pendegrast, of Hull's ship, could have been induced to have entered that board *alone;* they had not the individual courage to carry out the plan they had devised. It required the *collective* courage of all four to support each other in their dark actings. As Dupont said in his article on the 21st of May, "the sharper *appetites of juniors whose* INTEREST *would coincide with their duty.*"

Not long since, a board composed of Commodores Morris, Shubrick, Skinner, and Dupont, were constituted to prepare a code for the better government of the navy. Dupont seems to have appropriated the whole of that duty pretty much to himself, according to the confessions of his associates. The work was referred to the Attorney General, by the Secretary of the Navy, for his legal opinion ; and he decided it "null and void," having transcended its rightful jurisdiction. This, too, after a cost of many thousand dollars to the government.

The thirty-fifth regulation of this code deserves comment, from the fact that it had singular significance upon the council of "fifteen." It forbade the court to receive evidence of the previous good character and former services of the accused in mitigation of the punishment to be awarded, while it allowed evidence of previous *bad* character to be adduced. The board acted on this principle : it received and entertained every accusation, and admitted no evidence, however abundant, in defence of the accused. It ransacked the shelves of the department for musty old documents, from which they hoped to find charges against those they had *already* condemned ; and, according to Shubrick's statement, they made *free* use of these. They used its archives to abuse the government. When the country loses its true men, what else is there to save?

Hence, Dupont's system, after being pronounced in derogation of the powers of Congress, still made shining marks for its full efficacy in the operations of the council of fifteen. During the cruise of the Delaware, commanded by Commodore Hull, Lieut. Boyle was attached, with Dupont, Barron, and Godon. At midnight, when Boyle retired from the watch, Dupont took her deck. The foreyard and all her sails were soon carried away. Boyle was called, and found Dupont agitated and confused. He put the ship in trim, and she went on her cruising-ground. Here were three members of the board present; but Boyle alone proved himself an officer. This efficient man is now laid aside, a victim of the very men who had proved themselves incompetent in the service.

Some time after, Dupont was placed in command of the "Perry," for the East India squadron. He reported himself sick, on reaching Rio de Janeiro, of a chronic disease, and came home. Lieut. Ringold, also, once suffered from disease; and, although he had recovered, in the opinion of medical men, it was, in Dupont's judgment, a valid reason for putting him upon the shelf.

The gravest charges are on file in the department against Pendegrast, preferred by Lieut. May, February 13th, 1854. He complains of the inefficiency of Pendegrast in every particular. That at the very moment when the difficulties growing out of our affairs with Cuba rendered the Saranac liable to a naval engagement, she was wholly unfitted for fighting. Her guns even had not been exercised but once in six months; and they never mustered at fire stations, one single time, until the officers of the ship had been alarmed by fire, seven months after sailing. And, with this unprecedented and culpable neglect, being indifferent to the condition and efficiency of the ship, he sailed from Pensacola to San Juan de Nicaragua, to investigate the difficulty with the Prometheus, which was fortunately settled without an exposure of the ship's inefficiency.

Pendegrast has never been tried upon the charges, and they stand on the record disproved. Lieut. May is an officer of character and reputation, and is retained on the active list.

With these facts before him, the Secretary of the Navy, instead of acting under a high sense of official responsibility, and bringing Pendegrast to trial, and punishing him, if the facts were sustained, saw fit, with all the guilt upon him, to give him a seat in the "Navy Retiring Board," while officers have been dismissed or disrated in the navy, who have received swords and medals as the grateful appreciation of Congress for their fidelity and zeal in the service of the country.

Misroon, also a member of the inquisitorial council, has made misstatements under oath, before the naval committee, in reference to Lieut. Bartlett; and, with the complicity of Dupont, this valuable officer has been degraded in the service. Lieut. Bartlett, who had been detailed for active duty at the time of this infliction, was the first to introduce the great temperance reform in the navy, and was covered with eulogium for efficiency in duty by every distinguished official of the government with whom he has been connected.

CHAPTER III.

And now with what different emotions can we, Americans, recur to the name of Commodore Perry, though he is found among the list of that board of "fifteen"! There is a moral sublimity in the defiant and manly manner with which he has, in the frankness and candor becoming a gallant officer of the navy, disclaimed to other officers, both in and out of the navy, all participation or sympathy with the proceedings. "I wash my hands forever of the conduct, proceedings, and action, of the Navy Retiring Board," was the language of Commodore Perry to a prominent officer of the navy. Perry's achievements in the Mexican war, which rivalled those of his distinguished brother on Lake Erie, command our praise; his Japan Expedition, in which he effected a treaty with that nation, whose ports, for more than a century, had been sealed to all but the Chinese and Dutch, commands our praise; but the moral and physical bravery which he has displayed on this occasion challenges the gratitude, as well as admiration, of all honorable men and women; and the press everywhere commends the magnanimity, while the people, appreciating his merit, gladly take him out of this inquisitorial council, to reserve him for higher honors at their own hands.

Commodore Perry's own son was put out of the navy by that board. Since its action became history, it is astonishing to learn how its members threaten and defy officers to breathe suspicion against its exactions, lest they who are laid aside be dropped altogether. And Shubrick, we learn from reliable authority, wrote to Commodore Perry to know whether he had not severely censured the board. Perry replied very briefly as to his question, but denied the right of the hero of Mazatlan, Guaymas, and Craney Island, to inquire into his private conversation with gentlemen. Biddle, too, Perry's junior, the hater of science and learning, as his letter to Lieut. Maury shows, writes to the same import as Shubrick, when Commodore Perry despatches that gentleman by saying he wished no further correspondence with him. And the subsequent *silence* of Mr. Slidell, the relative of Commodore Perry, after he came to New York and conversed with Perry, furnishes the true version of the case in the United States Senate.

We are told that dismissed and disrated officers are not suitable to represent their own cases. That men, whose reputation and honor have been deeply wounded, deprived of their living, and prevented at the same time from embarking in any other pursuit, are not to be believed. Americans, we all know very well that such doctrine as this is political heresy of the vilest character. It is anti-American, anti-republican, and only fit to emanate from an emperor or autocrat.

These men, free from the obligations of oaths or conscience, have, under the direction and connivance of the Secretary of the Navy, tried their superiors, and exercised upon them their hate or their love, irresponsible to law, and in violation of the constitution. The President acted as they willed and directed. He endorsed the action of that board with as much zest as he did the contemptible action of Hollins upon the people of Greytown. And the redress that can be had from him you can very well decide. Never before have the rights of our citizens been so hazarded by public men, who indubitably proved that they were not to be trusted.

The *family* relation that board sustained was another odious influence in its clumsy manœuvring. The prominent actors were either connected by blood or marriage, and took excellent care to distribute the spoils through their own social circle.

Formerly three years were regarded as the shortest cruise for an efficient officer in command. Recently three officers have been appointed in six months to a single ship — a beautiful comment upon the efficiency of the service. Capt. Latimer, confessedly one of the most accomplished officers in the service, has had applications for sea duty constantly before the department. The highest among his peers declare him unrivalled in all the duties of the profession to which he has been devoted from early life, and say that his ship was ever equal to any emergency that could arise. He has been neglected and disrated, to give place to incompetent men, and the blow was struck by Stribling and Pendegrast, who are eminently notorious for want of discipline and efficiency. Capt. Latimer was never known to ask to be relieved from duty, but always for it; and upwards of twenty-eight years of active employment are replete with the richest memorials of his distinguished ability.

Capt. John H. Graham, now "furloughed," served in the memorable battle of Black Rock, opposite the enemy's frontier, in 1812. He was wounded in the leg while entering the burning barracks, and was saved by a sailor, who threw young Graham upon his shoulder, and carried him across the river, while his clothes actually froze to the boat. Nine of the twelve naval officers were killed and wounded. Gen. Porter, in his report of that battle, says: "If bravery be a virtue, — if the gratitude of the country be due to those who gallantly and desperately asserted its rights, — the government will make ample and honorable provision for the heirs of those brave tars who fell on this occasion, as well as for those who survived." Graham afterwards fought gloriously, upon his cork leg, at the battle of Lake Champlain.

Capt. Wm. Inman, retired, is also eminent for efficiency in the navy, and rigid in his exactions of duty.

Lieut. Gibson, the executive officer of the St. Louis, was nearly paralyzed by this unexpected blow of the board. He had seen about as much sea service as Shubrick, the president of the board, though born after he entered the service; and more than twenty-six post-captains, and seventy-nine of the commanders, had seen, who are retained on the active list.

Lieut. Brownell, who fought through the war of 1812, and was seven times victorious in engagements with the enemy, has had a like fate.

There is one other case — that of Capt. Uriah P. Levy — to which we must advert, as it is one of the most scandalous outrages in connection with the action of the Navy Retiring Board, and deserves the severest reprehension from every American citizen. As a reformer in the service, Capt. Levy deserves the gratitude of his country, and of humanity. He is the father of the system abolishing flogging in the navy; and through him that inhuman barbarity, which so long disgraced its annals, has been made to yield to reason and moral suasion.

This act was in consonance with American liberty, and with the progress and intelligence which belong to a free people. Without resort to that antediluvian means of enforcing discipline, Levy's ship was eminent for its order, neatness, and efficiency to duty ; and when the Vandalia returned to the United States, after a long and perilous cruise in the Gulf of Mexico, in 1840, it was the boast of its crew that there had been less personal chastisement in the whole cruise than the records of any other ship of war ever had in a single month ; and, while seamen were deserting Shubrick's and other ships, Commander Levy found no difficulty in retaining those under his control, simply because he respected character, and did not lose sight of the fact that he was dealing with American men. The Secretary of the Navy, then, was so gratified by this first essay of Commander Levy towards reform, that he ordered quarterly returns to be made to the department by all the navy, upon the principle adopted by Levy for the abolition of the "cat" and "colt."

Capt. Levy — whose biography is given elsewhere in this volume — is also distinguished as being the first to enforce upon his ship religious duty, without the aid of a chaplain, by instituting the custom of reading the Old and New Testament of our blessed Lord. Time would fail, to refer to all the patriotic and gallant men who have thus been outraged.

What relief can be procured for the suffering families of those officers who have been reduced to want by the action of the President of the United States, the Secretary of the Navy, and the Navy Board?

Another serious question is presented in relation to this matter: What is to be done for the innocent wives and children of some forty-eight dismissed officers, who are reduced to penury? What for those fifty lieutenants and masters, who, with six hundred dollars, and three hundred and seventy-five dollars, per annum, are left with large and helpless households depending on their maintenance, and without means of other employment? What for those brave men who have served their country thirty, forty, and fifty long years? Is there no arm of mercy to reach their impoverished and stricken homes? Will not the people hear their cry for justice? Will they not flee to their succor? Will the American nation suffer such injustice? Can Americans hear, without lively indignation, that such oppression has been inflicted upon the naval chivalry of the country?

Will Americans believe that two hundred and one "skulks" have been dropped or disrated from the navy, as the "wise reformer," Mr. Secretary Dobbin, has been pleased to call these officers?

The law was really a *government bill*, and the board was designed by Congress to protect their brother officers, — to act as a conservative body between them and the President, who was to inflict the degradation. The board, therefore, instead of performing the trust assigned by Congress, and shielding their brothers from unmerited disgrace, became the subservient tools of the Secretary of the Navy, who, like themselves, was a relentless persecutor, and who, to carry out his own caprice, adopted their views, and ordered the sittings to be secret, in defiance of every principle of justice and law.

Without complaint, it had long been known that the "board" had, by intrigue, sought and obtained more favors, more full pay, more pay for extra service, than all the victims they have made ever did together. But they still wanted "more;" and, to obtain their end, they took the places of their modest, meritorious seniors. Intoxicated with this power, they forgot their country, to make a navy to suit themselves.

The authority to remove military men, even by

the President, is a very delicate and dangerous exercise. It is rarely necessary to do so, particularly in the navy, without impartial trial, and a formal finding of a court-martial. Unlike the civil service, there are always others ready to discharge the duty temporarily. But, more than this, the profession of a naval officer is the business of his entire life, considered and adopted as an honorable tenure in the service of his country, and secured by law.

Dismission always implies disgrace, which is, in the judgment of all sensible men, greater by arbitrary decision than when flagrant wrong, by a fair trial, has proved the necessity for such sentence; and in this act not only have officers been subjected to an arbitrary and tyrannical action, but have also had it inflicted, in many instances, by juniors and inferiors in the service.

The precipitate and feeble conduct of President Pierce, devoid of dignity, discretion, or justice, in confirming the sentence of unmerited disgrace upon American officers, of whom he knew nothing, and was without the means of being correctly informed, ought to serve as a solemn warning to this people. Neither Congress, who passed the law, nor the President, nor the Secretary of the Navy, were imbued with that military and national pride which belong to those educated in the navy of their country, whom they have ingloriously set aside. And thus have consequences arisen, from the conduct of *civilians*, which must fire the spirit of every patriot in the land, especially when the nation takes into consideration the further proof of the efficiency and worthiness of these officers, which time will soon develop, and whom justice shall have vindicated and restored to their rights, when the people shall have made an *American* President. A chief magistrate is needed who can comprehend the wrong in a national as well as individual character, and will consider it an imperious duty to afford these two hundred and one officers all the protection and redress which lie within the compass of the constitution and laws.

It may be well to remark that all these officers, endorsed and approved by Commodore Perry, became victims of the board.

Suppose, Americans, you should go to the department at Washington, and look into the records for charges against those officers now *promoted* in the service, we tell you that you could find them.

And, while we cast no reflections upon any of these government officials, and wish to see them all elevated to distinction in the service of their country, we say, fearlessly, that there are many officers retained and promoted, who, if the records be *true*, are much more entitled, by every consideration of justice, to the same sentence which has been passed upon their more unfortunate brothers in the service.

CHAPTER IV.

The question also arises, why it was that such officers as Capt. Wilkes, who had seen no duty afloat for twenty-eight years, and had already had fifty or sixty thousand dollars from the government for his contributions to science, should be retained on the active list by the board, when Lieut. Maury was retired because he had seen so little sea service. It was possibly allowed by Biddle as a monument of mercy to learning; but more probably for some personal predilection, which did not operate in the cases of other scientific officers.

When it is remembered with how much difficulty, and at what dear pecuniary cost, many of these officers procured their original commissions in the navy of their country, the present case will seem peculiarly appalling. The hard earnings of their parents, the cost of years of sacrifice, deprivation, and toil, have been given, and given freely, to members of Congress, as a bonus for the midshipman's warrant.

The pride of country, the desire of name in its service, for that son on whom they had fixed their hopes for distinction and exaltation, has, in many instances, induced parents in our land, in humble circumstances, to forego comfort, and, oftentimes, the education of the other children, to minister to the grasping desire and corrupt exactions of members of Congress, in order to obtain this boon for a meritorious son ; and which would readily have been tendered, without solicitation, to the wealthy and influential of their districts, whose favor their selfish thirst for power and place would lead them to propitiate.

How much benefit, how much relief, would this money now be to the suffering families of the country reduced by the "Navy Retiring Board"! Will not members of Congress, who voted blindly for the bill, feel it a moral duty, at least, to redress the rights of these officers now, if they will not restore to them this unlawful pecuniary gain? Let such remember that the condition upon which the purchase-money was paid has been abrogated. The contract was for *life*, unless proved, by a *fair* trial, unworthy to serve under the national flag.

A member of Congress from New York State was asked for his influence in behalf of a promising young man in adverse circumstances. He said that he would interpose if he were paid five hundred dollars. The case thus looked hopeless ; for the applicant was poor, and such a demand was too much to exact of his father. The matter was laid before the family circle for discussion, and decided favorably for the son. The only five hundred dollars the father had in the world was paid this member, who, pulling out the blank warrant from his pocket, where it was at the first interview, filled it with the young man's name, and took his money. He is now a victim of the executive vengeance.

Has the remedy been provided by Congress to restore to health this paralyzed arm of the public service? It has not. The Senate passed a bill which gives these injured officers the benefit of a court of inquiry, which shall decide upon the action of the Navy Retiring Board ; and this court is to submit to the President of the United States its findings for his approval. If the sentence of the Navy Board is decided to be unjust, the President can renominate those dropped officers to the Senate for restoration, and place on the active list officers retired by the unjust proceeding of the board. If a dropped officer shall not be restored within one year from the passage of the law, he shall be entitled to one year's pay of the grade to which he belonged. The President, also, is empowered by this act to transfer any furloughed officer to the reserved pay-list, and make him, as before, eligible to promotion. To the President, therefore, the power will be given, by and with the consent of the Senate, to restore, within one year after the act shall have become law, any dropped, retired, or furloughed officer to the same grade he would have occupied had the Navy Board never had an existence.

The objection to this Senate act is, that it calls an officer to trial for mental, moral, or physical incompetency, upon unconstitutional grounds, after he has been convicted and punished. It allows officers to *submit* to an investigation into their past lives, simply because a cabal of designing men saw fit, without the authority of law, and for private reasons, to destroy them, and then fill their places. But it has other advantages, which no high-toned officer should overlook. It will, if made a law of Congress, oblige that Navy Board to appear before the court of inquiry, and compel them to expose the reasons which influenced their individual action.

In this point of view, we say, honorable men, who have nothing to fear from public scrutiny, would rejoice at the prospect of bringing their defamers to trial. And, with an American President, of any party, who will not dodge responsibility, the navy of the country would be reinstated, the honor of brave men vindicated, and some redress afforded for their past suffering.

But, Americans, that Senate bill we believe to be a mere pretence, which never will be passed if the same influence continues to prevail in the House which did in the Senate. Why? Because its ostensible friends know it to be such. The President has the same power *now* to nominate that he would have after the passage of the act, — so said Mr. Mallory to Mr. Bell; and who believes Mr. Pierce would stultify himself any more than he has done by nominating the very men he has condemned? Mr. Bocock, of the naval committee of the House of Representatives, is the pliant friend of Mr. Mallory and the board, and introduced the amendment to the Senate bill, to destroy the court of inquiry, by giving the President the power to nominate (which he already possessed), purposely to defeat its passage. He did it to protect the board from public exposure before the court of inquiry, and had already distinguished himself as the author of the clause in the law to drop officers.

Mr. Mallory, the person who devised the deep and villanous scheme to destroy our American men, is a *foreigner*, a West Indian, and his wife is a Spanish woman. What a commentary upon our nationality, to have a foreigner come and exercise the privilege of tearing our navy to pieces, and adding to the weeping and wailing of this people, who, four years ago, were laughing with national heartiness at the sure prospect of peace and progress!

A navy that has had a Stewart,— the Nelson of the service, — a Decatur, a McDonough, a Lawrence, and a Perry, of Lake Erie memory; a navy that for seventy years has braved the breeze in distant seas and in foreign climes, to be now overslaughed under our own flag, and by a foreigner, is enough to make the nation ring. Are all our heroes dead?

Another of the follies of the late Senate bill is the introduction of flag-captains, by Messrs. Mallory, Shubrick, & Co. Capt. Shubrick, the instigator, it is said, craves the admiralty, for which he is as unfit as he is unscrupulous in his efforts to obtain it.

Shubrick, then, by his own act, put himself in the safe line of promotion; and Commodore Morris' death has made him, with all his unfitness, heir apparent. Hence the ridiculous idea of the flag captaincy in the American navy. The material of our navy bears no comparison with that of other nations; and this is the reform we need to exalt the nation, instead of ruining its *personelle*. We want a navy to progress with our country's growth, in the quality of our ships and efficiency of our men. For a whole year there was but one single ship bearing our national flag in the Baltic Sea, while so much of our commerce needed to be protected. And, while our resources, properly managed, could make a navy to meet the world, we have but little improvement in naval construction in the last forty years. Why? Because the navy commissioners and navy bureaus have ruined the navy. These men, put in places which properly belong to civilians, have squandered millions of the nation's money, without benefiting the country or service in any sense whatever. Where is there any evidence of originality, any evidence of benefit, by the enormous outlays of these bureaus? We challenge these men to point to any improvement in naval architecture originating with them. All the improvements of any importance have been obtained from other nations; and were the United States to go to war to-morrow, we should find our men-of-war thirty years behind the advancement of all other maritime nations.

Thus, my countrymen, you have before you the history of the transactions of the Retiring Navy Board, which, like a dark cloud, hang over the proud and gallant navy of your country, which has reaped so many triumphant laurels, enkindled the fire of patriotism in the breasts of so many noble officers and aspiring youth, and spread the glory of her achievements and emulous prowess over the whole globe. The injustice, the stigma, of these transactions, will forever blot the annals of President Pierce's administration; because they are not for a day, but will go down, on the stream of time, to posterity, to tell the ignominious story of the late Navy Board, and to raise a blush on the cheek of our patriotic countrymen, who scorn such inglorious deeds, while, at the same time, they honor with increased estimation, and renewed plaudits of approbation, the suffering but noble-hearted and high-minded victims of a false policy and a cruel oppression.

AN AMERICAN HERO

THE VICTIM OF A CONSPIRACY.

CAPTAIN BARTLETT'S VINDICATION.

CHAPTER I.

Now, after the exposition given in the preceding chapter, can the public wonder at the atrocious outrage perpetrated upon so many distinguished Americans, under the administration of J. C. Dobbin, of the Navy Department? Can it wonder that a set of conspirators to rob and plunder the name and fame of good men, did walk into the department, and signifying to Mr. Dobbin that they were the proper parties to reform the service, set about the work, institute an Inquisition, create a clerkship to their board, and give Dobbin the appointment?

This is precisely what they did actually do! Chief Justice Gilchrist, in his unanswered argument in the case of the "Brig Armstrong," says, "*If the*

Painted by Wm. S. Jewett. Engraved by J. C. Buttre.

Washn. A. Bartlett

United States, in the plenitude of their power, see fit to submit the claims of a citizen to arbitration without his assent, ought they not to make the most full and ample provision, that he shall be fully and fairly heard, and that he shall have all reasonable opportunity to lay before the abitrator the evidence on which he relies? An award made, without the party having had an opportunity to be heard, rests neither upon law nor justice." "*The position,*" he adds, "*that every party should have an opportunity to be heard before the tribunal that is to pass judgment on his rights, needs no labored argument to support it. It has been repeatedly asserted by the most eminent jurists.*" In Regden *vs.* Martin, 6 H. & Johns., 403, the court said: "*That the parties ought to have notice of the time of meeting, is a position so strongly supported by common justice that it would seem not to require the aid of authorities. Every man ought to have an opportunity afforded him to be heard in defence of his rights.*" In Falconer *vs.* Montgomery, 4 Dallas, 232, it is said: "*The plainest dictates of natural justice must prescribe to every tribunal the law that 'no man shall be condemned unheard.' It is not merely an abstract rule, or positive right, but it is the result of long experience and a wise attention to the feelings and dispositions of human nature.* * * * * Besides, there is scarcely a piece of written evidence, or a sentence of oral testimony, that is not susceptible of some explanation, or exposed to some contradiction; there is scarcely an argument that may not be elucidated so as to insure success, or be controverted so as to prevent it. To exclude the party, therefore, from the opportunity of interposing in any of these modes (which the most candid and intelligent, but a disinterested person, may easily overlook) is not only a privation of his right, but an act of injustice to the umpire, whose mind might be materially influenced by such an interposition." In the case of Lutz *vs.* Linthicum, 8 Peters, 178, Mr. Justice Story said: "Without question, due notice should be given to the parties of the time and place of hearing the case; and if the award was made without such notice, it ought, upon the plainest principles of justice, to be set aside." In Elmendorf *vs.* Harris, 23 Wend., 628, it was laid down as a fundamental rule of construction in reference to every transaction in the nature of a judicial proceeding, that the contract of submission necessarily implies that the arbitrator is not authorized or empowered to decide the question in controversy, without giving the parties an opportunity to be heard in relation thereto.

We now proceed to the case of Lieutenant Washington Allen Bartlett, who, by the deepest malignity, jealousy, and injustice, has been dropped from the naval service of his country, by the late "Naval Retiring Board." And we shall cite this most remarkable one in its interesting detail, because it has *alone* been the subject of examination before the Naval Committee of the United States Senate, and will *alone* break and wither the whole action of that stupendous and most unparalleled iniquity.

Indeed, we have no choice but to use his case, for it is only through it, and Biddle's disgraceful letter to the distinguished Maury, that we are able to see behind the curtain of the Inquisition.

Lieutenant Bartlett was on duty upon the coast of Africa, as first lieutenant of the flag-ship, when the Council of Fifteen struck his name from the rolls of the navy! Not a single allegation of any kind, verbally or in writing, had ever appeared against him in the Navy Department, in any form. And we here insert the letter of the Secretary to Mrs. Bartlett, who, stricken down by the sudden and unexpected attempt to put disgrace upon the good name of her husband, writes, in the anguish of her soul, like a true woman, to know, *why* his fair fame as an officer has been outraged?

NAVY DEPARTMENT, *Sept. 30th*, 1855.

MADAM:—Your letter of the 18th instant has been received. The board of naval officers, recently convened in Washington, in accordance with the law, merely reported the names and ranks of officers who, in their judgment, came within the provisions of the recent act of Congress, but not the facts or the grounds upon which their action is based. No charges were preferred against any officer. You will perceive, therefore, that I am unable to comply with your request to know what the charges were against Lieutenant Bartlett.

I am, very respectfully,
Your obedient servant,
J. C. DOBBIN.

MRS. WASHINGTON BARTLETT, *New York*.

This, the only *official* notice to this hour received, accompanied by the endearing solace of her who best knew his worth, met him on active duty abroad, and instantly created the deepest and most unfeigned sorrow among all with whom he was associated. And so highly was Lieutenant Bartlett esteemed by officers and crew, as an officer, a gentleman, and a friend, that the *separation*, by those who witnessed it, is said to have been one of the most painfully affecting ever seen upon a frigate's deck, and resembled, from its inexplicable character, and the emotions thereby excited, a funeral at sea!

SECTION I.

We here insert, as corroboratory, the distinguished testimonials of his commodore, commanders, associates, and subalterns:

Testimonial of Commodore Crabbe, U. S. Navy.

U. S. SHIP JAMESTOWN,
PORTO GRANDE, *Oct. 23d*, 1855.

SIR:—I have received your letter of this day's date, containing a copy of a letter from the honorable Secretary of the Navy to Mrs. Bartlett, [the same published in the body of the memorial,] in relation to your retirement from the navy of the United States.

Although I have not received anything official from the Department upon the subject, yet the Hon. Secretary's letter to Mrs. Bartlett, and the reasons set forth by yourself, will, no doubt, justify me in relieving you from further duty on board this ship. In doing so, however, I cannot avoid saying that I deeply regret the loss of your services. Your gentlemanly and officer-like bearing, whilst under my command, has uniformly met my warmest approbation.

I am, with great respect, your obedient servant,

THOMAS CRABBE,
Commander-in-chief of U. S. Naval Forces, Coast of Africa.

To LIEUT. W. A. BARTLETT,
U. S. Ship Jamestown.

Letter from Commander F. B. Ellison, U. S. Navy.

HEMPSTEAD, LONG ISLAND, *January 17th*, 1856.

DEAR SIR:—In reply to your request that I would state my opinion of your efficiency as an officer, and your deportment as a gentleman, during our recent association on board the "Jamestown," where you served under my command, I with great pleasure say, that in every particular, as a zealous and capable officer, and a well-informed, intelligent gentleman, I regarded you as most exemplary. Commodore Crabbe frequently expressed himself to me in very warm terms of you, as a highly accomplished officer, and like expressions were made from all your messmates in the ward-room, showing a uniformity of opinion throughout the ship.

Sincerely trusting that the error which seems to have been made in your case may speedily be rectified, and that you may be honorably restored to your former position in the navy,

I am, very truly,
Your obedient servant and friend,
FRANCIS B. ELLISON,
Commander U. S. Navy.

W. A. BARTLETT, Esq.,
Washington, D. C.

Testimonial of Lieut. Commanding, James F. Armstrong.

U. S. FLAG-SHIP JAMESTOWN,
PORTO GRANDE, ST. VINCENT, *Oct.* 23*d*, 1855.

DEAR SIR:—In forwarding you the enclosed letter from Commodore Crabbe, relieving you from further duty in this ship, I beg leave to assure you of my deepest regret for the cause that has produced it, and for the interruption of an intercourse and association always confidential, harmonious, and friendly.

I shall ever esteem you, in your character, as an officer and gentleman, and, in parting from you, tender you my sincere wishes for your restoration to the service, and for your future welfare.

Very respectfully, your obedient servant,
JAS. FRANCIS ARMSTRONG,
Lieut. Commanding.

LIEUT. WASHINGTON A. BARTLETT,
U. S. Ship Jamestown.

Testimonial of all the Commissioned Officers of the U. S. Flag-ship Jamestown.

PORTO GRANDE, ST. VINCENT, *Oct.* 24*th*, 1855.

DEAR SIR:—We entertain too high an appreciation of your character as a gentleman and an officer, and too warm a regard for you as a messmate and friend, to allow you to leave us without saying to you, in the sincerity of our hearts, that we deeply regret that you are about to part from us, and, above all, the cause that takes you away.

In the difficult and responsible relation that you have sustained to us, as executive officer of the ship, you have ever, whilst discharging your duties with fidelity, borne yourself toward us with the utmost frankness, conciliation, and courtesy. And, in the more intimate and kindly relation, as a member of the little society that we form amongst ourselves, and which can subsist in harmony only by mutual cultivation of friendly feelings and the practice of friendly offices, you have endeared yourself to us by your uniform amiability of disposition, and by the desire that you have ever evinced to cherish the most cordial intercourse with us all.

We, therefore, beg to assure you that, in parting from us, you are taking leave of those who will ever remember you with pleasure, and who, whatever fortunes may betide you, will always continue your well-wishers and friends.

Ever, very truly, yours,

GEO. CLYMER,
Fleet Surgeon, ranking with Commander.
T. H. PATTERSON, *Lieutenant.*
EDWARD BARNETT, *Lieutenant.*
T. M. TAYLOR, *Purser (rank of Commander.)*
JULIAN MYERS, *Lieutenant.*
SAMUEL RICHARD SWANN, *Ass't Surgeon.*
JOHN L. HEYLEN, *Commodore's Secretary.*
JNO. E. HART, *Acting Master and Lieut.*
JAS. M. BRADFORD, *Acting Lieut.*
CHAS. W. THOMAS, *Chaplain*

LT. WASHINGTON A. BARTLETT.

Letter from the Junior Officers of the Jamestown.

U. S. SHIP JAMESTOWN,
PORTO GRANDE, ST. VINCENT, *Oct. 24th*, 1855.

SIR:—You are about to return to your home; in so doing, the members of the steerage feel it their duty to express to you their deep regret, and their sincere gratitude for the extreme kindness with which you have universally treated them, during the time they have had the pleasure of being under your command. You may be assured that, after your leaving us, you will ever be cherished in our memory with feelings of the highest regard and esteem, in your character as an officer and gentleman.

Sir, we bid you, with sorrow, a hearty farewell; with many wishes for your future welfare and happiness,

Believe us, very respectfully, your obedient servants,

N. B. CONCKLIN, *M. Mate.*
C. W. LAWRENCE, *M. Mate.*
VAL. HALL VOORHEES, *M. Mate.*
O. N. HENKEL, *M. Mate.*
H. B. JOHNSON, *C. Clerk.*

LIEUT. W. A. BARTLETT, *U. S. Navy.*

Now we challenge for these papers a comparison with any testimonials ever bestowed upon the most distinguished of our officers by his brothers in arms. They testify to his competency and efficiency in every relation in which he was called to act as an officer. And will it not be perceived from these testimonials that, considering the delicate and responsible position which the executive officer bears towards all *above* and *below* him, that they exhibit the clearest evidence that the frigate "Jamestown" was, under Lieut. Bartlett's administration, in the *highest state of efficiency?* Every officer and man would cheerfully follow the lead of one whom they held in such confidence and admiration; and to whom they could look in whatever emergency might arise on their cruise.

And this being the moment when Lieut. Bartlett ceased his naval services, it is proper here to review in part his naval career.

His immediate commanders during the Mexican

War were Commodore Lavallette and Capt. J. B. Montgomery. Their testimonials are sufficient without a single comment.

Testimonial of Commodore E. A. F. Lavallette on the services of Lieut. Bartlett in the Pacific Squadron.

PHILADELPHIA, *January 23d*, 1856.

DEAR SIR:—I received your letter of the 22d instant, in which you state, that "while absent from the country, serving as first-lieutenant of the flag-ship of the African squadron, it has pleased the late 'Navy Board' to present my name to the President to be stricken from the rolls as lieutenant in the Navy.

"I had the honor to serve under your command as a midshipman, and again as a lieutenant, commanding the armed prize brig Argo in the Gulf of California, and in the attack on Guaymas, and its occupation. On that occasion you did me the honor to assign me the most advanced post, on the night previous to the attack, out of supporting distance of the guns of the squadron, and out of sight, being covered by the island which separated me from the squadron.

"How did I bear myself on that occasion? Did I meet your expectations or not?

"From your knowledge of me, my abilities and acquirements, was or was I not an efficient officer of the Pacific squadron during the Mexican War?"

In answer, I have to state, that your foregoing statements of our operations in the Gulf of California are correct in every particular. Your conduct on that occasion not only met my approbation, by the activity, energy and skill which you displayed in getting your gun landed, merited—and the effect which it produced by your management, upon the works of the enemy entitled you to—the highest praise.

Your abilities and acquirements I consider quite equal to any of your grade, and very superior to very many of them. I certainly viewed you as an efficient officer of the Pacific squadron.

I am respectfully,

Your obedient servant,

E. A. F. LAVALLETTE.

WASH'N A. BARTLETT, Esq.,
Late Lieut. U. S. Navy, Washington City, D. C.

WASHINGTON, D. C., *February* 18, 1856.

MY DEAR SIR:—Your letter of the 6th instant was handed me, and should have been sooner answered, but for pressing engagements, which have occupied my time since its receipt. You state: "It has become necessary that I should exhibit to the Government, to Congress, and to the people, such concise testimony as I can obtain as to my efficiency and qualifications as an officer of the Navy—from which I have been most unjustly dismissed—and, therefore, I appeal to you to state in whatever manner and form you may please, whether I was or was not an efficient and capable officer in all particulars and at all times, as an upright, capable, and zealous officer of your ship and of the Navy; and whether, by act or deed, which may have come to your knowledge, I ever attempted, in any manner, to avoid responsibility, or aught which friend or foe could allege against me; or whether any circumstances of duty, or otherwise, ever impaired my usefulness or your confidence in my integrity and ability," etc.

I have quoted largely from your letter, in order to a more succinct and direct reply to the several inquiries contained in it.

In reply, therefore, I take pleasure in stating that during your long service—from November 1844 to May 1848—in the United States ship Portsmouth, under my command, with the usual opportunities enjoyed by naval commanders of forming a just estimate of the merits and qualifications of those serving under them, I have no hesitation whatever in bearing my testimony to your high mental and physical qualifications and efficiency as an officer of the Navy, and an accomplished sea-officer.

At all times, and in all circumstances, I found you ready and willing for the various duties assigned you, on shore and on shipboard, and ever prompt, zealous, and capable in the performance of them. I always regarded you, sir, as a most useful officer, not only in the proper line of professional employment, but as interpreter and translator of important official correspondence during the revolutionary movements in California and the war with Mexico which followed; your services were of signal importance to your commander, and (as regarded by him) to the public interests at the time.

When, in the course of events, after the occupancy of San Francisco, it became necessary to establish the magistracy of that place, the duties of alcalde were assigned to you, and discharged with a faithfulness and ability which claimed for you the commendation of your immediate commander, as well as that of the commander-in chief; and the people of the district, when required to elect their civil officers, manifested their high appreciation of your character and services in the magistracy, in according to you an overwhelming vote (over several candidates) for your continuance in office.

During your service under my command you certainly did possess my confidence as an upright, intelligent, and most capable officer of the ship and of the Navy.

Allegations were brought to my notice by officers of the Portsmouth, at San Francisco, in 1846, which you promptly met, by a demand for immediate investigation by court-martial or court of inquiry, which the exigency of the public service precluded at the time. I should have deemed it exceedingly unjust to you, sir, as well as to my own feelings, to have suffered any permanent impression to your prejudice, on my mind, until sufficient evidence had been adduced before a competent tribunal—until shown to be true.

I know of nothing that occurred during the cruise of the Portsmouth, or since, to the present time, that ought in anywise to diminish my friendly regard, or impair my confidence in your integrity, high capabilities, and usefulness, as a naval officer.

I trust, my dear sir, that you may speedily satisfy the Government, Congress, and the people, of your innocence of any and all allegations of a prejudicial character, which may have operated in any degree in procuring your recent dismissal from the Navy, and, by a speedy restoration, have it again in your power to render valuable service to your country, for which I regard you eminently qualified.

Very truly, I am your friend and obedient servant,

J. B. Montgomery,

Captain U. S. Navy.

W. A. Bartlett, Esq.

SECTION II.

The war having ended, and no further field for active naval service being presented, Lieut. Bartlett accepted the tender of the command of the

Ewing, in the service of the coast survey, to return to the Pacific Ocean, where he already had had eight years of active duty. How faithfully he performed these services is best exhibited by the appreciation of the distinguished superintendent of the survey, A. D. Bache, LL.D.

The late Lieutenant, Commanding, Wm. P. McArthur, being the hydrographical chief of the western coast, having deceased, in an eulogy delivered by Professor Bache to his memory at Washington, we find this reference to the eminent services of Lieutenants McArthur and Bartlett:

> The work which he accomplished will live for ever! Surrounded by circumstances the most difficult perhaps which ever tried the constancy, the judgment, the resources of any hydrographer, he vanquished circumstances. His reconnoissance of the western coast, from Monterey to Columbia river, and his preliminary surveys there, were made in spite of desertion and even mutiny—in despite of the inadequacy of means to meet the truly extraordinary circumstances of the country. Happy that in his officers he had friends devoted to him and to their duties—*especially happy in the officer next to him in the responsibilities of the work.*

And before the Naval Committee Professor Bache said:

> In justice to Mr. Bartlett, I should state briefly what those services were. He took the schooner Ewing, a small vessel, which had been used in the revenue service as a cutter, from New York

to San Francisco. Was active in pursuing the mutineers who attempted to drown Passed Midshipman Gibson, of the schooner Ewing. Went to Columbia river with Lieutenant Commanding McArthur, though it was understood that unless a second vessel were attached to the coast survey he was to return home. Was active in the survey of Columbia river and the reconnoissance of the western coast. The letters from Lieutenant Commanding McArthur express his sense of Lieutenant Bartlett's services, and refer to him for important information in regard to the coast, showing his confidence in him. He assisted assiduously in preparing the coast survey charts of the western coast at the office.

We will now advert for a moment to the services of Lieut. Bartlett at the mouth of the Columbia river, and his *successful* labors in opening to the commerce of the world that magnificent *water*-course, an *original* American discovery of the last century; where Vancouver recorded his extraordinary want of judgment, by placing the name of "Disappointment" upon that majestic headland which stands sentinel at its mouth, and upon which an American sailor had already placed the venerated name of "Hancock." That gigantic river, whose beauties are so vividly and truthfully daguerreotyped by Washington Irving, in his "Astoria," but whose importance to the commerce of the world, and facilities for use, were left to be exhibited by the united efforts of those energetic and skillful officers, McArthur and Bartlett.

This will be the more apparent when we state the well-established facts, that although the entrance to this mighty river had been in the hands of the English Hudson Bay Company forty years, and the South Sea Exploring Expedition, under its Lieutenant-Commodore Wilkes, had spent months in its waters, yet it remained for all practical uses as a great outlet of commerce, as hermetically sealed, through the *imaginary* dangers which were thrown around its entrance, as if its mighty waters had never found their natural course to the sea.

It will be remembered that Wilkes said it was necessary to take the channel of the Columbia with wind and tide both *adverse* (a physical impossibility) in a five knot current! After the loss of the Shark, whose commander, we suppose, attempted the nautical manœuvre described by Wilkes, and the report and chart of that remarkable commander was given to the public, the time for going in and out the channel actually *doubled!* The loss of the Peacock and Shark, of the American Navy, and the known fact that the Hon. Hudson Bay Company's commanders took forty or fifty days to find their way into the channel, and the same number to find their way out of it, had long elicited the interest of the commercial and scientific world. So far from gaining any advantage through Wilkes, the *smallest* vessel of the company actually lay eighty-four days near the mouth of the river (Baker's Bay), with the Shark's crew on board, before this "ancient mariner" dared to proceed to sea. And four years later, when the Ewing, with McArthur and Bartlett on board, appeared off the mouth of the river, in a snow-storm, on the 18th of April, 1850, the same *little* vessel of the Hon. Company's service, with the same commander, was met there, having been cruising off and on for weeks, though anxious to enter, through fears of the imaginary terrors of the entrance! The Ewing *boldly* took the channel, and the Cadboro' bravely followed suit. This was the *last* real detention that has ever occurred at the mouth of the Columbia. The advent of the Ewing proved the truth of Mr. Benton's prophecy, five years previously, when he said, in substance, that notwithstanding this *extraordinary* report of Wilkes, the time would come, within five years, when the entrance of the Columbia would be as practicable as a commercial channel, as the bay of New York!

In order to show the true force of these

marks, we place, side by side, the reports of Lieutenants McArthur and Bartlett:

September 25th, 1850, McArthur wrote Professor Bache:

Within the last eighteen months, more vessels have crossed the Columbia river bar, than had crossed it, perhaps, in all time past; and, during that time, no vessel has received the slightest injury, and but few have met with much delay.

I have examined all the charts that have been made of the Columbia river from the time of its discovery to the present, and find that there has been continued changes going on, *but at all times has there been a good deep channel* at the mouth of this river.

Report of Lieutenant Washington A. Bartlett, U. S. N., Assistant in the Coast Survey, in relation to the draught of vessels which can enter the south channel, Columbia river entrance, Oregon.

WASHINGTON, *November 30th*, 1850.

SIR:—In answer to your inquiries as to the draught of vessels which may, at any time, be carried into the Columbia river by the new south channel, I have to state that our late survey of that channel, and my personal experience in passing over the south bar, in vessels of deep draught, show conclusively, that vessels drawing seventeen feet can be taken over the south bar at quarter flood, or three-quarter ebb, without the least risk of touching, and twenty feet can pass at high water.

In making the preceding statement, it is proper to state that I have fully considered the "drop" which a vessel makes when in the swell of the bar, which is, however, much less in the south than in the old north channel, when the wind is in the usual northwestern quarter.

In the winter, or spring season, when the wind is in the south, or southwest quarter, there is a lively breaker on the south bar, at which time it will be smoothest on the north bar, and this southerly wind being fair for the north channel, there is no occasion to take the south bar in *southerly winds going in;* yet, with a moderate draught in a *sailing* vessel, the south channel is ever safest in coming out, although the wind may be "dead in" to the bar; the bar being so short and quickly passed, that it is not necessary to tack in shoal water.

The U. S. steamer, Massachusetts, and U. S. sloop-of-war, Falmouth, each drawing seventeen feet water, have passed the bar of the south channel into the Columbia river since our survey was made.

In addition, I would state that my experience at the mouth of the Columbia, has convinced me that the south channel is the practicable commercial channel of that river for certainty and safety, with the additional advantage of accomplishing the passage, to or from the river, without waiting for a particular wind. Ships frequently pass the bar inward, in fifteen minutes after receiving their pilot, and outward, in thirty minutes after getting their anchors.

A disabled ship, that can be sailed so as to have good steerage way, can pass over the south bar in safety, when it would be impossible to get her in by the north channel.

From the 18th of April to the 5th of August, 1850, there was no day that the south channel was not practicable for vessels, and was in daily use.

I crossed the bar (south channel), in the pilot-boat "Mary Taylor," during the "heaviest bar" that occurred within the above named period, beating out with the wind ahead.

SECTION III.

Commander Wilkes, whose total sea service in the navy, was but seven years and nine months! (which will account for his want of practical ability to obtain proper deductions from his own work), was made a post-captain by the Naval Board, though he has not seen salt water for the last fourteen years! while Lieutenant Bartlett's sea service was thirteen years and nine months, quite double that of the present Captain Wilkes! Such is "efficiency," in the acceptation of the Board! Had McArthur lived to this day, and remained on that service, he would most assuredly have been "dropped," or "furloughed;" for Lieutenant Maffit, of the same date, who had performed eleven years of like continuous sea service on the Atlantic coast, and admitted by all to be, like McArthur, without a superior in the service, has been "furloughed!" We confidently expect, however, that Maffit will be restored (and we know he should be on his own merits), because Mr. Dobbin, having known him from boyhood, takes a *personal* interest in him, and, in defiance of the Board's judgment, who had pronounced him "inefficient," immediately augmented his command from one to *three* vessels, an honor which has not yet been conferred upon any one of that inquisition, since it closed its sittings. The moment the Secretary gave three vessels to Maffit, he made him *Naval Commodore!* practically, ranking with the oldest officers in the navy.

The publications emanating from the coast survey office, relating to the hydrography of the western coast, the discoveries and minute examinations on the whole line of coast from Monterey to the Columbia, carefully compiled sailing directions, plans for lights, and other improvements for navigation, which have been put in operation by the government, and lauded by the people, the confidence with which Congress increased the appropriations to extend this meritorious work, will ever remain inscribed upon the public records an enduring monument to the energy and skill of McArthur and Bartlett.

In April, 1846, Commodore Sloat sent the "Portsmouth" from Mazatlan to California; on arriving there, Captain Montgomery supplied the wants of Captain Fremont, who had been hostilized by Castor, the Commandant-General of the Province of California. We quote from the letter of Captain Montgomery, to show how valuable, at that juncture, were the military and civil services of Lieutenant Bartlett:

Montgomery says:

"I have no hesitation whatever in bearing my testimony to your high mental and physical qualifications and efficiency as an officer of the Navy, and an accomplished sea-officer.

At all times and in all circumstances I found you ready and willing for the various duties assigned you, on shore and on ship-board, and ever prompt, zealous, and capable in the performance of them. I always regarded you, sir, as a most useful officer, not only in the proper line of professional employment, but as interpreter and translator of important official correspondence during the revolutionary movements in California and the war with Mexico which followed; your services were of signal importance to your commander, and (as regarded by him) to the public interests at the time.

When, in the course of events, after the occupancy of San Francisco, it became necessary to establish the magistracy of that place, the duties of alcalde were assigned to you, and discharged with a faithfulness and ability which claimed for you the commendation of your immediate commander, as well as that of the commander-in-chief; and the people of the district, when required to elect their civil officers, manifested their high appreciation of your character and services in the magistracy, in according to you an overwhelming vote (over several candidates) for your continuance in office."

From the moment of Montgomery's arrival at Monterey, on the 22d of the month of April, 1846, to the commencement of the war in that quarter, he was in active preparation to take instant possession of San Francisco, and the versatile talents of Bartlett were employed by his commodore to their fullest extent.

As Military Secretary and Translator, Civil Magistrate, and Judge of First Instance, with Admiralty Jurisdiction for the waters of San Francisco, "Collector and Superintendent of the Port," etc., Lieutenant Bartlett was found not only fully qualified by his previous business knowledge, but manifested great administrative ability, by the obedience of all classes shown to his government.

As Chief Magistrate of the Town and District of San Francisco, he exercised all the powers of a local "Cabildo," or "Mexican Ayuntamiento;" he caused the re-survey of the town, regulated and named the streets and squares; located markets; sites for public edifices; and granted lots to actual settlers, under the forms of the Spanish laws of the Indies and colonies, which have ever continued to rule over Mexican Territory.

Bartlett soon saw that the people were willing to obey their new rulers, if they could but be protected by them. And being well read in Kent and Wheaton, he knew where to ascertain the rights of the conquerors, and by reading such Spanish authorities, and consulting such traditional lore as the country afforded, he was able to protect the rights of the conquered.

The original appointment of Bartlett, was confirmed by the people at their first election of civil officers, on the 13th of September following. And when Commodore Stockton saw the harbor filling with ships, the town of San Francisco building up, he appreciated the talent and tact of Bartlett so highly, that he confirmed him in all his functions, as Chief Magistrate, Judge, and United States Collector; even though he then needed officers to conduct his military movements.

In February 22d, 1847, General Kearney arrived in San Francisco, and saw with gratification a well ordered community under perfect control, a civil court of "Common Pleas," and admiralty, proceeding with all the formality of an old New England county, a Court of Records, and Probate, a custom-house, and safe for the public funds, and a well-guarded prison for culprits. He could not but commend such order in the public service, especially since no complaint was laid before him, asking for reversal of a single decision or decree of the Hon. Judge and Collector, and which under the circumstances of the government and Mexican customs and laws, General Kearney must have entertained, had they been presented. And it is a singular fact, that at no period subsequent to this time, has there ever been any reversal of a verdict, judgment or decree, made by Bartlett.

After his election by the people, Judge Bartlett laid aside his naval uniform for the time, wearing only the staff and insignia of the magistracy. And it was under his authority as judge, that the first regular jury was empanelled, for the trial of any cause in California. Amongst other criminal cases tried, there were two seamen for piracy, or robbery on the high seas, who preferring the judge to a jury, plead guilty, and laid themselves at the mercy of the court. There was, too, an interesting civil suit, which had for years hung upon the Mexican docket, viz.: "Reedley, *vs.* the Hon. Hudson's Bay Co.," and no Mexican Judge had dared, because of the power of the British Government, to decide it against the Company.

The Plaintiff appeared in court, a jury was summoned, the case fully heard, and a verdict given against that Company, and the money was paid before an execution could issue against them. The applause was great in finding that an *American* had manifested proper appreciation for their just rights, and without regard for the animosity of any power, had accorded in the spirit of our free institutions, the fullest justice to whom it was due.

SECTION IV.

We can now discover why this young officer was acknowledged by all his superiors and peers to possess "high mental and physical qualifications and efficiency as an accomplished officer of the navy, at all times and in all circumstances ready and willing, on shore and afloat, and ever prompt, zealous and capable in the performance of the various duties assigned him. Whose services were of singular importance to his commander, and to the public interest."

In this connection, we shall continue to exhibit the civil service of Lieutenant Bartlett, and for the reason that it not only shows eminent ability as an officer of the government, but because it enabled him to execute the plans for improvements, which his service on the western coast had shown him to be necessary, and which the govment adopted at his suggestion.

In the publication of the coast survey, we find that Lieutenant Bartlett was the first officer who called the attention of the government to the absolute and immediate necessity for lighting the approaches to San Francisco, and a general plan for the western coast. The subsequent examinations for exact sites for these works, exhibit the closeness of his observations, as they were ultimately placed on the points designated by him in his original communication. It was natural, therefore, that the commercial interests of the western coast should look to him, to aid their delegations in Congress in procuring for that coast, such illuminations for the pathways of commerce, as science and high mechanical skill could produce. And to prevent being supplied to that important region of our coast, any system which scientific investigation had condemned, but which had been so universally and pertinaciously adopted on the Atlantic coast, by the late general superintendent (who, for forty years or more, controlled that department), and who, no doubt, conscientiously believed that no improvement could be made on the then existing system! And yet such were his fears that it might be overturned, that he reported officially to Congress, that light-houses, so far from being useful, had become *public nuisances!* Hence it was, that Lieutenant Bartlett determined to enlighten the hon. gentleman who then presided over the Treasury, on the vast importance of the subject to our commercial interest on that coast. The Secretary could not resist their adoption; he recalled the contracts already made on the old system, and reluctantly embraced the new.

Herein we discover the reasons why the Hon. Mr. Corwin should have selected Lieutenant Bartlett to proceed to Paris for further information, and to superintend the execution for the general introduction of the Fresnel system throughout the United States.

What was the result? Why plainly this, that Bartlett's reports from Paris—the only position where the examination could be made in detail—caused the Department to adopt the system generally on the Atlantic as well as Pacific coast. Congress having already passed a law giving the department the power to change or improve the lights, as the public interests should require, the advocates of the old torchlight system were zealous in their opposition to the improvements in France, and the Secretary of the Treasury, doubting the extent to which the Fresnel system could be carried, and being responsible for what he should adopt, sent Lieutenant Bartlett as an enlightened confidential agent, to Paris, in his behalf, and instructed him, in part, as follows:

TREASURY DEPARTMENT, *June* 16, 1852.

SIR: Congress having authorized the construction of light-houses at different points on the Pacific, the department contemplates furnishing them with the improved French lens, provided the needful appropriation can be obtained to cover the increased expense; but previous to giving any positive orders for the purchase of them, it wishes to obtain particular and detailed information upon all points connected with the subject, and for that purpose has appointed you to proceed to Paris.

You will, on your arrival, make yourself acquainted with the different manufacturers of these lens, and ascertain whether there is any choice between them as to the quality and excellence of their work and their respective prices. The department wishes you to procure the latter in detail.

With this you will receive a copy of a communication from the Light-house Board on the subject of the French lens. The department has not yet approved of this report; and it is not, therefore, furnished to you as a guide, but merely in case it may contain some details or information which might be useful to you. The department will make no determination as to the kinds or orders of the lighting apparatus and fixtures as recommended in this report, until after it hears from you.

It has been suggested that the sixth order lens could be advantageously employed in various small lights on the coasts and harbors of the United States, without making any other change except substituting them for the present reflectors. You will please ascertain on what terms this order of lens can be procured with a suitable mechanical, or other lamp, and without other fixtures or accessories of any kind; or if you find, on inquiry, any of the latter would be absolutely necessary, in order to make the suggested change, then to include the cost of them also; but to have nothing of the kind that is not absolutely necessary.

The department, after hearing from you as regards these—the smaller sized lens—and obtaining further information in connection with the subject of this size, may probably try the experiment with six or eight of the smaller light-houses, and if it succeeds, extend to a much larger number.

The department would also wish to have the statement of cost for any different kinds of materials which are, or can be used in the construction of these apparatus, such as bronze, copper, iron, etc., which might be indiscriminately used, with your views as to which would be most advisable under all the circumstances.

Your report will also include the kind and cost of all the needful items necessary for the use of the light keeper, as connected with the due care and operation of the light after it has been completed and put into use, including not only such items as will be permanently required for the above purpose, but likewise, those which are in regular consumption, estimating the supply of the latter for a period of one year.

CHAPTER II.

While the Light-house Board, by action of its Chairman and Secretary, Shubrick and Jenkins, have studiously kept Lieutenant Bartlett's name out of view in all their reports, they have made free use of his labors in those same documents, and his important services for the safety of our Navy and commerce are appropriated by them as the result of their own investigation. But when to induce the Secretary to give his confidence to the newly elected Board it suited their purpose to refer to the action of Bartlett in Paris. They write thus:

Treasury Department, Light-house Board,
November 17, 1852.

Sir: Your communication of Saturday last, with the accompanying report, papers, and drawings, from Lieutenant Bartlett, U. S. N., special agent of the Treasury Department in Paris, to procure illuminating apparatus for the light-houses on the western coast, have been received, and in reply I am directed by the Board to say—

1st. That the manner in which the duty of Lieutenant Bartlett has thus far been discharged, merits their fullest approbation, and that his report is full of information, and very explicit.

2d. That they recommend the Treasury Department to send

to Lieutenant Bartlett the sum of 48,500 francs, to meet the contracts made by him, as requested in his report to the Department. These contracts are, in the opinion of the Board, made on very favorable terms.

3d. That they recommend to the Treasury Department to authorize Lieutenant Bartlett to make contracts for the illuminating apparatus for the remaining lights recommended by the Board.

The Board has already taken steps preliminary to ordering the illuminating apparatus for Sand Key, and now being informed by Lieutenant Bartlett's report that the apparatus is finished, will complete the action contemplated.

I have the honor to be,
Very respectfully.
Your ob't servant.

(Signed,) WM. BRANFORD SHUBRICK,
Chairman Light-House Board.

The Hon. *Secretary of the Treasury.*

Again, the Secretary, in his second letter, addressed to Lieutenant Bartlett, writes:

Referring to the letter of instructions from the department, under date of 16th inst., I have now to state that the amounts which will be deducted from the contracts for building eight of the light-houses on the coast of the Pacific, in consequence of dispensing with the lanterns and reflectors, specified in said contracts, will enable the department to give a positive order for a portion of the contemplated supply of French lens; you are, therefore, authorized, after your arrival in Paris, and having made yourself acquainted on all the points alluded to in the above letter of instructions, to contract for a Fresnel lens, of a size not exceeding the third order, for the light-house on Fort Point, and, also, for the one on Alcatross Island, San Francisco Bay, and have them completed and shipped as promptly as possible.

And then, referring to the economy which should govern his operations, adds:

But the department, in this, as well as on all other points connected with your mission, *depends upon your best judgment and discretion being exercised*, in purchasing everything on the most favorable terms, consistent with a due regard to having proper workmanship and materials.

In the very teeth of this plenary power conferred on Bartlett by the Treasury Department, Lieutenant Misroon, when speaking for the Navy Board, before the Naval Committee of the Senate, affirmed "that Bartlett was ordered to no other duty than to enter into contracts for eight illuminating apparatus!" And Jenkins, secretary of the Light-house Board, who acted as the jackal, or lackey to the Navy Board, supports Misroon, in the face of his own instructions to Bartlett, of various dates, in 1852–3–4:

OFFICE LIGHT-HOUSE BOARD,
WASHINGTON CITY, *October 15th*, 1852.

DEAR SIR:—I have written to-day to M. Lepaute, in relation to the apparatus for Sand Key, to which you called my attention in your private note to me some weeks since.

If the apparatus can be had, I am authorized to say that the Board will give the necessary orders to have it forwarded without delay, and prompt payment provided.

I wish you would see M. Lepaute, and explain to him fully the difference between the light-house, as at present organized, and the previous mode of managing the lights of this country. We may want some third, fourth, fifth, and sixth orders of lenses, and I wish you would ascertain, from both Lepaute's and Letourneau's establishments, what are the prospects of our getting these different orders, and in what numbers, within the next year, and if there is any change of prices.

Messrs. Sautter & Co. have been informed, as well as M. Lepaute, that you will have the *direction, examination, and test of all these articles so long as you remain in Paris*, after which steps will be taken to obtain a proper person to attend to setting up and examining such as may be ordered. If these orders can be filled at an early day, another will follow immediately.

The implements, tools, etc., and a year's supply of the articles enumerated in the list No. 1, are desired to accompany the Sand Key apparatus when it is shipped.

The articles enumerated in lists No. 1 and 2, as well as the apparatus ordered, must be of the quality, quantities, and prices of the French administration, without they can be had for less.

If the little lighting lamps, called "Lucernes," do not cost more than a trifle each, you may order a number of them.

I wish you would forward us something of a practicable kind, relating to Colza oil. Any printed or manuscript notes on the subject, will be most thankfully received, and the expense of purchase refunded.

Your letter of the 12th, 13th, and 14th ultimo., to this Board, with inclosures, have been received, and your letter of the 14th ult., to the Secretary of the Treasury, has been referred to this office.

The Sand Key apparatus will, probably, be applied to the Cape Hatteras tower, to save time; but the order for the duplicate, with a lantern, can be changed, as you suggest, to a duplicate of the one for the Farrallones and Cordouan. The lantern should accompany it; but it is desired that no unnecessary expense should be incurred in constructing the lanterns, particularly now, that iron and copper are both so high. The desire of the Board is utility, with as little ornament, not necessary to the efficiency of the objects, as possible. The best lights, at the smallest expense, consistent with utility and economy.

And, if these are not sufficient, we are provided with the testimony of Professor Bache, together with Professor Henry, the distinguished scientific members of the Board, who have given prestige, in the public judgment, to that institution, and whom we know unite in their appreciation of the services of Lieutenant Bartlett, as conveyed in the following note:

WASHINGTON, *December 5th*, 1858.

MY DEAR SIR:—

* * * * * * * * * * * *

I have not seen Lieutenant Jenkins, or the Light-house Board, since my return to Washington, but expect to do so soon. When last here, your doings had given great satisfaction. For myself, I do not believe we could have succeeded, in any other way, so well, in setting our machine in motion, as in the way we took by suggesting to the Secretary of the Treasury to send you abroad.

Yours, truly,

Signed, A. D. BACHE.

LIEUT. W. A. BARTLETT, *U. S. N.*, *Paris*.

SECTION I.

Americans, note the fact that, when Bartlett was sent to Paris, this Light-house Board had not even been created by law; and, when it was, the Secretary of the Treasury, under whose instructions Bartlett was then acting, became, *ex officio*, the President of that Board! What, then, do we see? That, every subsequent act of the especial agency at Paris is communicated to that Board, for its approval, by the Secretary of the Treasury; and through which Board the Secretary *only* communicated with the agent ever afterwards.

Can any intelligent reader fail thus to see

that Bartlett was held responsible for the faithful execution of every suggestion of that Board, and the same discretionary power that was given when he derived the appointment was maintained to the last? His suggestions were adopted, his plans and contracts were approved; and the work, when finished, from time to time, was pronounced by the French engineers as of the finest possible execution. The expenditures for this delicate, yet substantial illuminating power, amounting to nearly three hundred thousand dollars, were paid only on his certificates of the exactness of the work, and in precise accordance with the wishes of the government. These bills being, in every instance, *less* than the originally approved estimate.

The importance of all this will be best shown by the Board's own *reports* to Congress, January 15th, 1853. The Senate session of XXXIId Congress, Vol. V. The Board having convened at the Treasury Department, on the 9th of October last, were duly organized by their President, the Hon. Secretary of the Treasury.

Since that date the Board has executed, under the direction of the Treasury Department, all the administrative duties relating to the management of the light-house establishment.

It relies upon the officers to direct their first attention to the fulfillment of the wants of the navigator, for whose benefit the establishment exists.

In an economical point of view, it is of equally great importance. This subject has occupied the attention of those charged with the management of European lights for many years.*

---

* Three years previous to Lieutenant Bartlett's mission to Europe, a conditional or indirect order had been given to Mr. Henry Lepaute of Paris to construct a proper lens light for Sand Key, Florida, and another for Carysfort Reef, on that coast, by the late J. W. P. Lewis, Marine and Light-house Engineer, who had obtained the passage of a special act of Congress for those lights. The opposition of the then existing Light-house Department to this great improvement was so intense, that it succeeded in causing the Carysfort Reef lens to be sold at auction, at the New York Custom House, for $600, although the Government had, indirectly contracted to pay $9,000 for it; and as by this act Mr. Lepaute had lost all hope of being repaid for that beautiful work (and did finally, when in 1853 the Government received possession of it, actually lose over $3,000 dollars in expenses), he of course suspended work on the order of Sand Key. But Lieut. Bartlett, on reaching Paris, having tested the work as it stood in the *atelier*, and pledged himself personally to Mr. Lepaute to procure its sale to the Government if he would but finish it, Mr. Lepaute did so on Lieut. Bartlett's individual credit.

As the new Light-house Board had got to work in November, Mr. Bartlett's report upon it to the Secretary of the Treasury, and asking its purchase, was sent to them, and enabled them to put it up at once in Sand Key, the work of the Chairman and Secretary of the Light-house Board.

There is one other circumstance in connection with this light which must be told, as it shows that from the very beginning Mr. Thornton A. Jenkins, who, although a Lieutenant in the Navy and Secretary of the old and new Light-house Board, was not only determined that Lieut. Bartlett should not have any public credit for his work, but was also determined to cheat him by a trick out of his rights to be paid his "reasonable" expenses while serving in Europe.

Lieut. Bartlett had filed a bond in the Treasury for $15,000,

Estimates to be of any value should be based upon a faithful examination of the different works by competent and disinterested persons.

The lights authorized to be built on the Pacific coast were transferred to the management of the Board on the 22d December, 1852.

The officer charged with the purchase of the remainder of the lights contracted for on the western coast, having received his instructions from the Secretary of the Treasury direct, it remains for the Board to see that they are faithfully carried out, and that the lights be supplied with them without unnecessary delay.

---

signed by Wm. H. Aspinwall and Henry Grinnell, and Drake Mills, as security for his faithful disbursement of the public money. Jenkins has Bartlett's approval of Mr. Lepaute's prices for the Sand Key apparatus, approved by the Board; then obtains from the Treasury the exact sum of money requisite to pay it, having it charged to Lieutenant Bartlett's account, as a disbursing officer of the Government, and remits it to him, made payable to Mr. Lepaute's order, and asks Bartlett to send back the vouchers to the Department; Bartlett, never dreaming, from the tenor of the letter, that he was charged with the money, sent back the vouchers, leaving the name of the paying officer in blank; this voucher is now in the Treasury Department, with the blank filled up in Jenkins' handwriting, as if paid by the "Secretary of the Treasury." Why, but to prepare himself to contest Bartlett's right to have his expenses refunded, to an amount equal to three per cent. on the expenditures, provided his expenses should amount to that sum?

That Lieutenant Bartlett was the agent, responsible to the Treasury Department for the money expended for refitting Hatteras light with its new illuminator, is incontrovertible, *vide* the following official letter:

TREASURY DEPARTMENT,
OFFICE OF COMMISSIONER OF CUSTOMS, *January 12th*, 1854.

SIR:—Your account for fitting Cape Hatteras light with first order of illuminating apparatus, has been adjusted and closed on the books of the Treasury.

Respectfully yours,

Signed, H. J. ANDERSON,
Commissioner of Customs.

LIEUT. W. A. BARTLETT,
Agent for fitting Cape Hatteras light, etc.

The Board, having the benefit of Bartlett's reports on his investigations abroad, showing the high point of efficiency and economy to which the system had arrived, stated to Congress, "that they would proceed with the gradual introduction of a better description of illuminating apparatus, the superiority of which is no longer to be questioned, by adopting a system of instruction founded upon scientific attainments and practical knowledge."

When Lieut. Bartlett left Paris, he had superintended, inspected, approved, and shipped to the United States, to the order of the Light-house Board, sixty-three Fresnel luminators, several of which, especially of the great light off San Francisco, exceeded in power any light ever previously constructed in any part of the world, having the power of six thousand six hundred Argand burners concentrated in a single beam! It now flashes upon the mariner every consecutive minute from sunset to sunrise!

A duplicate of the same power he also constructed for the Atlantic coast. Hon. John Y. Mason, Ex-Secretary of the Navy, and Minister to France, who, in company with other members of the diplomatic corps, and distinguished savans of Europe, including Fresnel, surviving brother of the inventor, Messrs. Reynaud and Degrand, engineers of the French Light-house Department, often attended the exhibitions of Lieutenant Bartlett, attesting the power of these lights; and the Hon. Mr. Mason thus addressed the Secretary of the Treasury:

UNITED STATES LEGATION,
PARIS, *September 2d*, 1854.

DEAR SIR:—Lieutenant Bartlett, of the United States Navy, is about leaving Paris, on his return to the United States. It gives me great pleasure to bear my testimony to the care and vigilance with which this gentleman has performed his responsible duties, since I have been here, and to express my admiration of the splendid lights which have been manufactured under his supervision for the coasts of the United States.

I do not believe that there are, in the world, superior mechanical structures for the safety of commerce than those which have been prepared here, under the superintendence of Mr. Bartlett. The chief credit is, unquestionably, due to the faithful and skillful manufacturers, but no small share is, in my judgment, due to Mr. Bartlett, who has displayed zeal, industry, and intelligence, in the performance of his duties. I hope that you will not consider me obtrusive in thus expressing my admiration of the lens lights, prepared here for the exposed and dangerous coasts of my country.

I have the honor to be, most respectfully,

J. Y. MASON.

HON. JAMES GUTHRIE,
Secretary of the Treasury, Washington.

Having disposed of this assertion, that the duties of Lieut. Bartlett were limited, we now advert to another statement of Misroon, speaking for the Naval Board, that he (Bartlett) claimed expenses for constructing sixty-three light-house illuminators ; but he was ordered to attend to no other duty than to enter into contracts for eight illuminating apparatus. This is absolutely and most unqualifiedly *untrue.*

And this is met by the official letter of the Auditor of the Treasury, to which we call the attention of the reader.

WASHINGTON, *April 21st*, 1856.

SIR:—I am in possession of your letter of the 18th inst., requesting me to furnish you copies of all the reports made by me in the settlement of your accounts as the special agent of the Treasury Department, for the purchase of light-house apparatus, etc., during the years 1852, '53, 54, and '55.

The reports made by me in the settlement of your accounts, are on file in the office of the Register of the Treasury, which is the appropriate office to obtain copies.

You also ask, if I will state whether there is anything in the accounts rendered by you, or in the correspondence relating thereto, calculated to impugn your personal or official honor; and whether your accounts were not rendered in a full and business-like manner.

In the settlement of your accounts, there was not anything that, in the slightest degree, tended to impugn your personal or official honor.

Your accounts were rendered in a full and business-like manner.

Respectfully, your obedient servant,

T. L. SMITH

WASHINGTON A. BARTLETT, Esq.

SECTION II.

And we ask now, who are the public *bound* to trust, the sworn auditor of the government, whose business it is to investigate and pass upon the accounts of all its officers, and which in this, as in all other cases, were again inspected by the Comptroller of the Treasury, or that Jacobin slander of a secret Inquisition, whose purpose it was to *create* a spot to blast the victim they had marked out for their destruction.

Remember, Americans, that this same cabal did ten years ago *signally fail* in a similar attempt to injure the fair fame of the same gallant officer. Why was he the subject *then*, of their low, petty, ill-natured, unmerited slander, but because of the rising character of the man, his genius, his enterprise and promise, which at that day on the "Portsmouth," excited the envy common to vulgar minds.

It is sufficient for us to say, that after the indisputable testimony of the sworn Auditor of the Treasury, whose language we repeat, "*that in the settlement of your* (*Bartlett's*) *accounts, there was not anything that, in the slightest degree, tended to*

Engraved by J.C.Buttre.

N. Ranney

OF MISSOURI

impugn your (*his*) *personal or official honor*," that we shall not enlarge upon this subject, except to say, that Lieutenant Bartlett was sent abroad by his government, with powers and duties for his employment, and a discretion in their exercise, with which it would have honored the oldest in the public service of the country to have been charged. That he performed them with signal ability, to the entire satisfaction of two administrations of different political sentiments, we know. That he was sent upon a mission which was to enlarge by his capacity and industry; that he was found equal to the task. Upon his labor and researches great public improvement, which gives protection to the navy and to commerce along the vast coast of the United States, has resulted. Two little lights in the Bay of San Francisco had not long shown this improved illuminating power, before Lieutenant Bartlett had caused sixty-three to be constructed, and shipped to the United States. These have now expanded until upwards of three hundred illumine and bless the pathway of the mariner!

It was not supposed that the original orders would have extended to such a vast work, and over so long a period of time. Nor could it have been supposed then, how much expenditure it would involve. He was to be paid his "reasonable personal expenses," provided those expenses should not exceed three per cent. upon the amounts expended on that business. This would have admitted for personal expenses, a sum of nearly four thousand dollars. He faithfully executed his work, and is commended *throughout* for all his proceedings. And presents an account for his expenses, in *accordance* with his instructions. These expenses covering nearly twenty-seven months. The travel from Washington to Paris, *viâ* England, and general expenses abroad, amounted in the aggregate, to the sum of four thousand and eleven dollars. Of this amount, the auditor passed to his credit, the sum of three thousand seven hundred and fifty two dollars, and eighteen cents. And here we remark, that every public minister, indeed, almost every agent of the government, who ever presented an account, has had some items suspended or rejected. But, who but a "Council of Ten," or an "Inquisition of Fifteen," would dare, for this reason, to call their high integrity in question?

Lieutenant Bartlett's account was settled at the treasury, with a balance in his favor; although the Hon. Secretary of the Treasury exercised the power of construing his predecessors' instructions, with a narrowness of view illy according with the magnitude of the powers conferred by them. And while he limited Lieutenant Bartlett's expenses to an amount not exceeding three per cent. on the amount which that officer had himself disbursed abroad, instead of allowing his reasonable personal expenses not to exceed three per cent. on the amount expended in the business! and which the department knew, by its own records, to be near three hundred thousand dollars.

Bartlett made no claim as of right; he rested upon a liberal interpretation of his instructions. He knew that he had faithfully performed his duty; he knew that a *sum larger than three per cent. had been saved the government on every contract;* he knew that a less sum of money than the contract called for had paid it; for, with these savings, he had defrayed these very personal expenses, without calling on the Department to do so.

One hundred and ten dollars and sixty-two cents was the full amount of money required to be taken from the treasury, to pay Lieutenant

Bartlett's personal expenses! The balance had been paid, by his savings on the amounts placed in his hands, to cancel contracts. And, had no part of the whole amount, which was placed to his credit by the auditor, been arbitrarily withheld by the Secretary of the Treasury, there would still have been but one thousand and thirty-nine dollars drawn from the treasury, on account of his expenses!

The Secretary allowed but three per cent. on ninety thousand four hundred and thirteen dollars, and ninety cents, while the books of the Register of the Treasury show that Lieutenant Bartlett actually disbursed and accounted for one hundred and two thousand three hundred and ninety-four dollars, and eight cents; and while he claimed no commissions, he had a right, in the common sense view of the matter, as well as in the opinion of eminent jurists, to claim his "reasonable expenses." He did this and nothing more. It was the *Board*, and not Bartlett, who suggested, in their report to the Secretary, the propriety of paying commissions, on the amounts disbursed by Bartlett, as "a partial reimbursement," and which drew forth from the Secretary the following letter:

TREASURY DEPARTMENT, *January 3d*, 1855.

SIR:—I have read the inclosed communication from Mr. Bartlett, upon the subject of his claim for expenses, to and from Paris, and whilst there.

Mr. Bartlett, being an officer of the government, and appointed to go to Paris, was promised, as his letter of appointment shows, his expenses in going and returning, and whilst there, not to exceed the sum of three per cent. on the amount disbursed, as expressed in the letter of appointment. The account, being stated on the principle of allowing three per cent. on the amount disbursed, is not properly stated. It should be stated by allowing the expense, in strict compliance with the letter of appointment, not to exceed three per cent. This will require a re-statement of the account, and, when his vouchers are not sufficient, you will apprise him, and allow him time to make them right.

I am, very respectfully,

JAMES GUTHRIE,

Secretary of the Treasury.

H. J. ANDERSON, Esq., Commissioner of Customs.

Here, we find that astute and mighty official expresses his opinion that Bartlett really did have a letter of appointment!

SECTION III.

But the Secretary was not ignorant of what duties Bartlett had performed, as we find this letter had previously enlightened him.

I (Mr. Bartlett) requested the Secretary "to have in view the fact that I superintended, inspected, and shipped, to the United States, for the Light-house Board (which is not less a part of the Treasury Department), *fifty-five* illuminators for the Atlantic coast (including Hatteras, etc.), and costing over eight hundred thousand francs, for which *no expenses of agency or superintendency have been incurred, in any quarter, and* CERTAINLY NOT CLAIMED BY ME." *

He understood, perfectly well, that *sixty-three* of these Fresnel lenses had, under the supervision of Bartlett, been constructed from 1st September, 1852, to 1st September, 1854; a greater number than any other country has ever constructed in *ten years!*

---

* At the time Lieutenant Bartlett was serving abroad, the State Department had occasion to send a *sealed dispatch to Madrid*, via Paris. Ex-Governor Winslow, of North Carolina, now a member of Congress, was selected for this special mission; he was absent from the United States just *sixty-nine days!* and his expense account was audited, after the regulation of some items, and paid by the Department, as follows:

For expenses, ...	$617 00
For pay, sixty-nine days, at $6 00	$414 00
Total	$1031 00

Or, fourteen dollars ninety-four and one-fifth cents per day.

Lieutenant Bartlett was on foreign service of *real responsibility*, from June 16th, 1852, to September 18th, 1854, a period of eight hundred and twenty-one days, at the following cost to the government:

For his pay, as a Lieutenant in the Navy, being set down in the Navy Register, on "special service in Europe,"

For two years and three months	3375 00
For "partial reimbursement of his expenses," . . .	2712 42
Total	6087 42

$6087 42 ÷ 821 days = $7 41 per day, *or, less than one half the daily expenses of the Hon. Ex-Governor for carrying a dispatch!!!*

Had the whole amount of Lieutenant Bartlett's expenses been paid, it would have amounted to nine dollars and ten cents per day, for *pay and expenses!*

Having shown something of the military and civil character of Lieutenant Bartlett in the service of the country, we find peculiar pleasure in directing Americans to his claims as a philanthropist. Here, as in other relations, he furnishes the most undissembled evidences of a genuine feeling for his fellow man.

In the Winter of 1846 and '47, it is known Lieutenant B. was chief magistrate of San Francisco, where, in aiding and assisting the settler, and frequently in protecting the houseless, he was not less eminently useful to that young community, than in the preservation of law and order. During his magistracy, breadstuffs became so enhanced in price, by the action of speculators, as to threaten immediate famine among the suffering poor. Bartlett, foreseeing the result upon that class, became himself immediately responsible to a large amount for flour, binding the importer to

---

At this very time, the Secretary of the Treasury was allowing to officers of the *army*, who were superintending public works, such as the extension of the Treasury Building, and the Custom House, and Light-house Inspector, at Portland, or any other superintendency in the civil service of the Treasury, a sum equal (including his army pay), to eight dollars per day. Would an addition of one dollar and ten cents per day, for such *foreign* service as Lieutenant Bartlett rendered, with the remarkable economy and saving he produced, have been an extravagant sum?

deliver it in single barrels only, to all comers at a fixed low price, until all families should be supplied. And thus brought upon him the grateful appreciation of that large and helpless class of emigrants.

On another occasion, Bartlett, while chief magistrate, received a letter from the venerable Judge of Sacramento, giving intelligence that some eighty-five men and women were then perishing in the snows of the Sierra Nevada, sixteen having escaped after many weeks' detention. Bartlett called the people together, and in the most affecting address to their humanity, besought their aid for these sufferers, largely leading the subscription. The appeal was successful, and with provisions, blankets, and clothing, chief magistrate Bartlett selected and dispatched this relief through Midshipman Woodworth, son of the poet, late a Senator of California; and by this timely interposition of Bartlett, these people were saved.

When commander of the "Ewing," in the Pacific, Bartlett encountered a British ship from Panama, bound to California. As its commander responded "all well," Bartlett ordered his vessel "filled away," when a shout went up from two hundred suffering souls on board, "water, water, water!"

These people were on short allowances of half pint per man, and the barbarous commander did not wish it known to a United States vessel which had outsailed and passed him at sea.

Bartlett instantly ordered the unfeeling commander to "back his top-sails," and wait until he placed provisions and water on board, sufficient to supply the pressing wants of these people, which was speedily done. The whole country will remember the appeals of Lieutenant Bartlett through the Washington and New York papers, in behalf of the sufferers of the Cape de Verde Islands; as well as his address before the Corn Exchange in that city, in which, in addition to his own large contribution to this charity, Bartlett tendered his own personal services to take the provisions himself to that unfortunate people free of all charge. And he did not go simply because passing vessels were found through which this assistance was forwarded, thus saving the necessity of fitting out a ship for the especial purpose. Thus did Bartlett perform his promise to the people when he left the "Jamestown!" And although called suddenly home, broken in the service by conspirators against his fame, and deprived of his pay, he stopped at the *Canaries*, sent money on shore, and by his indefatigable exertions with friends and acquaintances, caused a supply of the necessaries of life to be at once dispatched to the starving Islanders, from the nearest points. At Madeira and at Lisbon he made similar appeals, and such was the estimate in which he was held as a distinguished naval officer of the United States, that food in immense quantities at once went to that land of starvation and woe. The American Consulate at each of these ports, and the American Minister at Lisbon, long after Bartlett's return to the United States, tendered him the thanks of the people and the Government for the successful efforts of a wise philanthropy in saving from death so many of the human family.

The archives of the Portuguese Legation in New York city furnish these facts. It was by Lieutenant Bartlett's interposition, aided by Dr. Clymer, fleet-surgeon of the African Squadron, that famine was stayed, and the pestilence removed from them.

Americans, if Rome decreed a civic crown to him who had saved the life of but one citizen, what should have been the reward to one like Bartlett, whose record proves him a rare benefactor of his race?

And yet, while in the performance of acts like these, which elevated his *national*, as well as personal character, we find a small lieutenant, devoid of any consequence through his services, and without a solitary claim upon the respect or gratitude of a single junior, exercising his unmitigated selfishness and envy, by daring to assail, in the secret councils of an inquisition, a man like Bartlett, whom the God of nature has made his superior.

And this same Misroon, the implacable enemy of Lieutenant Bartlett, has maligned the character of that officer, by assailing his personal and official reputation, and in the face of the most irrefragable proof, asserted that Bartlett was without friends in the Pacific Squadron, or the *association* which belonged to officers of his rank.

No friends! No social intercourse! Let us see! Bartlett commanded the "Argo," an armed prize in the Gulf of California, and subsequently, another brig, also a prize to the "Portsmouth," and as such, was continually consulted by Shubrick, for the local information of the coast which he possessed, and was a constant guest at his table, as he was at every table in the squadron.

Lieutenants Chatard, Heywood, Selden, Wise,

Montgomery and Henry Lewis, M'Cree, Stanley, Maddox, Tansil, M'Lanahan (killed at San José), Duncan, Carter, Stephen H. Rowan, Bullock, the gallant and deservedly popular commander of the "Cahawba" steam packet-ship; Fleet-Surgeon Dr. Charles Chase, Captain Watson, M. C., Lieutenant Revere, Pursers Rodman M. Price (the present Governor of New Jersey), Spieden, the late Dr. Powell, etc., etc., etc.; Mr. John Parrott, and Mr. Bolton at Mazatlan; Mr. Larkin at Monterey, and Lienenduff, Howard, Mellus, etc., etc., at San Francisco, American consuls and merchants, at whose houses and tables Lieutenant Bartlett was ever a welcome guest. These, with scores too numerous to mention here, were then his friends, and remain so to this day.*

---

* Young Midshipman Downs, the brother-in-law of Misroon, who joined the Portsmouth at Misroon's solicitation, has become ever since the warm and intimate friend of Bartlett, and subsequently visited him at Key West, to renew the association, and recur to their travels in the Pacific and Mexican services.

There are other ways besides, which society recognizes as the true test of friendly consideration! We have seen the notes and obligations for money, which Bartlett holds over the sign manual of his brother officers. And Lieutenant William Gibson, Captain J. C. Rich, marine corps, Lieutenant Hart, Dr. Hill, Lieutenants Hanell, Harrison, Perry, and others, will attest that no officer ever called on Lieutenant Bartlett for pecuniary aid, who did not receive it.

SECTION IV.

In this connection we will for a moment ask the reader's attention to the proof.

An American consul died suddenly at his post. His nephew was the companion of Bartlett on the ship. No money could be found belonging to the deceased to reimburse the funeral expenses. In a foreign land, where all parties are strangers, these expenses have to be provided, even before the interment of the body.

With no visible means, the small pay of the nephew did not justify his assumption of the debt, and no one appeared who was willing to take the responsibility.

Bartlett alone stood forth, the firm friend of the sufferer. "Draw your bill," said he, "on any party whom you regard as your uncle's friend in the United States. I will endorse it, Baring's agent in this Island will so negotiate it, and you can have all the money you require for this purpose. Should your friend be unable to meet the bill in New York, I will instruct my agent to do so, the moment it arrives!"

By this disinterested act of Bartlett's, the name

of a man honored by his country with a commission in a foreign land; a name appreciated in the literature of his own country; a name dear to American citizens, and hosts of friends, was preserved from desecration and slander, and the honor of our flag was preserved, in the estimation of all who have an American "heart!"

And the strongest evidences of this regard, has since been manifested to Bartlett, by the friends of the distinguished dead. At another period of this same cruise, the one in which he served abroad, when broken at home, an officer lay ill, and the surgeon declared the necessity of his immediate return home. He was without money, and under the circumstances, a doubt arose, as to drawing it from the public chest. To relieve the depressing influence this was making on the invalid, Bartlett came to his side, and begged him to banish all anxiety on that account, promising all the money needed to restore him to his friends. It was, however, decided that the sum was due from the government. But, the generous tender, and its effect upon the officer, is, to this hour, a subject of his grateful eulogy upon Bartlett.*

* In the winter of 1851 and '2, Bartlett was one day at the navy agent's, in New York, when two interesting youths called, and

Lieut. Washington A. Bartlett belongs to the family of Josiah Bartlett, who *first* appended his name to the Charter of our Independence. He was appointed Midshipman in the Navy by General Jackson, January 1833, while the Department was under the administration of Hon. Levi Woodbury. Well instructed in mathematics, nautical astronomy, and navigation, he was immediately selected by Commodore Wadsworth as his "aid," and sailed in the Vincennes to the Pacific. There he joined Capt. Lavallette, and after active service for two years, rejoined Commodore Wadsworth, who had shifted his flag to the Brandywine.

---

exhibited orders to proceed "without delay" to Norfolk, to rejoin the "San Jacinto," being midshipmen. They stated they were suddenly detached (from cause unknown to them), at New York, and having exhausted their pay in fitting out a new mess, were in arrears for board, and without means to reach Norfolk. The case was modestly and feelingly presented, but without eliciting aid from the agent of the government, who informed them that he had no authority to advance for such expenses, and they must telegraph to the department. But how could they, without a dollar! Bartlett followed them out, having heard with emotion their pathetic, but simple story. He knew the necessity of prompt obedience to orders, and sympathizing with their condition, he at once tendered the money, and urged their quick departure. These young officers gave their note for immediate payment from Norfolk, which was done, and it was not until the business transaction was being consummated, that they knew their benefactor as Washington A. Bartlett, a brother officer!

During this period, Midshipman Bartlett attained proficiency in the Spanish language, assiduously devoting those hours to study which his comrades were wont to give to recreation. An incident occurred shortly after Bartlett entered the Fairfield, under Captain, now Commodore Lavallette, which furnishes the strongest evidence of confidence reposed in that young officer by his superiors, as well as the necessity, of understanding the native tongue of a people with whom we are daily associated.

Commodore Wadsworth, of the Vincennes, and Captain Lavallette, of the Fairfield, each twenty-four guns, had forced General Mina, who carried an admiral's flag on board the Columbian frigate Columbia, of sixty-four 42-pounders, and 600 men, into a treaty, which guaranteed to our flag the possession of the ship until the meeting of the Columbian Congress in 1834. General Mina, with his staff, and 500 artillerists, was also to leave the ship, which had long closed the Guayaquil river against American commerce, and made almost piratical exactions upon our citizens. The American ships, fearing treachery, or an attempt to escape, had been prepared for action since entering the river; but after the treaty was signed, the Vincennes proceeded to visit the city of Guayaquil, and announce the favorable result to American commerce. No sooner had she got out of sight (being night) than a revolt took place on the Columbia, and the time was occupied in silently placing her in a perfect state of defense. These proceedings were watched by the Americans on board the Fairfield, but the hour of surrender by the treaty was not to be until nine o'clock next morning.

At 8·40 a boat was sent by Captain Lavallette to the frigate, to inform her that at nine o'clock a prize officer would be sent to receive her, and watch the landing of the crew. The answer returned was, that Mina no longer commanded, that a colonel and naval commodore now held control, that no treaty would be recognized, and that they were prepared to stand to their guns.

Captain Lavallette now called to Midshipman Bartlett, and in the firmest, clearest tone of voice, said to *him*, in presence of all on board, "Proceed to the Columbia, and say to whoever may be in command, that unless when the bell strikes two (or nine o'clock) I see her boats manned, and her crew leaving the ship, and you inform me that you are in command, as her prize officer by five minutes past nine, I will open my fire on her, 'and sink her, boys, we must; or she will sink us.' *Stay on board*, when you get there," continued he, "and let me see you on her rail as quickly as possible, saying yes or no."

Bartlett landed on the deck of the frigate without resistance, in the presence of the old veteran follower of Bolivar, and his scores of officers, and immediately, like a high spirited American youth, delivered his message and defiance. Its boldness astonished commander and officers, and after a short consultation, before the "bell struck two, or nine o'clock," the commander said to Bartlett, "*The artillery will land as you direct, and the sea officers and men, with the ship, are yours, to save the effusion of blood.*"

After a prompt execution of this order, Bartlett inspected the ship, and found the most ample resources, and preparation for battle had been made. The magazine passage was strewed with loose powder, which was immediately flooded, and all fires forbidden.

The wonder was, that they had not instantly blown up the ship, with Bartlett on board. It is very rare that a young midshipman has an opportunity to deliver such a message from a twenty-four gun ship, of 200 men, to a frigate of sixty-four guns and 600 men! Its success, too, was still more remarkable, which nothing but the indomitable energy and American heroism of Captain Lavallette and his officers could have accomplished.

SECTION V.

The late Lieutenant, Commanding, W. P. McArthur (who distinguished himself, and received three wounds in Florida), and Colonel Morrison, who so gallantly led the Illinois regiment in their desperate fighting at Buena Vista, under General Taylor, were Bartlett's messmates at that time, in the Fairfield. The gallant commander, H. W. Morris, of New York, then a lieutenant, commanded the second division of the Fairfield's guns, and this surprising victory over a superior force was obtained by the surpassing firmness and efficiency of American men.

Suppose, now, Bartlett had not spoken the language of the people, no matter how great his other qualities, he could not have been sent on this fearful mission. Instead of returning to the United States in the "Fairfield," Midshipman Bartlett lengthened his cruise to four years and over, and on rejoining the "Brandywine" again, became aid to the commodore, with whom he determined to continue, until he should haul down his flag.

In that period of revolution and counter-revolution in Lima and Peru, generally, the commodore was detained there. And while his ship lay at Callao, his "aid" was constantly exposed on that celebrated robber and assassin's course, the "road to Lima," while bearing the commodore's dispatches to and from the ship; which duty, like all others, he fulfilled to the letter and spirit.

There are eminent merchants now in New York, who can bear *testimony* to the valuable services of Commodore Wadsworth and his officers, during the Gamorra, Santa Cruz, Salavery, and Arbegosa wars in Peru. At one period for weeks, the "Brandywine" had about two hundred ladies, gentlemen, and children guests of her officers.

In August, 1837, Lieutenant Bartlett was ordered to the receiving ship of Capt. Montgomery, when an intimacy and friendship between this admirable Commander and the youthful subaltern was formed, which has never faltered in the succeeding series of years. We remember the name of Montgomery embellishing the naval history of the country in the successful part he bore in Perry's victory on Lake Erie.* The service of a receiving ship was not, however, suited to one of the professional ambition of Bartlett, and we soon find him transferred to the frigate "Fulton," the second, under Captain, now Commodore Perry, and the letter given by this distinguished officer to Midshipman Bartlett, to present to the Board of Examiners, indicated the warm personal regard which it is well known that gentleman now bears towards Lieutenant Bartlett. Having been detained by illness in New York, when the Fulton sailed to Washington, he next reported himself, as ordered, to Commodore Ridgely, for duty at the navy yard, and to attend the lectures of Professor Word, preparatory to examination. This

* Such was Captain Montgomery's confidence in the judgment and skill of Bartlett, that when one night in the Pacific, into which he had not been himself, a night of the deepest darkness, with baffling winds and hidden dangers on all sides, he communicated his anxiety to Lieutenant Bartlett to be in port before morning. "If I command the ship," said Bartlett, "I will certainly go in; though I have not seen it for ten years." "That is sufficient," said Capt. M., "take the ship, sir." And at daylight, next morning, great was the astonishment of the people to find a large American ship in port, and being just before the Mexican war, caused much surprise among the Mexican officers of the place.

ordeal he passed at Philadelphia, in 1839; and without the aid of any connection with Commodores or Washington officials, Bartlett took No. 7 in a class of 32! He was immediately selected by Lieutenant Commanding Glenn with a party of young officers, to survey "southern harbors," and when finished, we find him the succeeding year prosecuting that service under Commander Powell. While on this expedition, Bartlett was promoted to an acting lieutenancy, and made the executive officer of the steamer "Poinsett," while under Powell's command. It was then that the superb survey of Tampa Bay, Florida, was made by the officers of the "Poinsett; the most magnificent sheet of water which had then been surveyed by American officers south of the Chesapeake. Captains Glenn and Powell have ever borne testimony to the skill, ability, and zeal which Bartlett rendered to the service in these surveys of the southern waters of the United States.

SECTION VI.

In 1842, Bartlett was ordered to the coast survey, under that most distinguished hydrographer, Commander Gedney, and was, for two years, actively engaged with him in the prosecution of this great work, between New York and Delaware Bay. The exposure of life to imminent peril, in these coast works, is best known to those who are familiar with the subject. And any well-informed naval officer knows that it requires more than the usual science of seamanship to become an accomplished surveyor, or hydrographer. There is a quick perception and ready judgment called constantly into exercise, in the physical difficulties which occur at every step, and which must be overcome by the strongest resolution to submit to whatever risk the occasion might present. For such duty, Bartlett has ever been seen to be highly efficient, and when he left that service, in 1844, he bore the highest evidences of the confidence and esteem of his superiors. He was next attached to the naval rendezvous, at New York, for some months, when he was ordered to the "Portsmouth," as sailing-master, but he soon became the junior lieutenant, and made the cruise of three years and ten months in the Pacific ocean, and, during the entire Mexican war, was on the West coast of Mexico, or some part of California.

It was on this cruise of the "Portsmouth,"

that Misroon, one of the Inquisition, acted as the executive officer of the ship. Lieutenant Misroon there showed so total and selfish a disregard for the comfort of others, that every watch officer sought the earliest opportunity to escape his contact. Lieutenants Shenck, Forrest, and Carter, left the ship the very first opportunity. And it is a singular fact that, among all the active officers of the ship, that joined her at Portsmouth, Lieutenant Bartlett was the only one who adhered to his post, and, although he did not like the personal bearing of Misroon, his habits of subordination (the surest test of the future influence of an officer) were such, that he never, for a moment, forgot his own dignity, or the respect duty required him to render to the executive of the ship, without regard to *the personnel of the man* who filled that position.

In making this exposition of the character and services of Lieutenant Bartlett, the author has had not only the data, but the *vouchers* before her for every item that has been stated. And she asserts, without the fear of refutation, that so overwhelming is the proof of the scrupulous integrity and honor of Lieutenant Bartlett, that no unprejudiced mind can resist the conclusion, after investigating this evidence, that he has been basely wronged by the unscrupulous action of a cabal, instigated by unprincipled and envious revilers!

We do not believe that a higher integrity ever characterized the settlement of any official accounts under this government than has been displayed by Lieutenant Bartlett. And if, after an entire knowledge of all the facts in this connection, it could have been pronounced otherwise, then those of General Washington, during the American Revolution, would not have passed unscathed!

It is a crying shame, a burning shame, that this American citizen has been so outrageously maligned and persecuted in the service of his country! And as the honor of that country is identified with the character of its true men, so has the nation been dishonored by those who have trampled down its naval heroes, and in a spirit of merciless recklessness, without contrition or remorse, consummated an act which would not have been tolerated under any despotism of Europe!

Our fathers saw the triumph of *right*, and left to their sons their speaking actions. Shall that heroic generation be slighted now? To give peace and liberty, American men struck tyrants and hurled back their thrones! They founded liberty on the enfranchisement of the mind. They counted not parties, but principles, and rejected restrictions, distinctions, and exclusions! We have the witnesses of that great age when we started as a nation into life, and he that halts now in condemning that action which has wantonly outraged the personal and political rights of Lieutenant Bartlett and his associates in the naval service, condemns and rejects the very men who gave to the whole world America!

CENTRAL AMERICA.

CHAPTER I.

It was our fathers' wish to keep the administration of this government in an American sphere. They wanted no colonial or territorial dependence. They wanted to maintain the Union, and therefore asserted the right of the American people to the exclusive control of their own matters. They said, in the constitution they left us, that Congress could sell the public lands, that it could admit new states, but not a word was mentioned about organizing any government without the rights of a state.

Under this constitution we Americans have signally prospered, while our influence has exerted a mighty power over all the civilized states of the world. There is not a nation with which we have not a commercial and political relation. There is not a country in which our enterprise has not entered, nor an ocean on which our ships do not float. American genius is more or less impressed upon every people and clime, and mutual interest and sympathy bind us to mankind. We have no need now, Americans, to fear to assume the principles which have guided us thus triumphantly; nor can we limit those principles within our own borders. Our example, our ideas, our discoveries, our inventions, our habits of life, our social, political, and religious institutions, must ultimately extend our form of government. And to see our maxims securely applied to other people; to see our laws, the settled principles of equality and justice, administered throughout Christendom; to see our industry and enterprise exacting equality everywhere, could not but create an honest exultation within the breast of every true American.

We, then, my countrymen, have a mission to perform, out of our country; we have to throw our weight, in behalf of equality and justice, over the countries of the world, and to guard with a vigilant eye the principles of Protestantism and Americanism, that our own strength shall increase, our own resources expand, and an additional impetus be given to our moral, commercial, and political greatness.

On the 1st of July, 1823, Central America formed a federal republic, called the "United Provinces of Central America," doubtless designed to accord with our system of government, and adopting our constitution as its guide. The succeeding year, they emancipated all the slaves in the republic, amounting to about one thousand, and indemnified the owners for the pecuniary loss. The constitution of this republic was ratified in November of that year, and the first federal congress was convened the 1st of September, 1825. But this union did not bind the states together like those of the United States of North America. It did not prevent the effusion of blood. And their constitution was but "a passive instrument, powerless for good, and only active for unimportant or pernicious purposes." The unchecked force of numbers, influenced by bad, designing men, soon annihilated the union, by making the small states tributary to the larger; a fate, Americans, we shall surely feel, if ever our own beloved Union shall be cursed by separation.

On the 20th of July, 1838, in the thirteenth

year of the Central American republic, Congress met for the last time under the constitution, and the states returned to their former political system. In 1840, General Francisco Morazan, "the Washington of Central America," made an effort to restore the union of these states; but the Jesuit priesthood united with the Indians, under Carrera, in opposing the liberties of the people, and expelled the "father of his country" from his native soil. Morazan subsequently returned, in 1842, to Costa Rica, where he was murdered; and this consummated the destruction of that unfortunate republic in Central America. And, Americans, mark the fate of that country, and you will see, in its feebleness, suffering, and horror, but a faint picture of what these United States will encounter, if ever the traitors within our borders shall sever the bonds which now hold us as one people.

A light from heaven has now guided a son of our American republic, to open the way for the beautiful flag of the free, to deliver that misguided people, and bring them out of the humiliating condition to which tyranny and priestcraft have subjected them. Gen. William Walker, now President of Nicaragua, a citizen of the United States, has commenced, and we trust will not fail, to renovate that land. He was born in Nashville, Tennessee, and his age does not exceed thirty-three years. His personal appearance is not commanding, by any means; being of small stature, without the prepossession of address or manner. But there is an expression of meekness, accompanied by a nasal tone and sluggish utterance, which would arrest attention in any assembly; and these peculiarities made young Walker a subject of interest at a very early age.

He was remarkable, as a boy, for the ardor of his friendships, the amiability of his disposition, and his obliging character towards his companions. If a "hard sum," or an "awful lesson," was exciting his young friends, Walker was eagerly sought to remove the difficulty. He was never known to be at recitation unprepared, and was so sensitive of his reputation at school, that the slightest mistake or blunder he might make would affect him to tears. He rarely then was known to laugh, although he often participated in the amusements of his companions.

But, to give the secret of Walker's rise from the modest school-boy of Nashville to the presidency of Nicaragua, we must tell you he had a *good* mother, an American woman, who loved God and her country, and by gentleness, affection, and purity, exemplified and inculcated into the mind of her son the faith and doctrine of our Protestant Bible. He thus, as the eldest of four children, became the reliance of his widowed mother, and by the amiability of his disposition, and the sweetness of his temper, supplied the place of a daughter to her as a companion.

Walker was educated a Christian youth, and made a proficient in Christian law. This stimulated him to spread American principles, and enlisted the sympathy of his fellow-men in his new and important mission of introducing a new administration and laws, exciting enterprise, and proclaiming human rights and freedom in that darkened land. He was originally intended for the ministry, but a visit to Europe interposed, and he remained in Paris two years to prosecute the studies of law and physics. He returned home, and connected himself with the editorial corps of his country, first at New Orleans, where he was connected with the *Crescent*, and then with the *Herald*, at San Francisco, California.

His independence, as well as ability, soon made

him a terror to evil doers; and an article reflecting upon the judiciary in California caused him to be arraigned for contempt of court. He was condemned, and made to pay a fine of five hundred dollars, and suffer incarceration.

This tyranny excited the just indignation of even that community, and every public demonstration was made to encourage Walker in his advocacy of the liberties of the people. When he afterwards appeared before the legislature to demand the removal of this unjust judge, he awakened the confidence and respect of the assembly, although he failed to secure the expulsion of his enemy.

Gen. Walker's first military effort was directed to conquer Sonora, in northern Mexico. But the brig was seized in which his party were to embark, by the interference of the government. This momentary detention was followed by greater success on the part of Walker; and, landing in Lower California, in October, 1853, he was soon declared president of that country.

The motive which influenced Walker was frankly exposed, namely, to take possession of Mexico, by first securing the provinces of the north. The invasion of Sonora was then made. His numbers became reduced by desertion and starvation, and he and his surviving men, clothed in tattered garments, were compelled to retreat. This expedition occupied seven months, when Walker returned to California, and resumed his occupation of editor.

In August, 1854, a company, formed for commercial purposes, organized in California, and set sail for the gold regions of Central America. After an absence of some months, it was proposed to augment their forces, and send for Walker, to enlist in negotiations with the Spanish American republics. A grant of twenty-one thousand acres of land was offered this party to enlist in the democratic cause, and the siege of Granada. Walker demanded fifty-two thousand acres, and would consent to nothing less. This proposition was accepted, and after five months of preparation, attended by formidable opposition on the part of capitalists, he embarked early in May, 1855, upon the enterprise of colonizing these states by American means, and on American principles. Sixty-two persons composed this entire expedition, armed each with a rifle, revolvers, and knives.

The scenes of massacre and carnage which followed the dissolution of the union in Central

America, demonstrated that these people were unfit for self-government. In Nicaragua and Guatemala, particularly, the strife had become most fearful with the Indian and negro, in opposition to the old Spanish races.

Two years ago, Castellan, a republican democrat, without the support of wealth or power, attempted to redeem his oppressed countrymen, by introducing the principles of freedom. He was opposed by Chamorro, a haughty aristocrat, who, by intrigue and wealth, secured his reëlection, against the will of the people. Castellan and other political opponents were then thrown into prison. The Supreme Court was abolished, and these men finally banished from the country.

Castellan fled to Honduras, where, under the protection of President Cabänos, the friend and patron of human rights, they conceived the idea of revolutionizing Nicaragua for the sake of liberty. Castellan and his associates returned and triumphed. He became Provisional Director, which office he held until his death, September, 1855.

The priesthood, the most powerful enemy to the rights of the people in Central America, as everywhere else where they prevail, now united with the autocrat Chamorra, to defeat the liberals; and this proud demagogue obtained almost the entire state of Nicaragua. At this crisis Chamorra died, and, amidst the savage ferocity which followed among his chiefs, who assumed the quarrel, General Walker entered, and arrested the career of bloodshed by the immediate restoration of peace and order.

Gen. Walker repaired to Leon, the capital of the state, exhibited his contract, and reported himself ready for action.

The ministry had steadily opposed the coming of the Americans; and Walker, disgusted by their delay to give him a formal recognition, was about embarking for Honduras to aid the patriot Cabänos against Guatemala, when a courier was despatched entreating him to stop, and the next day the Americans enlisted in the cause of Nicaragua.

CHAPTER II.

THE battle of Rivas was the first to engage the fifty-eight Americans who were then under Walker. He added to that number one hundred natives, who fled at the first fire, leaving the Americans to encounter five hundred of the enemy alone. The fight continued several hours, and while the Americans left double their own number of the enemy dead on the field, they remained without the loss of a hair of their heads. Walker, seeing the odds of *eight to one* was too great an exposure, made for a house where the enemy was sheltered, and drove them out and occupied it. These *Chamorrins* then held a council, and decided to dislodge them; but every attempt was made futile by American shot, which was poured into each as he attempted to approach. At night, however, the Americans fought their way out, and retreated to Virgin Bay.

This Rivas battle inspired the Nicaraguans with such awe of American arms, that they regarded it certain death to go within three hundred yards of their rifles. Gen. Bocha *owned* one hundred and eighty killed in that fight, and the conduct which the Americans displayed under such fearful odds soon encouraged the democratic party to hope for success under the intrepid Walker.

The battle of Virgin Bay followed next. Here, again, the fifty-eight Americans, with one hundred and twenty natives, were all Walker's force, while the servile party had five hundred and forty. Beside, they had cannon, and were protected by timber, while the Walker party were exposed in the streets. But these enemies to freedom were again routed. Gen. Walker was struck by a spent ball in this battle, and other Americans escaped in a no less remarkable manner.

The Americans, after making a good impression at Virgin Bay, proceeded to San Juan, where, with death meeting them at every turn by cholera, this little American band remained, encouraged by the example of their brave commander. From San Juan del Sur, Walker, with his troops, proceeded in October to Granada, where some fighting was done, fifteen of the enemy being killed, and seven taken prisoners. The Americans were fired upon from the Romish church; and, on approaching it, found men, women, and children, to the number of eighty souls, chained, in abject misery, whom the Americans instantly released.

Lieut. Col. Gilman, and twenty-five Americans, were now detailed to obtain the fort, a mile east of the city, which was armed by forty men; and on the morning of the 13th October, 1855, the battle of Granada was fought. Gen. Walker, discarding the natives, had but one hundred and ten men, with whom he took the Grand Plaza, captured all their artillery, and, after killing but ten men, from three hundred to four hundred surrendered as prisoners. In this engagement, but *one* American was slightly wounded.

Walker's power was now *felt*, and he was then military commander in the vanquished Sebastopol of Nicaragua. On the day succeeding the battle of Granada, the native citizens met, and adopted resolutions offering Walker the Presidency of Nicaragua. This he declined in favor of Gen. Corral.

Col. Wheeler, the American Minister, was then consulted, and requested to take to Gen. Corral, at Leon, a proposition of peace. Wheeler at first declined, under the fear that it might compromise his government; but, becoming satisfied that it did not, he proceeded at once to Rivas. Corral was absent; and, after a few hours, Wheeler ordered his horses, to return, when he was told he could not leave, and armed soldiers were placed at his door. Thus detained for two days, his friends became alarmed at his absence, and sent a special messenger to Rivas, who, unable to enter, was informed by a native woman, true to the instincts of humanity, that the American Minister was a prisoner.

The steamer *Virgin* immediately proceeded to Rivas by the quickest water course, and fired four heavily-loaded cannon on Saint George, the nearest point to the town. Col. Wheeler then informed the governor, through the Minister of War, that, if he was detained another day, his friends would attack Rivas, and exterminate its population. This produced the desired effect, and Wheeler obtained his passports, and an escort of one hundred men to the ship.

Reinforcements now began to pour into Nicaragua from California. Col. Fry and Mr. Parker H. French arrived in October, accompanied by brave and spirited men. They were too late to participate in the conquest of Granada, but there were still enough to engage them in Nicaragua. Col. Fry and Mr. French took passage in the Virgin, at Virgin Bay; and, determined to take San Carlos by surprise, sent the captain and two men ashore, requesting the immediate surrender of the fort.

They were seized and made prisoners, and the steamer was fired into by twelve-pound shot five times. The American riflemen, detached from Walker, under Capt. Turnbull, were then sent ashore, to take the fort; but their ammunition got wet by the rain, and they were obliged to retreat to Virgin Bay. About an hour after these men left, the New York steamer *San Carlos* arrived, and was hailed from the fort before reaching it; and an eighteen-pounder was fired into her, instantly killing a mother and child, residents of California, and otherwise committing serious outrages upon the ship.

A few days later, while these passengers were waiting for transit at Virgin Bay, a troop of horsemen surprised them, and fired seventy shots over their heads. The excitement now was appalling, and passengers fled in all directions, while many were subsequently caught, and deprived of their revolvers. These two steamers, *Virgin* and *San Carlos*, then made for Granada, and placed their passengers under the protection of Col. Wheeler, the American Minister.

While this outrage was being perpetrated on passengers at Virgin Bay, Gen. Walker was in Granada, organizing the army, of which he was made general; and in sixteen days from his entrance into that city, peace had been made, and a new government organized.

Why did Walker thus become the liberator of Nicaragua? We answer, because his integrity inspired confidence with friends and enemies; and when he refused the Presidency, it carried conviction to the minds of the people that he would not deceive them to glorify himself.

On the 19th of October, Gen. Corral was inaugurated President of the country. A public thanksgiving was made for peace, and oaths taken to perpetuate it. "Look at that man Walker, sent by Providence to bring peace, prosperity, and happiness, to this blood-stained, unhappy country," was the language of Padre Vijil, who subsequently was sent on a mission to the United States, for the recognition of Nicaragua's independence. Walker and Corral reviewed the army on that day ; and it certainly must have gratified any American to behold the promising prospect of that country, in an American citizen claiming to teach the people the rights and the benefits of democratic freedom.

By every monthly steamer from California, adventurers flocked to Central America ; and from both sides of the continent Walker's forces were steadily augmented, until they had grown from fifty-eight to upwards of one thousand men. Nor were these emigrants confined to mere adventurers, without education or fortune. On the contrary, men imbued with the true spirit of American progress, who could look to the future, and see America's magnificent destiny, were found identified with the "Nicaragua Expedition."

The devastation of war was sadly visible over all Central America. Granada, upon whom a new era had then dawned, was reduced from thirty thousand to about eight thousand. Walker was soon placed in emergencies which prove the real character of men, and settle the question of fitness for mental and moral responsibility. A man named Jordan had fired at a native when intoxicated ; and, under the belief that the man would recover, Jordan was sentenced by court martial to leave the country. Subsequently, the man, however, died, and Walker ordered Jordan to be shot, next morning, by a file of twelve rifles. The mother of the boy went down upon her knees, and implored Walker's clemency. Padre Vijil and others also begged the same, on their knees. But Walker was inexorable. He had made this stern decree to satisfy justice, and no power could dissuade him from its execution.

Treason was now discovered in the President of the country, and he too was made to pay the penalty of the traitor. Gen. Corral, to whom Walker yielded the chief magistracy, and who, with the Bible in one hand and the treaty in the other, had promised to sustain and respect the government, was proved to have been plotting its entire destruction. Treasonable design on the part of Corral was proved by a fair trial, and he was sentenced to be shot. Walker approved the finding of the court and sentence; and, on November the 8th, at two o'clock, he ordered Corral to be led to the great square, in the presence of the garrison, and die the death all traitors should die. Rivas then was made President of the country.

At this time, new reinforcements came to Walker's aid; and a letter to him from Col. Kinney, proposing to recognize Gen. Walker as commander-in-chief of the army of Nicaragua, provided Walker would recognize him as Governor of Mosquito Territory. Walker thus characteristically replied: "Tell Mr. Kinney, or Col. Kinney, or Gov. Kinney, or by whatever name he styles himself, that, if he interferes with the territory of Nicaragua, and I can lay my hands on him, I will most assuredly hang him."

The American minister, Mr. J. H. Wheeler, officially recognized the new government of Nicaragua, and he was officially received by President Rivas on the 10th of October. On the 17th of November, the *Nicaragueuse* newspaper was started; and, with an independent press, and a free constitutional government, it became at once an important object to have it recognized by all the states of the world, but, above all others, by that of these United States. Col. Parker H. French was consequently sent as minister plenipotentiary to this government. This placed the administration in its usual attitude of weakness before the world; and, the authorities at Washington becoming alarmed about Central

American matters, the District Attorney of New York, Mr. McKeon, was directed to guard us against fillibusteros with a vigilant eye. Here, Americans, with the Cuban affairs and the burning of Greytown staring us in the face, the administration suddenly becomes frightened at a very harmless fact!

In the mean while the government of Nicaragua, learning the treatment awarded to its accredited minister, immediately dismissed or suspended all official communication with Mr. Wheeler, the American minister, and revoked the appointment of Mr. French, that he might return to Nicaragua. The refusal of Mr. Pierce's administration to recognize this ambassador was based upon the unwarranted conclusion, in view of the facts, that Walker's government had not been acknowledged by the people of that republic. Col. French, instead of a reception befitting his mission, was arrested on the charge of enlisting soldiers, and the steamer *Northern Light* detained from her regular trip, and passengers taken from her. But American acumen was quick to discern the utility of Walker's government, and the people, undaunted by the petty refusal of Mr. Pierce to sanction American rule,—

which promised reform in a foreign land,— pressed on with alacrity to Nicaragua, under those inalienable rights which are the heritage of American men.

The early explorations in the gold regions of Nicaragua were made under the temporary establishment of peace, and satisfactorily demonstrated that, with the advantage of such machinery as is used in California, the product from them would be infinitely greater. With the common rocker, from five to ten dollars a day were at once realized. The climate of Nicaragua, too, is inviting to settlers; the fevers do not prevail there, as in California; the air is cool and salubrious, and labor is rarely impeded at any season of the year.

Nothing can surpass the beauty of the natural scenery of Nicaragua. Its plains, valleys, and volcanoes, the plumage of its birds, its beautiful verdure, and the ever-varying hues of its mountain ranges, present attractions for habitation rarely pointed out to man. Then the richness and variety of the products of its soil are not less noted; and, with the exception of *cotton*, there is not a vegetable growth in the United States of America that does not flourish in Nicaragua.

What is there, then, Americans, to arrest or check

the advancement of this new republic under Ameri can men? Nothing but interior impediments, arising from the want of education among the people. Labor is cheap. It is on the very road of commercial travel, and between our Pacific and Atlantic states. In point of geographical locality, with an ocean each side, in the great centre of trade, Nicaragua must become a great "highway" of commerce throughout the world. Now, what she needs is the right kind of population. To obtain this, Americans must have the *bona fide* evidences of *interest*. With its auspicious position, its gold, and its American protection, we shall see American settlers increasing from year to year.

The government of Honduras has made grants already to the Honduras mining and trading company, of New York. The daily discoveries prove the universal presence of this metal.

After California was discovered, England became alarmed at the travel across the Central American isthmus, and thought there would be another effort to get a ship canal between the oceans; and, to arrest Americans in taking exclusive advantage of this central route, England brought about the unique treaty of 1850, made by Mr. Bulwer on the part of Great Britain, and Mr. Clayton in behalf of the government at Washington. This "Clayton-Bulwer Treaty" ostensibly settled this disputed region; and, under this idea, it was confirmed and ratified. The states of Central America supposed it was a full redress for their past grievances; but too soon they discovered the whole affair was a failure, England asserting her claim to the "Ruatan Islands" and the "Mosquito coast." It is useless here to inquire into the fallacy of this claim. It is clearly proven she never did of right possess it; and recent negotiations at London have resulted in the entire withdrawal from this pretension.

The effect of our government's refusal to recognize the independence of Nicaragua through Mr. French was very disastrous. Guatemala, Honduras, and Costa Rica, immediately followed the example, and refused all correspondence with Walker's government. Col. Schlessenger was sent as commissioner to Costa Rica, to inquire into the reasons of its refusal to recognize, stating that Nicaragua desired peace with all the neighboring states. He was treated with scorn, and driven from the country. Gen. Walker instantly declared war against Costa Rica, and the most energetic measures were taken to avenge the insult. The Costa Rican government then authorized its president alone, or in union with other states, to take up arms against Nicaragua, and "*drive the foreign invaders from the soil.*" The militia of Costa Rica, amounting to nine thousand, were called into action, and one hundred thousand dollars were immediately raised for their support. The army commenced its march to Nicaragua before the design was known to Gen. Walker. A printing press was taken along, and daily bulletins issued of their progress.

Schlessenger, an unprincipled German, was selected by Walker, more from the spirit of retaliation than personal regard, to head the forces sent against Costa Rica. This force amounted to two hundred and seven in number, commanded by Schlessenger, when he left Virgin Bay for Costa Rica. These were composed of two American companies from New York and New Orleans, and two other companies of Germans and Frenchmen.

The guides left this little band on reaching Costa Rica; and the brutal conduct of Schlessenger to the troops, requiring them to march under a torrid sun and lie by under a cool moonlight, and innumerable acts of cruelty and cowardice, soon disgusted the Americans, and inspired their deepest resentment. He showed, besides, marked difference in his treatment towards Americans and the other troops. A German, for example, who had committed an act which in military law merited death, was scarcely reprimanded ; while a New Yorker came near being shot for picking up a piece of bread as he was walking. The fear of American fire only prevented that act of the ignominious coward.

CHAPTER III.

THE battle of Santa Rosa is in all respects the most disreputable engagement which ever occurred upon this continent, or was associated with the American name. Santa Rosa was the hacienda occupied by Schlessenger and his forces when they fired upon the enemy. The Americans took their position in the front ranks, and while the battle was raging, Schlessenger appeared at the corner of the house behind the New York troops, and, in utter consternation, cried out, "There they are, boys! there they are!" Then, retreating, exclaimed, "Campaigne, Francaise!" and ran with his best speed, followed by the Frenchmen. The Germans caught the influence, and, dashing their weapons on the ground, fled likewise. The American party remained unmoved and undaunted, and as soon as the real intentions of the enemy were discovered, Lieut. Higgins gave the order to fire,

Engraved by J. C. Buttre.

Thos. H. Clay

OF KENTUCKY

and never did an angry volley of shot go out with a greater *will*, or do more effective execution.

The enemy fell back, but, on reloading, pressed nearer to the gates of the hacienda, when the brave Parker, engaged in checking them, was shot to the heart. Cahart, another brave American, now took his position on the plaza, and shot the enemies' leader as he rode up and down their *lines*, and who three times before had fired his rifle into the American ranks. By this time, Major O'Neill, who had gone after Schlessenger, returned, saying "he wanted to be with the company who would fight;" and the New York company then, seeing the enemy approaching with such fearful odds, withdrew, under O'Neill's sanction.

Here note the fact that this New York company was the only one which fired a volley in that action! These forty-four men were reduced to twenty-two by the action, and were the last to leave the spot. The enemy, too, on this occasion, beside being double Schlessenger's force, were picked and tried soldiers, who had before fought the Americans at the bloody battle of Rivas. The troops in the American camp were entirely unprepared for this engagement. And it was not remarkable that rowdies and raw recruits should run, when their leader took them by surprise and set the example.

The whole management of this expedition to invade Costa Rica was defective, and served to warn Americans from taking arms again under an incompetent leader, like Schlessenger, or relying for coöperation upon men without principle, experience, or patriotism. Schlessenger was caught, and tried by court-martial on two indictments, One was, that he had acted the traitor when Walker sent him as minister to Costa Rica, and that he betrayed his country to that government. The other was, cowardice in deserting the American army in that country. Before the court, however, had consummated the trial, Schlessenger suddenly disappeared, and joined the ranks of the enemy.

After Schlessenger's defeat by the Costa Ricans, no effort was made to impede their invasion of Nicaragua, and about three thousand concentrated at Granada. The havoc of property, and the murder of wounded American citizens residing at Virgin Bay and San Juan del Sur, are among the acts of the most atrocious barbarity on record. The Americans, however, found some little redress for these outrages, a few days later, when Col. Green, with but fifteen men, met two hundred Costa Ricans, killed twenty-seven and dispersed the remainder, only losing one man and wounding two others of that little party of Americans.

We next find the Costa Ricans entering the city of Rivas, on the 7th of April, to take possession. Gen. Walker, on hearing this at Granada, determined to expel the enemy from Rivas ; and, with only five hundred men, including one hundred natives, he made preparations, in a *single day*, to attack the enemy in their stronghold, with a practised force of two thousand seven hundred men. With this democratic party, Walker surprised the enemy by coming in by a route which they had never suspected. But when the troops were seen, as they ascended the eminence to approach the city, the enemy poured down their batteries with tremendous violence, which the American forces returned with such fierce energy and rapidity, that in five minutes they had the entire possession of the plaza. The Costa Ricans fled to their barricades, and, concealing themselves for protection, continued to fire. Then, too, they had the advantage of a cannon, which made them more formidable. The

Americans, having none, determined to seize it. The design was no sooner formed than Lieut. Col. Sanders gave the order to fire on the Costa Ricans, and, regardless of danger, he and his brave followers rushed in and captured this fatal weapon of war. They took it to the corner of the plaza, and placed it under the management of Capt. McArdle, a ready and accomplished artillerist; and in a few minutes that engine, which was destined to destroy Walker's forces, was playing fatally over the enemy.

Infuriated to madness, the Costa Ricans tried to recover their gun, but the Mississippi rifles drove them back to concealment. A body of these riflemen now stationed themselves on a house-top, and during the engagement killed, at least, one hundred of the enemy. Seeing the American party invincible, the Costa Ricans, with three hundred remaining, retreated towards San Juan del Sur, where they were met with a reinforcement of two hundred and fifty from Virgin Bay. As soon as Gen. Walker was notified of their approach to San Juan del Sur, he sent a body of men to protect that part of the town in which the American rangers were stationed; and after signal execution on their part, the Costa Ricans again were repulsed, with slaughter. More than one hundred dead bodies of the enemy were left to tell the story, while *two* of the noblest of the democratic party became victims in this action, — Lieut. Morgan, of Gen. Walker's staff, and Lieut. Doyle, of the army.

This fighting was excessive, and showed the determined spirit by which the Americans were actuated. They fought from morning to night, and when the enemy ceased hostilities it was soon discovered to be a *ruse* to reinforce themselves. Lieut. Gay, who subsequently died from excessive exertion and useless exposure to danger, was the man to detect the trick; and it was decided to rout the Costa Ricans from the place they so much coveted.

Ten officers, beside three privates, armed with rifles and Colt's revolvers, equipped themselves for the expedition, and entered the building of the foe to determine on a plan of operation. As soon as they did, they gave the signal and fired, and drove the enemy to the fence without any loss, except a single wound upon one gallant officer, Capt. Breckenridge. The opposition was at least one hundred, but these thirteen Americans, with bullets flying all over them, persisted, and accomplished their purpose of dislodging the enemy, without the loss of a single man, killed or wounded.

The enemy still obstinately attempted to maintain their ground, and in the continued action Capt. Hueston was killed. Thirty of the enemy now paid the atoning penalty for this brave American spirit who had fallen, and the remaining twelve carried such havoc into the Costa Rican ranks that they once more desisted, and sought safer quarters.

Retreating and assailing continued, until, after a loss of ten more of their number, the Costa Ricans again reached the old cathedral, from behind where they renewed the assault on the Americans. Lieut. Gay, who was in the first battle of Rivas, and in all the future engagements of Nicaragua, was now compelled to lay down his life. He who projected the engagement died in its triumph.

The English and Germans held Minié rifles, which they used dexterously; and it was by those foreign jacobins, who had joined the despot's party in Central America to put down liberty and trample upon human rights, that most of our American citizens were killed.

The Walker party, in this second Rivas engagement, was not one fourth as great in number as the

Costa Ricans. Beside, all the barricades and fortresses were with the enemy. Gen. Walker, for hours, in this battle, moved about on horseback, unmoved and undismayed, reposing confidently upon the justice of his cause, and sustained continually by the sublimity of his victories. The staff of Gen. Walker demonstrated extraordinary courage and daring, and, with the exception of the brave Capt. Sutter, they all died gallantly and desperately asserting the rights of human freedom. Col. Kenew, also the volunteer aid of Gen. Walker, was not less noted for his prowess in arms; while the native force in this battle, under their distinguished leader, Col. Machado, who fell in the engagement, certainly deserved the highest commendation for their eminent courage.

This engagement of the 11th of April, 1856, is one of the most remarkable in the history of Central America. The Costa Ricans had actually killed at least six hundred of their number; how many wounded and deserted was never ascertained. Their quick retreat and abandonment of Rivas tell the unfortunate result to them. And now look at the disparity again. The Americans came off with fresh laurels, having had but thirty killed, and the same number wounded.

By this time recruits came in numbers from New Orleans, New York, and California, to reinforce the Americans by joining the Nicaraguan army, while public meetings in the United States, and the voice of the press, united in pæans of praise for the brave deeds of Americans on foreign soil. Hostilities now seemed to cease towards Gen. Walker by the northern states of Central America, and the proclamation of President Rivas was accepted by San Salvador, Honduras, and Guatemala, in the most amicable spirit. The enlistment of soldiers was therefore stopped in these states, and the new levy ceased; and, the Rivas government of Nicaragua being acknowledged, the surrender of that country to Anglo-Saxon liberty seemed to have been made.

There are those, unquestionably, among us, who censure the idea of American expansion, and would squeeze the very thought from the minds of the people. But, Americans, you may search the records of history, in vain, to find that any people were ever condemned or defamed for their conquests. Why have Cæsar, Alexander, Charles the Fifth, Charlemagne, and Napoleon, been held in admiration by the human race? Simply because they extended their conquests into foreign territories. And while American youth will study the histories of those heroes with interest and pleasure, they will never be inspired with enthusiasm for the opposite class of men. And this sympathy, instinctive with Americans, for any people struggling to be *free*, carried brave men to the Mexican army, to the Russian army in the Crimea, as well as to Nicaragua, when they beheld their own countrymen, imbued with the true spirit of liberty, and nerved with Anglo-American energy, unsheathing the sword upon that soil to accomplish what years of bloodshed might not otherwise have done for that people. Walker has done for Nicaraguan liberty what Lafayette, De Kalb, Pulaski, Kosciusko, had done for American liberty, and for such considerations. Who, then, can repress patriotic emotion, or deep sympathy for his triumph?

When the people of Nashville, Tennessee, the place of Walker's birth, heard of his brave deeds, they met to testify their joy, and bore witness to the singular purity of his character, and his high mental and moral endowments. They had watched his movements with filial solicitude, from the Chemora and Castellon revolutions to the battle of Rivas, which secured to Nicaragua independence; and when it was demonstrated that Walker had covered himself with glory, there was no measure to their generous admiration.

After the battle of Costa Rica, on the 11th of April, to which the friends of liberty in the United States looked with so much apprehension, Gen. Walker, without ammunition, remained on the spot until next day, and then marched with music to Granada unmolested, leaving the Costa Ricans to evacuate the town.

And now, my countrymen, you may inquire whence the determined hostility of the Costa Ricans to the government of Nicaragua. It was the result of British instigation to drive out the Americans, which English and French agents encouraged, after the government at Washington refused to accept Mr. French. When, then, the fortunes of Gen. Walker seemed about to end, England made offers of thousands of her arms to prejudice the natives against Americans, and, if possible, to get the control of Central America. The conduct of the President of Costa Rica was unparalleled, in denying Americans the right to engage in foreign service, and ordering them when taken prisoners in all cases to be shot. The attempt, then, of Costa Rica to control and prescribe the action of Americans, was enough to call upon every citizen of the land to bid our people "God speed" in Nicaragua

CHAPTER IV.

Is it nothing, Americans, to see a son of this soil opening two hundred and fifty thousand acres of land to the agricultural pursuits and industry of freemen who may choose to go there and occupy it? Is it nothing to see two millions of people being regenerated from papal ignorance and degradation? Is it nothing to see this portion of the Western world affording its facilities for commerce, by bringing together the extremes of trade, which will benefit mankind?

When we consider that British power nerved the Costa Ricans with twenty-five hundred fighting men, to punish Americans for bringing Nicaragua to the desire for independence, and that France and Spain aided the effort, what American would hesitate to give every proper encouragement to Walker? From the moment we acquired California, too, the isthmuses of Nicaragua and Panama have been important to us.

In 1811, Congress declared the Territory of Florida to be necessary to the United States, and passed a resolution to keep it out of the hands of foreign powers. On the 15th of January, the same day the President approved the act, Congress authorized Mr. Madison to take possession of that territory, and, if required, to use the army and navy of the country to defend it; and such civil and judicial power was given as would protect Americans in all their rights of person, property, and religion.

My countrymen, no effort was withheld by England to deprive this Union of Texas; and, to prevent the acquisition of California, which she wanted to colonize, her squadron followed ours with a vigilant eye. When, then, she saw Nicaragua almost in American arms, she set about aiding the Costa Ricans to put Americans down. Can we ever forget how England treated our fathers in their colonial independence? And yet, what has added so much to her greatness as our nationality? Had we never possessed California, England could never have penetrated the gold mines of Australia. What right, then, had she to interfere, because an American hero appeared by invitation in Nicaragua, to fix a higher glory upon his own glorious institutions, which open the main chance alike to all the sons of the soil?

It was England's interference that dissolved the union of the Central American states in 1838, just as she is now attempting to separate these United States to-day by intrigue and treachery on the question of slavery, about which she cares nothing, but to use as an instrument of discord to destroy our beautiful system of government. England bound herself by treaty to abandon Central America; and yet, in the face of her solemn engagement, she has maintained ascendency over the Mosquito territory, held on to the Bay Islands, and encroached on Honduras; and, two years after the Clayton and Bulwer treaty was ratified, we find the queen issuing a warrant to erect these islands into a British colony!

Now, Americans, do you not consider it right to extend the protection of your laws to a people who invite you to take up their cause? Do you not, in the self-relying, self-denying spirit of your ancestors, wish to see the principles of self-government, upon which they planted this confederacy, made impregnable to tyrants in other lands? In this sense, every American is a pillar to support the edifice of freedom, and to prepare this people for the perpetuity of Protestant liberty. Look at the length and breadth of our country, beginning with a slip upon the Atlantic, and moving on until it has met the roar of the Pacific. We have Mexico, nearly equal to our original dimensions. We have secured the territory of the West. And when we see what American energy and American principles have already done in Central America, and consider how our own territory is to be defended, we have no reason to doubt that our stars and stripes will yet float over the Pacific gate of the Nicaragua transit; because we cannot believe that Americans, now, will ever allow the key of the Gulf of Mexico to fall into the hands of savages. They will not consent that the Central American states, essential to the commerce of the United States, shall ever be owned by their enemies. They will not allow any foreign power to arm Spanish colonists to murder their kinsmen; which has been the work of European despotisms, who hate our interests, and tremble at the consequences of seeing Central America yield to Anglo-American intelligence, liberty, and laws. And, sooner than witness the unprovoked assault our people have sustained at Nicaragua and Panama, it would be better far to repeal the neutrality laws, and let Americans defend their own personal rights.

Gen. Walker intercepted the letters intended for the Consul General of Costa Rica in London, proving that England furnished arms to the enemies of Americans. Beside, the whole British West India squadron went to the San Juan del Norte to testify that government's sympathy, and is there still, because Americans struck down the foe in Nicaragua, and defended the people who were panting for freedom. The route to California was also endangered by the English squadron at the mouth of the river.

Now, my countrymen, mark the Jesuit trick! These bloody Costa Ricans never declared war at all against Nicaragua, but against the Americans in that state, thereby denying them the power to defend the rights of human freedom. Americans, then, were shot when taken, their houses burned, their bodies consumed to ashes; and still, as citizens of the United States, claiming protection from no other government. Think you that our Washington, could he rise from the deep slumber of the grave, would refuse his sympathy to the heroic Walker and his adherents? Read his words!

On the 1st day of January, 1796, in reply to the minister of the French Republic, on the latter presenting the colors of France to the United States, George Washington pronounced these noble words: "Born, sir, in a land of liberty; having early learned its value; having engaged in a perilous conflict to defend it; having, in a word, devoted the best years of my life to secure its permanent establishment in my own country, — my anxious recollections, my sympathetic feelings, and my best wishes, are irresistibly excited, whensoever, in any country, I see an oppressed nation unfurl the banners of freedom."

Had Gen. Walker taken possession of Nicaragua merely to keep the peace, he would have been justified by the precedent and practice of other nations. At least three countries in Europe are now occupied by the foreign troops of England, France, and Austria. Nothing could exceed the enthusiasm of the people, as the stars and stripes were raised at the American legation; and all the subsequent acts of Gen. Walker, after the establishment of the Rivas government, and the acknowledgment by the natives that he was their deliverer, confirms the prophecy of Padre Vijil, a few days before Walker entered Granada, when he said, "Our only hope now is in Heaven and Gen. Walker."

Walker has been censured for the execution of Corral, most unjustly. Did not Corral himself select the Americans to try him, having no faith in his own countrymen? And the two most intimate associates of Corral, who attended him to execution, are now the warmest friends of Walker.

When the presidential election again came around, the candidates all sympathized with democratic freedom; but Walker was called, in preference to all others, to the presidency; and, from the day of his inauguration, Nicaragua acquired a position, from which, we believe, she will never willingly recede. After the defection of Rivas, who, it is remembered, absconded with his cabinet on the 21st of June, Gen. Walker, in virtue of the authority placed in him by the treaty, appointed Fermin Ferrer president pro tempore; and he, Rivas, and Salizar, all were candidates for the suffrages of the people, as well as Walker. But, while Walker was elected by nearly sixteen thousand votes, the aggregate vote of the other three did not much exceed seven thousand.

This election occurred the 10th of last July; and, on the 12th, Walker took the oath of office. The ceremonies were very imposing. The American flag and those of Nicaragua and France were in front of the stage, an open Bible and crucifix placed on it, and a cushion laid upon the floor, on which President Walker knelt reverently, and took the oath of office. On the platform sat the provisional President, Ferrer, the bishop, Col. Wheeler, and some of the field officers and their staffs. An appropriate valedictory was delivered to the people by President Ferrer, and an inaugural by President Walker which would have honored any President of our own country, divested, as it was, of all useless verbiage, all specious professions, but carrying an intuitive conviction into the minds of the people that they had at last found a man in whose integrity and honor they could confide.

The assembly then proceeded to the church, according to their old custom, where the Te Deum was performed, with the usual ceremony of blessing the President, to which Walker submitted. Some may say, "Why did he do this, being a genuine

Protestant?" We answer, because reason and the Word of God justified the necessity of temporarily tolerating useless rites, which ignorance and papal prejudice had fastened upon the people. In this way he might hope to enlist their good-will, and gradually develop the benign influences of light and liberty, and prepare that down-trodden race to discard the infatuation of Jesuit priests, and the consequent degradation to which they are subjected. And until the population of Central America, or anywhere else, shall have become *Americanized* by *Protestant faith, they are unfitted to tread the* American soil as citizens; and we earnestly deprecate the idea of the annexation to our own territory of a race of savage idolaters, as the greatest national calamity that could befall us.

In all subsequent difficulties by which the safety of the government of Nicaragua and President Walker has been perilled, the same determined courage has signalized the man. He executed Salizar when he was proved a traitor, and issued an exequator to the British consul when he detected his complicity. The want of resources, and the consequent desertion of American troops, have at times since looked fatal to republican hopes; but, whatever may be the result, it is glorious to recount the brave deeds of Americans upon that foreign soil; and it will ever invest it with interest, to know that it is enriched by the blood of American martyrs, which, ultimately, must germinate the eternal principles of truth and freedom.

And, while we are astonished at the unequalled valor of our brave men in a foreign land, we find in their gallant and patriotic doings fresh evidences of the spirit with which they would meet the enemy on their own soil, if called to defend the national honor of their country, her rights, her altars, her homes, and her liberties.

We deprecate war, and believe it is opposed to the benevolent principles of Christianity, and we trust no occasion shall ever arise to plunge us into its cruelties; but, if this inevitable necessity should come, it is a blessing to feel that we are armed with brave defenders, millions of freemen, ready to repel the invader, and triumph mightily over the foe. Central America is yet in the mists of papal ignorance and delusion, through the influence and tyranny of a heartless, domineering priesthood, which must first be put down, and their power annihilated, before any free government can hope for permanent endurance, and the true sun of liberty rise to bless and gild the horizon of her hopes.

THE ROMISH SYSTEM A POLITICAL CORPORATION.

CHAPTER I.

By the Declaration of our Independence there are certain imprescriptible rights, derived from God, and of which man cannot be deprived by a majority, or have weakened by any conditions imposed by society. These are rights everywhere. They are necessary elements of free agency, and without them God is not worshipped at all. God has given to man the Bible, and the possession and use of this are man's inalienable privileges. The Romish church has, in its general councils, restrained the printing, translation, and circulation, of the Bible; and, by this restriction, has invaded the natural and indefeasible rights of man.

The American constitution, which guarantees these religious principles, and the state constitutions formed since its adoption, have reäffirmed this safeguard in these words: "All men have a natural and indefeasible right to worship God according to the dictates of their own consciences." "No man can, of right, be compelled to attend, erect, or support, any place of worship, or to maintain any ministry, against his consent; no human authority can, in any case whatever, control or interfere with the rights of conscience; and no preference shall be given by law to any religious establishment or mode of worship." This is the *constitutional* definition of religious liberty.

The constitution, then, is republican, and, by these prescriptions, Protestant; and hence the liberty, the intelligence, and the unequalled blessings, of the people of the United States, over the downtrodden, priest-ridden populations of the Roman Catholic countries of Europe, and of South America and Mexico. Romanism is an arbitrary and irresistible power over its subjects; and the man or woman who becomes its voluntary devotee renounces the most precious rights of freedom, and cannot be otherwise than mentally debased. So, whoever thus surrenders these constitutional rights into the hands of the priest cannot be a good American citizen, nor free in any true sense. The "indelible brand of slavery" is put upon every child who is born under the dominion of the Romish church, by its sacrament of *baptism*. And the fourteenth canon on baptism is thus: "Whoever shall affirm that, when these baptized children *grow up*, they are to be asked whether they will confirm the promises made by their god-fathers in their name, at their baptism; and that if they say they *will not*, they are to be left to their own *choice*, and not to be *compelled* in the mean time to lead a Christian life by *any other punishment* than exclusion from the eucharist and other sacraments, until they repent,—let him be *accursed*."

It is by *force*, then, not by *moral* means, that this obedience is enjoined; and the promises made by the godfathers are to be obeyed, or the subject is to be forever "excluded from the eucharist and other sacraments." It is made not only the seal of bondage, but also the seal of salvation. And nurses and physicians, and the laity at large, are authorized to administer baptism to the dying infant, while the priest, in order to enforce these shocking popish rites, often leaves the mother suspended between life and death, to save her babe from the fate of a heretic! This is the first delusion practised upon an individual, as it is also the death-blow to the first principles of liberty.

The next device to destroy the liberty of the individual and of nations is *auricular confession.* This papal injunction is so called because the *priest alone*, without any authority from heaven or natural right, puts forth a claim to know all the secrets of all the people. This is the most dangerous feature of the Romish church to the liberties of our country, and plainly proves it to be a mere political corporation to advance its power. This invasion of the primordial rights of man, and his responsibility to God only, is an alarming violation of human agency, as a free citizen, and the safety of the states. It is putting the people and their rulers under the priesthood. This confers an omnipresent espionage, by which the Pope of Rome can gain the secrets and control the *votes* of every Papist elector, and becomes a priestly political power over the millions of his subjects in all parts of the United States. This secret power of the confessional has enabled the priesthood, wherever it has prevailed, to extort legacies from wealthy individuals, to dictate wills, to subsidize the wealth of provinces, as well as to govern magistrates and monarchs ; and is the means by which that ambitious hierarchy has always ruled the countries and states in which it got a foothold. The dogmas for self-examination in the Book of Devotion, by the authority of the Roman Catholic priesthood in the United States, and in use all over our land, are enough to destroy all kinds of liberty God ever gave to the mind of man.

The power of the confessional, too, over morals, is incredible and astounding. The "Christian's Guide to Heaven," issued under the sanction of Archbishop Kendrick, of Baltimore, is so vile, so shocking an outrage upon decency and morals, that none other than a Romish Jesuit could conceive it ; and even the men who print and circulate it have desired its suppression. This book says : "If you have anything upon your conscience which you have *a particular difficulty in confessing, cease not, with prayers and tears, to importune your heavenly Father* to assist you in this regard, until He gives you grace to *overcome* the *difficulty.* Let your confession be *entire* as *to the number of your sins*, and such circumstances as quite change the nature of your sins, or notoriously aggravate them." The fifth chapter of the Council of Trent, on Confession, commands the most secret kind of "mortal sins" to be confessed, as indispensable to forgiveness. Can Americans need more than this to open their eyes, and see the ruin of the *heart*, the ruin of conscience, the ruin of female virtue and modesty; the ruin of the sanctity of the family, by invading its privacies, and creating, whenever it pleases, discords; the ruin of liberty, and the subjugation and final ruin of the country? Hence we see how that hierarchy has jesuitically contrived to pry into the secrets of the people, to know their thoughts, feelings, acts, intentions, and desires.

One question, among others in their odious books asks a woman if she loves any of the priests. How does she answer her good confessor? Tell Americans, ye holy fathers! In the fourteenth session of the Council of Trent, it is written in the decree of penance thus: "It is plain the priest cannot sustain the *office* of *judge* if the cause be *unknown* to them, nor inflict equitable *punishments* if the sins are only confessed in *general*, and not *minutely* and *individually* described. Those who do otherwise, and knowingly conceal any sins, present *nothing* to the divine goodness to be *forgiven by the priest.*" Again, the sixth canon is as follows: "Whoever shall deny the sacramental confession was instituted by the divine command, or that it is necessary to salvation ; or shall affirm that the practice of confessing to the priest alone, as it has ever been observed from the beginning of the Catholic Church, and is still observed, is foreign to the institution and command of Christ, and is a human invention, — let him be accursed."

Now, Americans, what is this but putting the priest, as judge, in God's place ? It is forcing a man or woman to unveil the inmost secrets to a mere creature, which act of confession belongs and is due to God alone. Here, in our beloved country, there are upwards of two thousand priestly confessors to-day, into whose ears are poured the *entire* secrets of the wife, and sister, and daughter, who have breathed, not only their words and actions, but the very thoughts, feelings, and desires, when *alone*, to the celibate confessor ! ! ! Blush, husbands, brothers ! Be amazed at this extorted confession and intrusion into your family privacies and secrets, under the garb of religion, and which not even a Gabriel, much less mortal authority, has a right to assume or exercise ! Do we wonder, are we startled, at the depth of depravity which flows like a polluted stream out of the confessional? Here, too, into the ear of this same confessor, are poured the secrets of all the villains connected with that church, who have incited mobs, stolen their neighbors' goods, oppressed the poor, cheated and lied at the ballot-box; and then to return, the very next day, to act over again the same guilty practices, because, the priest having given absolution, the white-washed culprits can take a fresh start on the march to crime, until the "bag of sins" is filled again, for the priest in the confessional to cast into the reservoir of oblivion, and, by absolution, give another new start. And so, in alternate repetition, the confessional, by the united action of the priest and the guilty culprit, aids the police, multiplies subjects in courts of justice, the penitentiary, and prisons, and, like Othello, does the state some service.

In all the devices of human ingenuity, none has ever been found so effective, on this earth, to advance the crafty schemes of a potentate, and to entrap and fasten the will, and control the interests, temporal and spiritual, of mankind, as this masterpiece of Satan, the invention of the confessional.

But, however dangerous the *confessional* is, it is only one part of the machinery employed by the political corporation of Rome in effecting its designs to bring the world to its feet.

CHAPTER II.

The suppression of the freedom of the press is another. When, in 1460, the art of printing, through the genius of Faust, was invented, it was like an angel of light suddenly bursting through the mists of darkness which had so long covered the earth. The first fruit of this sublime invention was the printing of the Bible. This immediately awakened the alarm of the papal hierarchy; for it was a sign of a successful invasion upon the fortress of imposture, more mighty and portentous than the attack of all the irresistible hordes of Attila upon the city of Rome. A struggle at once commenced with this light of genius and liberty against despotism; and, from that time to the present, the apocalyptical despot, in league with the other despots of Europe, has shown his determined antipathy to the freedom of the press.

Milton represents Satan in his passage over

chaos, looking toward paradise, and spying the sun in his "meridian tower," and makes him exclaim,

> "To thee,
> O sun! but with no friendly voice, I call,
> To tell thee how I hate thy beams."

With the same instinctive aversion and irreconcilable hatred, this hierarch of Rome exclaims against the press; and whenever he has occasion, and revolutionary symptoms appear, he thunders from the Vatican his bulls. In this act, he only imitates his inexorable predecessors, and carries out the decrees of Romish councils.

We will here present the canons upon which the decrees against the press are based.

The great Council of Lateran, held at Rome A. D. 1515, under Leo X., session tenth, enacted thus: "We ordain and decree *that no person shall presume to print, or cause to be printed*, any book or *other writing whatsoever*, either in our city [Rome] or in any other city, unless it shall first have been carefully examined, if in this city, by our vicar and the masters of the holy palace, or, if in other cities and dioceses, by the bishop or his deputy, with the inquisitor of heretical pravity for the diocese in which the impression is about to be made; and unless, also, it shall have received, under our hands, their written approval, given without price and without delay. Whosoever shall ever presume to do otherwise, beside the loss of the books, which shall be publicly burned, shall be bound by the sentence of excommunication." And, in another part of this decree, they further say, "that the transgressing printer was to pay two hundred ducats, to help to build St. Peter's Cathedral at Rome," and "to be suspended for a year from his trade," &c.

The Council of Trent affirmed this decretal, and enacted, Rule 1st: "All books condemned by the supreme pontiffs or general councils before the year 1515, and not comprised in the present index, are nevertheless to be considered as condemned." The *creed*, as adopted by every Roman Catholic, requires all "to receive undoubtedly all things delivered, defined, and declared, by the sacred canons and general councils, and particularly by the holy Council of Trent."

Here, then, is the destruction of all liberty to print, read, or think, enforced and sealed by that council. "Concerning the index of books, the most holy council, in its second session, under our most holy lord, Pius IV., intrusted it to certain select fathers to consider what was needful to be done in case of divers censures, *and books either suspected or pernicious*, and then report to the holy council; and, having heard now that their labors are completed, but yet seeing, on account of the variety and number of said books, the council cannot minutely judge in the case, therefore it is decreed that whatever is determined by them shall be laid before the most holy Pope of Rome, so that it may be completed and published according to his judgment and authority."

This is the authority or decree in council to sanction the act of the Pope and the committee. So the "committee on the index" went to work to draw up a list of "prohibited books." It is a very large volume, and the book can be had but in few of the libraries of America. In this book, ten "rules" are added, which the Pope approved and the church receives. Every succeeding Pope, to Pius IX., has ratified it. The second of these rules will show something of this tyranny: "The books of heresiarchs, whether year above mentioned, or those who have been or are heads or leaders of heretics, as Luther, Zwingle, Calvin, Balthaser, Pacimontanus, Luenchfeld, and other similar ones, are *altogether forbidden*, whatever be their names, titles, or subjects."

The fourth rule is this: "Inasmuch as it is manifest from experience that, if the Holy Bible, translated in the vulgar tongue, be indiscriminately allowed to every one, the temerity of men will cause more evil than good to arise from it, it is on this point referred to the judgment of bishops and inquisitors, who may, by the advice of the *priest* or *confessor*, *permit the reading of the Bible in the vulgar tongue*, by *Catholic authors*, to those whose faith and piety they apprehend will be augmented, not injured, by it; and this permission they must have in *writing;* but, if any one shall have the *presumption* to read or possess it without such written permission, he shall not receive absolution until he have first delivered up such Bible to the ordinary. Booksellers, however, who shall sell or otherwise dispose of Bibles in the vulgar tongue, or any person not having such permission, shall forfeit the value of the books, to be applied by the bishop to some *pious* use, and be subjected by the bishop to such other penalties as the bishop shall judge proper, according to the quality of the offence. But regulars shall never read nor purchase such Bibles without license from their superiors."

The fifth rule allows "books of heretics, containing but little of their own, to be used by Catholics, *after having been corrected by their divines*."

The sixth rule says: "*Books of controversy between Catholics and heretics of the present time, written in the vulgar tongue, are not to be indiscriminately allowed, but are to be subject to the same regulations as the Bible in the vulgar tongue*."

The tenth rule is thus: "*In the printing of books*, or rather the writings, the rules shall be observed which were ordained in the tenth session of the Council of Lateran, under Leo X. Therefore, if any book is to be printed in the *city of Rome*, it shall be first examined by the Pope's vicar, and the master of the sacred palace, or other persons chosen by our most holy father for that purpose. *In other places*, any book or manuscript intended to be printed shall be referred to the bishop, or some skilful person whom he shall nominate, and the *inquisitors of heretical pravity of the city or diocese in which the impression is executed.*"

"Moreover, *in every city and diocese*, the house or place where the art of printing is exercised, and also shops of booksellers, shall be frequently visited by persons deputed by the bishop or his vicar, conjointly with the inquisitors, *so that nothing that is prohibited may be kept or sold.*"

"If any persons shall *import* foreign books into the city, they shall be obliged to renounce them to the deputies. *Heirs*, or executors, shall make no use of the books of the deceased, nor in any way *transfer* them to others, until a catalogue is presented to the deputies, and obtained *their license*, under pain of confiscation of the books."

"Finally, it is enjoined on all the faithful, that no one keep or pretend to read any books contrary to these rules, or the prohibited index." "But, if any one shall keep or read the works of a heretic, *he shall instantly incur the sentence of excommunication*, and those who keep works interdicted *on another account*, beside the mortal sin committed, shall be severely punished at the will of the bishops."

Thus are the consciences, the intellects, trammelled, and the access to knowledge shut out from the sight of Americans, who are subjects of the Romish church. Think of this, O, my countrymen, think, and protect *your* schools for the education of your children!

What says the decree of the Holy Council of Trent, on the mere edition of God's Holy Word? Why, plainly this: "That considering no small advantage may accrue to the Church of God, of all the Latin editions in circulation, some one should be *regarded* as authentic, doth ordain and declare, that *the same old* and *vulgate edition*, which has been approved by its use in the church for ages, shall be held authentic in lectures, sermons, expositions, and disputations, and that *no one shall dare or presume to reject it, under any pretence whatever.*" And further, "That in matters of *faith and morals*, no one, confiding in his own judgment, *shall dare* to wrest the Sacred Scriptures *to his own sense of them, contrary to that which hath been held, and still is held, by Holy Mother Church, whose right it is to judge of the true meaning and interpretation of the Sacred Word*, or contrary to the unanimous consent of the fathers, even though such consent has never been published."

Now, Americans, do not forget to note this solemn fact, that what this Romish system styles the "vulgate," or "old *Latin* version of the Bible," is filled with interpolations, additions, and subtractions, and the falsehoods of the Apocrypha, and treats with entire contempt the original Greek language of that blessed book, which alone is able to make us "wise unto salvation."

This Roman policy *forces* upon its church a spurious Bible, and ordains it a *standard* opposed to God's Word, and makes it also *exclusive*, in order to carry out its own accursed purposes. It *forbids* men and women to *think* for themselves. You will further find, on the thirtieth page of their index of "prohibited books," that they actually *forbid the reading of any Bible in any translation* Not merely the *Protestant*, but the *Roman* Bible, and this only under the sanction of their church, thus: "*Biblia Vulgari quocunque Idiomate conscripta*," which means, *the Bible, in whatever idiom written, is prohibited.*

CHAPTER III.

Now, let the hierarchy of Rome, in the United States, to-day, rise up, if they dare, and deny that the decrees and rules which we quote here from their councils and papal authorities are not true; are not rigidly enforced by them upon every subject of their priestly influence! Let any lover of his country deny that this power tramples liberty in the dust! Pope Gregory XVI., in his encyclical letter addressed to the faithful of the world, August 5th, 1832, at the time of his coronation, wrote thus:

"*Towards this point tends the most vile, detestable, and never to be sufficiently execrated liberty of booksellers, namely, of publishing writings of whatever kind they please; a liberty which some persons dare with such violence of language to denounce and promote.*" "The *Apostles*," he continues, "*publicly burned a vast quantity of books.*" "This matter occupied," says he, "the attention of the fathers, *who applied a remedy to so great an evil by publishing a salutary decree for compiling an index of books in which improper doctrines were contained.* We *must exterminate* the *deadly mischief of so many books*; for the matter of guilty error will never be effectually removed unless the *guilty* elements of depravity be consumed in the flames." "The Holy See has striven *throughout all ages* to condemn suspected and *noxious books, and wrest them out of men's hands. It is clear how false, and rash, and fruitful of enormous evil to the Apostolic See, is the doctrine of those who not only reject the censorship of books as too severe and burdensome, but proceed to that length of wickedness as to assert that it is contrary to equal justice, and dare to deny to the church the right of enacting and employing it.*"

It needs no telescope, Americans, to discover now why Pope Pius the Ninth, the successor of Gregory, has had his foreign hierarchy at work, to get the Bible out of your public and free schools, and to expunge passages from school-books, which treat of the Reformation, and rights of men to be free to worship God as they choose. It is no wonder, now, why they dare to commit the blasphemy, and insult the Christian community, in publicly burning the Bible in New York, and other places in our country.

The right to worship God, Americans contend, none can take away, unless it interferes or involves the rights of other men. This religious right is spoken of in the constitution as a *civil* right, which it neither gave nor can take away. The constitution protects this right of free worship; and declares, in direct terms, that, "when any form of government becomes destructive of these ends, the *people have the right* to alter and abolish it." It asserts the necessity of *revolution*, if these rights are undermined. The tyranny of forcing men to accept, without choice, the doctrine and faith of the Romish church, submitting to the tyranny of the confessional, making a Romish priest the judge and lord of conscience, is an invasion upon the just political exercise of American men. The Romish catechism says, that "the priests hold the place, the power, and authority, of God on earth." The practical effect of the confessional is to put all men who confess to them in their power, and at their disposal. Hence the danger to American liberty. Out of the Romish church, they teach, there is no salvation. In it, remember, Americans, there is no liberty.

Jesuitism, says De Pradt, embarrasses itself very little about means,— scruples are trifles. The decisions of the Council of Trent *are laws* with all the Roman Catholics. The broad seal is set by this last great council, and over the whole earth every Romanist is under the following obligation: "I also profess, and undoubtedly receive, all other things delivered, defined, and declared, by the sacred canons, the general councils, and particularly the holy Council of Trent." The hierarchy impose on the civil power, by this oath, to punish heretics; to exterminate them, in order to give their lands to Catholics; while, in return, great indulgences are given to their persecutors.

Baptism, by their catechism and theology, makes subjects of the church; and, being so, the church has ordained means to punish them.

No Protestant in our land would dare to refuse his son or daughter the right to unite with Papists, although they knew it would shut the Bible from their sight, make the *pardon of the priest their means of salvation*, require them to *confess* their inmost secret sins to wicked men, and send them into "voluntary slavery" of the most abject and degraded character. Why? Because the system is beguiled under the name of *religion.* And it is an invasion on Protestant liberty, on our constitutional republican rights, to abridge personal choice.

The political system of Rome is subject here, as in all other countries, to the Roman *head* of the church, whom the foreign hierarchy are *sworn* to support and obey by the most solemn oath, in things temporal and spiritual. They are even bound to put to death, when ordered, any heretic in a Catholic family, and deny them the right to lie down in the same family grave-yard.

History, as well as the evidence of the present day, is full of these facts. De Pradt says: "*Catholicism is not organized like other worships.* The latter have no *common centre;* no exclusive source from whence flows power in every religious society. They have no Rome, nor precedents of Rome, nor pretensions of Rome. The exaltation or depression *of these worships is of no importance* in the political order of states. It *is not so with Rome;* everything in Catholicism tends to Rome. The Pope is chief of one hundred and twenty millions of followers.

Catholicism cannot have less than four hundred thousand priests. The idolatrous worship of that church and its priests is spread everywhere. The Irish *priests* in America *are more obsequious* to Rome than the German or French priests, who are placed nearest to her. *Reverence is increased* with distance. Rome, viewed at a distance, is a colossus. *The Pope counts more subjects than a sovereign; more even than many sovereigns together. These have subjects only on* THEIR OWN TERRITORY. *The Pope counts* SUBJECTS ON THE TERRITORY OF ALL SOVEREIGNS. *These command only the exterior. The Pope penetrates deeper. He commands the* interior. *The seat of his empire is placed in the conscience itself. If the whole world were Roman Catholics, then the Pope* would command the world. What a power! What would it leave to others? In a word, he would shake the world, and shroud it in midnight darkness. *He did it, for ages, in respect to Europe. Not to know how to foresee, is not to know how to govern or judge the world.*"

The writer who gave this graphic description of the political system of Popery was an *Abbe* of the Pope, and knew the exact meaning of all he said.

If ever Rome has the power in this country,

which she is striving, by the aid of all Catholic Europe, and certain blind, selfish American politicians, to attain, the treasonable war will be waged under the name of religion. Rome knows her political men, and her zealous agents in the United States, almost to a unit; and she knows her resources, also, to a dollar. She waits only for strength to her increasing resources, and the multiplication of her numbers, for her successful aggression on the ballot-box, and her acquisition of the civil power. When ripe, eventually, and in successful domination, she will confiscate our lands. She will pay her devoted political aspirants, as the *price of their treason*, in papal *votes*. She will enlist the zealous devotion of all the Catholic Irish, and priest-ridden foreign Papists, through the dangerous and unlimited power of priestly absolution in the confessional, and the dispensation of indulgences by the Pope.

The bull is published, and is irrepealable, in America, to-day, in which "the great hunter of men" raves through the earth, and lays his *curse* and his *claim* on all the civil and religious rights of man, not even leaving a *grave* for a *heretic*. He claims jurisdiction over armies, navies, seas, lands, treasures, coasts, &c. The Pope could order the extermination, by a crusade, of heretics within any province under his undisputed control. What hinders him but the iron will and the majority of Americans, from putting in operation the persecuting principle inherent in the very system of Popery?

Has not the Pope palsied and ruined every country where his power could be felt? Look at the kingdoms and states of Italy,—Lombardy, Florence, Tuscany, Genoa, Naples,— so flourishing, once, in maritime prosperity, and all the arts of genius! Look at Spain, Portugal, France, Austria, Mexico, the states of South America!

Why that tyrannical oppression of the beautiful valleys of Piedmont? Why that bloody triumph of the Vatican over the martyred Waldenses and Albigenses? Why has this spirit of persecution extinguished every rising effort for liberty, trodden crowns in the dust, and drenched Europe and the earth in blood? If the Pope, at any time, relaxed his grasp of empires, and his tortures of the Inquisition,— if, at any time, the fires at the stake have been put out, and the groans of slaughtered victims have ceased to fall on the ear,—to what is it to be ascribed but to the want of unrestrained power, and the energies of some Luther, some Elector of Saxony, some conquering arm of Marlborough, Charles XII., or a Napoleon? Did the Pope attempt to tread on the liberties of Venice in the seventeenth century, and is he a lamb to-day? If he spared not Venice then, why does he spare the United States to-day? For this simple reason, the want of strength and a majority. For it is the boast of the hierarchy, that its principles and character never change.

Du Pin, the papal historian, furnishes the most striking picture of the Papacy in the seventeenth century:

THE HISTORY OF THE INTERDICT OF VENICE, FULMINATED BY POPE PAUL V.*

"The difference of the Republic of Venice with Paul V. is one of the most important points of the ecclesiastical history of the seventeenth century; not only by reason on the subject of the dispute, but also much more on account of the great number of questions which were agitated on occasion of that difference, by the most able divines and lawyers of that time. The Senate of Venice made two decrees in the beginning of that century; by the first of which

* From Du Pin's Ecclesiastical History, Vol. viii. Book ii. Chap. 1. Century 17th.

it was forbidden, under severe penalties, to build hospitals or monasteries, or to establish new convents or societies, in the state of Venice, without the permission of the senate. By the other, which was made the 26th of March, 1605, a law made in 1536 was renewed, confirmed, and extended over all parts of the state, forbidding all the subjects of the republic to sell, alienate, or dispose in any manner whatsoever, of immovable goods in perpetuity, in favor of ecclesiastical persons, without the consent of the senate; upon condition, nevertheless, that if any legacies of immovable goods were bequeathed, those goods should be sold within two years after, and the purchase given to discharge those legacies. There happened at the same time two criminal affairs, which concerned the ecclesiastics. *Scipion Sarrasin*, canon of Vicenza, who had taken off the seal of the magistrates, affixed to the Episcopal chancery, at the request of the chancellor, the see being vacant, was seized by the senate, and put into prison, for having insulted one of his kinswomen, whom he intended to debauch; and some time after, Count Baldolin Valde-marino, Abbot Feveza, being accused of many enormous crimes, was imprisoned by order of the senate. The Pope, Paul V., being persuaded that the decrees and enterprises against the clergy encroached upon ecclesiastical jurisdiction, complained of them to the ambassador of Venice, and demanded of the senate, by his nuncio, that the decrees should be revoked immediately, and the ecclesiastics imprisoned by the authority of the senate delivered into the hands of his nuncio, to be tried by ecclesiastical judges; threatening to interdict the republic, if he was not obeyed immediately. The senate answered, the 1st of December, 1605, that they could not release prisoners accused of crime which belong to the recognizance of the secular judges, nor revoke the laws which they had a right to make, and which they believed necessary for the good of the state. The Pope, having received this answer by letters from his nuncio, and by word of mouth from the ambassador of Venice, despatched on the 10th of December two briefs; the one addressed to Marin Grimani, Doge of Venice, and the other to the republic, by way of monitory, exhorting the state to revoke their decrees, which he thought contrary to the canons, and prejudicial to the liberties of the church; declaring that they who made these laws, or caused them to be executed, had incurred ecclesiastical censures, from which they could not be freed but by revoking those statutes, and reëstablishing affairs in their former state. He commanded them, under the penalty of excommunication, *latæ Sententiæ*, to revoke them, which, if they refused, he protested that he should be obliged to put in execution the penalties annexed to such offences, without any other citation; being not willing that God should call him to account one day for having thus failed in his duty, and not being able to dissemble, when he saw the authority of the holy Apostolic See infringed, the ecclesiastical immunities trampled under foot, the canons and holy decrees neglected, and the rights and privileges of the church subverted."

The Pope sent these briefs to his nuncio at Venice, with orders "to present and publish them; and acquainted the cardinals, in a consistory held the 12th of that month, with the subject of complaint he had against the republic of Venice, and with what he had done thereupon. Nevertheless, the republic appointed Leonardo Donato, procurator of St. Mark, to go express, and treat of this affair in the quality of ambassador at Rome. The nuncio, not having received those briefs till the day after Donato had been chosen ambassador, thought he ought to put off the publication of them, and wrote to the Pope, who ordered him to present them. The nuncio received this order on Christmas eve, and presented, the day following, the briefs to the counsellors assembled to assist at a solemn mass, in the absence of the Doge Grimani, who was extremely ill, and died the day following. His death was the reason why the briefs were not opened, the senate having ordered that no affair should be transacted, but that of the election of a doge. The Pope, on his side, wrote to the nuncio to protest to the senate that they ought not to proceed to a new election, because it would be null, as made by excommunicated persons. The nuncio pressingly demanded audience to make this declaration; but the senate would not give it him, it being not customary to receive any memorials from the ministers of foreign princes during the interregnum, but compliments of condolence. The electors were not a long time in choosing a new doge. The 10th of January, 1606, Leonardo Donato was advanced to that high dignity. All the ambassadors went immediately, according to custom, to visit the new doge, and pay him their compliments. But the nuncio would not visit him. The doge did not omit writing to the Pope, according to custom, to notify his election to him; and the Pope received his letter. The first affair which was transacted at Venice, after the election of the doge, was the difference of the republic with the Pope. It began with nominating the Chevalier Duodo in the place of Leonardo Donato (who was elected doge), ambassador at Rome. After this the briefs were opened; and when the senate saw what they contained, before they returned an answer to the Pope they determined to have the advice of some divines and lawyers. The lawyers whom they principally considered were Erasmus Gratian, of Udina, and Mark

Antonio Pellegrin, of Padua; and the famous Fra-Paolo Sarpi, of the order of the Servites, was appointed the divine of the republic. It was also resolved not only to consult the doctors of the university of Padua and of Venice, but also the most able lawyers of Italy and Europe, who sent them their opinions, with the laws of the other kingdoms and churches of Christendom, which had any relation to the affair in question. Then the senate, after having understood the opinion of the doctors, returned this answer to the Pope, the 28th of January: 'That they heard, with a great deal of grief and astonishment, by letters from his holiness, that he had condemned the laws of the republic (observed with success for many ages, and with which his predecessors had found no fault), as contrary to the authority of the holy Apostolic See; and that he regarded those who had made them (who were men of piety, and had well deserved of the see of Rome) as persons who broke the ecclesiastical immunities; that, according to the admonition of his holiness, they had caused to be examined their ancient and modern laws, and that they had found nothing in them which could not be ordained by the authority of a sovereign prince, or which infringed on the power of the Pope; because it is certain that it belongs to a secular prince to take cognizance of all societies which are founded within his own jurisdiction, and to take care that no edifices may be raised which may prejudice the public safety, when there are in a state as great a number of churches and places of devotion as is sufficient. That they never refused giving leave to build them; the republic even contributing thereto very liberally on her part. That the law prohibiting the alienation of the goods of the laity forever in favor of the ecclesiastics regarding nothing but temporal affairs, it cannot be pretended that they have done anything by that against the canons.

That if the Popes had power to forbid the ecclesiastics to alienate in favor of secular persons the goods of the church without her consent, it might be lawful for princes to prohibit seculars also to alienate theirs in favor of the ecclesiastics without their permission. That the ecclesiastics lose nothing by their decrees, because they receive the value of the immovable goods which are given or bequeathed to them. That this alienation, weakening the state, is not less prejudicial in spiritual than temporal concernments. That the senate cannot believe they have incurred any censure by making these laws, since princes have by a divine law, from which no human authority can derogate, the power of making laws in temporal affairs. That the admonitions of his holiness have no effect but in matters that are purely spiritual, and not in a temporal affair, which is in all things separate, and wholly exempt from the pontifical authority. That the senate does not believe his holiness, who is full of piety and religion, will persevere, without knowledge of the cause, in his menaces. That these were an abridgment of the senate's reasons, which their extraordinary ambassador would give him to understand more largely.'

"The Pope, having received this answer of the senate, declared to the ambassador that he could not relax his severity if they did not revoke their laws, and deliver into the hands of his nuncio the prisoners. He complained still more of another decree they had made upon the emphytheoses,* and caused his complaints to be delivered by his nuncio to the senate. As he knew they would give him no satisfaction thereupon, he gave orders for another brief to be presented, the 10th of December, to the senate, whereby he required that the two prisoners should be delivered to his nuncio, under the penalty of excommunication. The

* A term of law for a long lease, from ten to a hundred years.

senate answered that they would not divest themselves of the right which they had to punish the crimes of their subjects, which they had always enjoyed from the establishment of their state, with the consent of the sovereign pontiffs. The extraordinary ambassador of the republic came to Rome, and represented to the Pope the reasons of their proceedings; but nothing was able to move his holiness. He caused a monitory to be drawn up against the republic of Venice, and having communicated it to the cardinals in consistory, the 15th of April, he ordered it to be published and fixed up in the public places at Rome. This monitory imported that the senate of Venice being not willing to revoke the laws which they had made in prejudice of the ecclesiastical authority, nor to deliver their prisoners, he declared these laws to be null, and pronounced the doge and republic of Venice excommunicated, if, within the space of twenty-four days, to begin from the day of the publication, they did not revoke, break, and annul, the aforesaid laws, and actually deliver the canon and the abbot into the hands of his nuncio. That till such time as they should pay obedience to this order, he forbade them to bury in consecrated ground those who happened to die; and that if, within three days after the twenty-four were expired, they did not comply, he laid the whole state under an interdict; and forbade all masses and divine offices to be celebrated, except in such cases and places as were privileged by common law. And that he deprived the doge and senate of all the goods which they possessed in the Roman church, or in other churches, and of all the privileges or indultos which they had obtained from the holy see, and especially from those which they had to proceed against clerks in certain cases. The monitory was addressed to the patriarchs, archbishops, bishops, their vicar-generals, and to all the clergy, secular and regular, having ecclesiastical dignity in the state of the republic of Venice.

"The senate, being informed that the monitorial bull was published, recalled their extraordinary ambassador, forbade all ecclesiastical prelates to publish or set up the bull of the Pope, and commanded that all they who had copies of it should carry them to the magistrates of Venice. The Pope, on his side, recalled the nuncio who was at Venice, and dismissed the ordinary ambassador of the republic. At the same time the chiefs of the council of ten sent for the superiors of monasteries, and of the other churches of Venice, and declared the intention of their sovereign to be that they should continue to perform the divine offices, and that no one should leave the ecclesiastic state without leave, assuring those who staid of protection; and declaring that they who departed should not carry with them any of the goods and ornaments of the churches. They commanded them, in case any brief was sent to them from Rome, or order from their superiors, to send it to the magistrates before they read it. And the governors of all the cities of the state were enjoined to give the same orders in the places of their jurisdiction. The superiors immediately all promised to obey the orders that had been given them, and to perform divine service as before. A council was held upon what was proper to be done concerning the monitory of the Pope. Some gave their advice to appeal from it, as many princes, and the republic itself, had done on the like occasion. But others believed there was no occasion for having recourse to this remedy, pretending that the briefs were notoriously null of themselves. This opinion was followed, and nothing was done, but a mandate made in the name of the doge, addressed to all the ecclesiastics of the republic, wherein he declared that, having received advice of the publication,

April 17th, at Rome of a certain brief fulminated against him, and the senate, and sovereignty of Venice, he thought himself obliged to employ his cares in maintaining the public tranquillity, and supporting the authority of the prince. That he protested before God he had not omitted any means of informing and laying before the Pope the strong and convincing reasons of the republic. But that having found his ears closed, and seen the brief he had published against all kind of reason and justice in opposition to the doctrine of the Holy Scripture, the fathers and canons, and to the prejudice of the secular authority which God has bestowed upon sovereign princes, the *liberty of the state* and the public repose, and to the great scandal and offence of the whole Christian world; he held that brief to be not only unjust, but also null, unlawfully fulminated in fact, and contrary to the rules of law, and that he would use the same remedies which his predecessors and other princes have used against the Popes, who abused the authority which God had given them to edification, and passed the bounds of their power. And this he was the more inclined to do, forasmuch as he was certain that this brief would be looked upon in the same light, not only by all the subjects of the republic, but also by the whole Christian world. That he was persuaded they would continue, as before, to take care of the souls of the faithful, and to perform the divine offices, being fully resolved to persevere in the Catholic and apostolic faith, and the respect which is due to the holy Roman church. This mandate, dated the 6th of May, 1606, was immediately published and set up at Venice, and in all the cities of the state.

"As the term of twenty-four days allowed by the briefs approached, and the *Jesuits*, who had received particular orders from the Pope, showed plainly that they were inclined to observe the interdict, and would at least abstain from saying of mass, they were commanded, on the 10th of May, to give an express declaration of the measures they designed to take. They acknowledged then that they could not celebrate mass during the interdict, and that if the senate obliged them to do it, they chose rather to retire from Venice. Upon this answer, the senate resolved to send them away, and appointed the grand Vicar of the Patriarch to receive the ornaments of their churches, and gave them order to depart immediately. They went out that evening, carrying each of them a consecrated host about their necks; and being put into two barks, retired to Ferrara. The Jesuits in the convents which were in the other cities of the republic departed also. As it was manifest that the Capuchins, Theatins, and other regulars, after the example of the Jesuits, were resolved to observe the interdict, the senate published a decree, the last day of the term, by which all those who refused to celebrate the divine offices, in the accustomed manner, were enjoined to retire out of the jurisdiction of the republic; upon which the Capuchins and Theatins departed also, and the other religions were placed in the government of their churches. The Capuchins of the territories of Bresca and Bergamo stayed, and continued to perform divine offices, like the other ecclesiastics, secular and regular, of the republic.

"The nuncios of the Pope, who were in the courts of Catholic princes of Europe, endeavored to exclude from divine service the ambassadors and envoys of Venice; but their attempts were fruitless. They continued to be treated as they used to be, and were admitted to prayers, assemblies, and the ecclesiastic ceremonies, as heretofore, in France, Spain, Italy, and Poland. The ambassador of the republic assisted in person at Vienna, in the first solemn procession of the Holy Sacrament, which was made by the Jesuits. But the nuncio, who was not present for fear of meeting the ambassador, gave out such menaces, that the ambassador did not think fit to be present at the two following ones. Though the interdict was not observed in the states of Venice, it occasioned *tumults* and *seditions* in several places, which the senate, having attributed to the suggestions of the Jesuits, made a decree, the 14th of June, whereby they declared that the Jesuits should never more be received for the future in any place of the state of Venice, and that this decree should never be revoked, before there had been first read the whole process in presence of all the senate, which should be composed at least of a hundred and four score senators, and unless there were five for one who voted for the revocation.

"Nevertheless, the Christian princes interposed to accommodate the difference betwixt the Pope and the Venetians. But these would not hear any proposition of accommodation before the Pope had taken away the interdict, and the Pope demanded before all things the revocation of the decrees. The ambassador of the most Christian king exerted himself more strongly and efficaciously than any one else in bringing matters to an accommodation, and at length effected it. The *King of Spain* assured the Pope that he *would assist him* with all his forces, and that he had given orders for that purpose to his ministers in Italy. But these promises had no other effect than to retard the accommodation, and had like to have kindled a war in Italy. Some unknown persons having set up in the state of Venice a placard by which the republic was exhorted to separate herself from the Roman Church, the senate commanded that search should be made after the author of it, and protested that their intention was never to depart from the Catholic religion, nor the obedience due to the Holy See. They published afterwards several orders to maintain a war, in case they should be attacked. The Pope, on his side, solicited the princes of Italy to put *himself* into a condition to *attack* the Venetians, or to defend himself, if he should be attacked by them. On each side preparations of war were made, but the dispute never came to an open rupture. It was not so in the war which was carried on by the pen; for a very great number of writings were published on both sides, with heat, vivacity, and learning. Though the affair had a lowering aspect, and all things threatened a rupture, the ambassadors of France did not cease, nevertheless, to negotiate an accommodation."

CHAPTER IV.

We learn from his history that the Pope, only two centuries ago, excommunicated a whole people for exercising the right to punish, by civil jurisdiction, two ecclesiastics, for drunkenness, murder, and other crimes, and for prohibiting the erection of monasteries and nunneries. These matters belonged to the state government alone. The courts of the church had no right to try civil cases, or inflict temporal punishment, without infringing on the liberties of the people, and violating the laws of God. The Pope demanded that these criminals of the republic of Venice should be tried by *him* in his ecclesiastical court, and threatened an instant interdict if prompt obedience did not ensue. The monasteries were polluting and ruining their country; and the senate passed salutary laws prohibiting their future erection, without the consent of the legislature, and regulating the bestowment of property on the clergy, who were securing the

Engraved by J.C. Buttre.

A. B. Ely.

OF BOSTON MASS.

A. G. S. or Presiding Officer of the Order of the United Americans in the United States.

treasure and soil of the country in their own hands. The Pope would not *allow* the state to *govern* his subjects, though they resided in it.

The Jesuits—observe, Americans!—left Venice to espouse publicly the cause of the Pope as a military foe to Venice; and the oath of allegiance to the Pope, by every Jesuit bishop and priest, will lead to the same results in this country whenever the blow is struck openly for Popery.

"The Pope," says Du Pin, "solicited the powers of Italy to put him in a condition to attack the Venetians, or defend himself if attacked by them." Thus the Pope, the head of the church, placed himself at the head of the army, to crush the republic of Venice for punishing two priests who had been found guilty of incest and murder.

The Jesuits then were the *soldiery* of the Pope, and left their country to join him in arms. But, to the glory and praise of Jehovah, there were some patriotic spirits in Venice who stood up for liberty, and who showed their love for the rights of the people by punishing their priestly persecutors, and annihilating their convents and monasteries, as Spain and Portugal had done before them.

All men, if their minds are not demented, love

freedom; and when Roman Catholics have become sufficiently enlightened and caught the true spirit of liberty, they have burst their chains of bondage, and risen up in Romish countries, as they did in the Reformation of Luther, and recently have done in Sardinia, New Granada, and partially in Mexico. It is by the spread of knowledge and the influence of true liberty that the hierarchy of Rome will, at last, fall. A system so false and pernicious, a power so grasping, a despotism so at war with human rights, so bloody and insufferable, cannot last forever. The people of the earth will, in the fulfilment of scriptural prophecy, comprehend that God has given them the *will* to be free.

The Church of Rome claims to be infallible, and that it has an unquestioned right to enforce all its rules and tyrannical oaths upon its subjects. It declares damnation on all out of its visible communion. It dares to claim universal spiritual and temporal dominion, — a more arrogant and impious pretence than ever Zenghis-Khan or the most wicked or victorious tyrant ever claimed. In the decretals by Pope Gelasius to the Emperor Aurelius, it is written thus:

"O, august emperor, there are two by whom the

world is chiefly ruled, — the sacred authority of the Popes, and the kingly power; in the which, that of the *priests* preponderates, inasmuch as in the divine examination they will have to answer to the kings of men." "Be well aware, therefore, that in these matters you depend upon their judgment, and they cannot be subservient to your will; *forasmuch as you see that the necks of kings and princes are put under the knees of priests;* and that, when they have kissed their right hands, they believe themselves to be partakers of their prayers." The heading of the chapter is in these words: "*It is necessary to the salvation of all the faithful in Christ, that they be subject to the Pope of Rome, who has the power of both swords, and who judges all, but is judged by none.*" "Moreover we declare, assert, *define*, and pronounce, that it is altogether necessary to salvation for every human creature to be subject to the Pope of Rome."

What a preposterous decree! What arrogant blasphemy! The Pope pronounces himself to be God's vicegerent on earth; to dispose of church and state, heaven and hell; to determine the eternal salvation or damnation of the souls of men! In perfect consistency, he gave a grant to Spain of America, even before its discovery. This grant, never having been revoked, is in full force; and Mr. O. A. Brownson, his Corypheus in America, says that the Pope holds it as his possession! And, with the Pope's increasing millions of subjects, his accumulating revenues, his subtle secret and open emissaries, his numerous and constantly multiplying papal schools, seminaries, colleges, nunneries, and monastic establishments, and all his swarming priests and Jesuits, is there not, my countrymen, ground for apprehension and serious alarm? No matter whether our politicians and unsuspecting and busy people see this danger; no matter whether the hope of accomplishing a particular end be fulfilled now or centuries to come; the springs and ramifications of this system, often concealed, and wholly unlike all other human inventions, are in powerful operation, and its agents labor assiduously to effect this end.

Pope Pius V., in his bull to Queen Elizabeth, in which he deprives her of her kingdom, and releases her subjects from allegiance to her government, said: "He who reigns on high, to whom is given all power in heaven and in earth, hath committed the Holy Catholic and Apostolic Church, *out of which there is no salvation,* to one alone on earth, namely, to Peter, Prince of the Apostles, and to the Roman Pontiff, successor to Peter, to be governed in the fulness of power. *This one man he hath appointed prince over* ALL NATIONS AND ALL KINGDOMS, *that he may pluck up, destroy, scatter, ruin, plant, build.*"

The bull against Henry of Navarre and Prince of Condé, by Sixtus V., says: "The power of the Roman Pontiff passes an uncontrolled sentence on all; casts down the most powerful from their thrones, tumbles them down to the lowest parts of the earth, as ministers of the proud Lucifer."

Among the *definitions of papal power received* and in use in the Romish system, we find the twenty-seven sentences or dictates of Pope Gregory VII.

"8. The Pope alone can use imperial ensigns.

9. All princes must kiss the feet of the Pope only.

12. That it is lawful for him to depose emperors.

17. That no chapter or book is canonical without his authority.

19. That he himself ought to be judged by no man.

27. That he may absolve the subjects of unjust men from fidelity to their princes."

Pope Leo III. says, "That the church, his spouse, had given him the *mitre* in token of things spiritual; the crown, in token of things *temporal:* the mitre for the priesthood, the crown for the kingdom, making me a *lieutenant* of Him, who hath written upon his thigh and his vesture, King of kings and Lord of lords; *I enjoy alone the plenitude of power, that others may say of me, next to God, and out of his fulness we have received.*"

These doctrines are brought to America, and, although not written in our statute-books, nor proclaimed from the top of the capitol, yet every "cross" on the splendid cathedrals and popish chapels in this country; every elevation of the "host" by the bishops and priests before the eyes of the crowding multitudes which throng them; every sermon on the Sabbath which teaches implicit obedience to the Pope; every oath of every Jesuit and prelate, and all the solemn binding vows of the millions of their adherents, proclaim, as with the voice of a trumpet, these dangerous and unchangeable edicts.

In the book called "*Three Books of the Sacred*

Ceremonies of the Holy Roman Church," printed at Cologne, 1571, it is seen how the Pope reigned in his days of greatest temporal splendor. These were his orders:

"1. The Emperor shall hold the Pope's stirrup.

2. The Emperor shall lead the Pope's horse.

3. The Emperor shall bear the Pope's chair on his shoulder.

4. The Emperor shall bear up the Pope's train.

5. The Emperor shall bear the basin and ewer to the Pope.

6. Let the Emperor give the Pope water.

7. The Emperor shall carry the Pope's *first dish.*

8. The Emperor shall carry the Pope's *first cup.*"

This is the man who claims to be the successor of St. Peter, the follower of our blessed Lord and Saviour Jesus Christ, who said to his disciples, "Silver and gold I have none!" O, the pride, the ostentation, the guilty ambition, of this Roman god, "sitting in the temple of God, and calling himself God!"

The religion of Protestants in America, as well as the constitution, oppose not the hierarchal pretensions of Rome only, but all *established* religions on earth. Both Protestantism and the constitution deny the right of the legislatures to enact laws against the freedom of conscience or private judgment. They deny that the majority has any power over the minority in these matters which belong to God alone. No mortal has this right; and whoever assumes it, be he monarch or priest, is a base and impious tyrant, against whom rise up the laws of heaven, and the conscious reason of man.

They who peopled our soil, and fought on the battle-fields of the Revolution, — the illustrious and heroic representatives of the first American Congress, who legislated our freedom, with Washington at their head, — felt the strong impulse of Protestant principles, and imbued the immortal instrument of the constitution with those principles, and thus established the glorious edifice of civil and religious liberty. Every true American patriot changed his allegiance to every foreign government, and denied the right to any civil authority or priestly usurper to trample on these native principles, or legislate away the rights of conscience. This denial, by the American inhabitants, with the exception of the Roman Catholics, was made even before the adoption of the constitution. But the papists have never dared to deny their allegiance to the foreign hierarchy of Rome, and therefore have never denied to the priesthood, or to the Pope, this usurped right to *control the conscience*, or to *think and decide* as they may dictate, in all matters of religion. Why? — Their dogmas forbid; the pivot of the lips of the priest, on which their salvation or damnation turns, and all the inextricable and deep web of superstitious mummeries in which they are immersed, sealed by "infallibility," forbid. Their *souls*, and consequently even the *disposal of their bodies*, are not their own. Freedom of conscience being in the hands of the priest, and the priest in the hands of the Pope, all the papists in this country, unless a little too much Americanized, form one great army, and move as a unit under the dictation of the priest. They are here, therefore, what, in spirit and in the principles of their system, they were under Raymond, Godfrey, Tancred; what they were at the siege of Rochelle under the cardinal minister of France, when, for twelve tedious months, the Protestants endured their unrelenting persecution and cruelties; what they were when the fires of Smithfield, under the reign of bloody Mary, lighted up England, and multitudes of Protestants perished; what they were on St. Bartholomew's night, when they murdered more than sixty thousand Protestants; what they were under the Inquisition; what they are in Rome, in Italy, in the armies of the Austrian and French tyrants, bayoneting the patriot sons who venture to breathe the aspirations of liberty; what in Spain, in Portugal, and wherever the priests hold their conscience, and dictate their ready obedience and movements.

CHAPTER V.

The Pope's power, which grants pardon, forgives sins, past, present, and to come, is in full force here. He pardons rebellion and high treason; dispenses with oaths, promises, or vows. And, though a subject take one thousand or five hundred thousand oaths to support the civil government, if it is not a Roman Catholic government there can be no possible security for his allegiance.

Is there an American who will say, in the face of these facts, that the system of Popery is favorable to civil and religious freedom? Is there one who will deny that its dogmas and practices are opposed to the principles of that constitution, which are dear to freemen as their hearts' blood?

Not merely the Pope, but the priests, can forgive sins. The priests are the monarchists; they are the *hierarchy* of Rome; they are the church, and the church is the foe of *divine truth and human liberty*.

19*

When Rome ceases to be consolidated, its system has ended. It has no vitality, but through the great *tyrant*, who "calls himself God," and rules on the ruins of religion, liberty, and law. Protestants, on the other hand, cannot consolidate, in the same manner, under one supreme head, who unites church and state. They own no such head. The Pilgrims of Plymouth, the Huguenots of South Carolina, the disciples of Wm. Penn, the Hollanders who colonized Manhattan, were all alike Protestants. But it was their freedom to think and choose each the mode of worship it adopted, and they were each and all resolutely and unanimously united in the founding of American liberty.

Bishop England, a most crafty Jesuit, in his book transmitted from Rome, 26th March, 1833, speaking in praise of the Pope's encyclical letter against liberty, says: "In the venerable successor of St. Peter I behold the former active, zealous, and enlightened prefect of the propaganda, *whose deep interest and laborious exertions in the concerns of the Church of the United States* have been so beneficial." He further says, "that stripping the Holy See of its *temporal* independence would inflict a deep wound on religion." And, in addressing the cardinals, whom this same Bishop England styles "the venerable and eminent senate of the Christian world," he further wrote: "That the grain of mustard-seed (the Papal Church in America), cultivated with success, under the auspices of Pius the Sixth, has mightily grown to a rapid tree, and, protected by Gregory XVI., is now extending its branches above an enlightened community, reposing in peace under its shadow."

To show further that this political corporation of Rome does what it dares and can do to subvert our liberties, we ask you, Americans, in conclusion, to read the letter of Bishop England, written from Rome, upon American nationality, soon after the news of the burning of the Massachusetts convent reached that city, and which was published under his direction, in Charleston, South Carolina.

"How often," says he, "do I wish my voice could be heard across the Atlantic, proclaiming to your meetings what I have seen and heard since I left you! *A people valuing freedom, and in the plenitude of its enjoyment, destroying religion, nay, having nearly effected its destruction, by reducing to practice here the principles which the Veterists and Conciliators contend for among you.*

" *The Americans are loud in their reprobation of your servile aristocracy, who would degrade religion by placing it under the control of a king's minister;* and could your aristocracy and place-hunters form the state of Catholicity here, *they would inveigh against the Democrats, who would degrade religion by placing its concerns under the control of a mob; and I am perfectly convinced they are right.*

"I am convinced that if these gentlemen of the Irish hierarchy, who are suspected, and I fear with good *reason*, of being favorable to Velotistical arrangements, had each one month's experience *of the operations of the principle here, their good sense, and piety, and zeal for religion, would compel them to suffer inconvenience rather than commit the fate of the religion of millions under their charge, and myriads yet unborn, to the influence of that most destructive principle*, to release themselves and their flocks from the unmitigated persecution they now suffer. *The people here claim and endeavor to assume the same power which the clauses and conditions would give the Crown among you*, though *not* to the same extent. *The consequence is that religion is neglected, degraded, despised, and insulted, with impunity.*"

This bold assertion of Bishop England against "responsibility *to the people as the great principle of the American system,*" is confirmed by that of all other leaders in the design upon American liberty. The *Catholic Telegraph*, published in Cincinnati, the contemporary of Cardinal England, spoke thus of our republicanism: "The system *may be very fine in theory, very fit for imitation on the part of those who seek the power of the mob, in contradistinction to justice and the public interest. But it is not of a nature to invite* the reflecting part of the *world, and shows, at least, that it has evils.*"

This *foreign emissary* and his coadjutors, the Jesuits and agents, who are under a bond to the Pope, *dare* to announce to our faces that the burning of one convent in New England, by a mob, "*is one fact in condemnation of the system of American institutions, confirmed lately by numerous other proofs.*"

Bishop Flagett, of Bardstown College, Kentucky, gives to his patrons abroad this plain hint at their ULTERIOR POLITICAL DESIGN, *and that no less than the entire subversion of our republican government.* In regard to the difficulty of Catholic missionaries with the Indians, he says the greatest is, "*their continued* traffic *with the whites*, WHICH CANNOT BE HINDERED SO LONG AS THE REPUBLICAN GOVERNMENT SHALL SUBSIST."

Do Americans know that, *at the point of the bayonet*, every individual must *kneel* or retreat, at the sight of a *Catholic procession* of the idolatrous "host," in every country in the *American* world, as well as papal Europe, where the power of the Romish system prevails? What though Papists are idolatrous; what though Bishop England says "NOTHING IS MORE OFFENSIVE TO CATHOLICS THAN A TRANSGRESSION OF THIS PRINCIPLE," that is, kneeling to a popish procession? What though it is the custom among the European slavish masses to worship a "wafer," which the priest (who secretly laughs at the credulous ignorance of his dupes) tells them is converted, by a few mumbling words which he utters, into a *real* God; what though the priests close the Bible, and their poor blind subjects know no better than to permit this despotism? Are Americans to be compelled to take off their hats to such a ridiculous deception,—to consent to be fools, and kneel down to such a monstrous imposture? And yet an Irish Papist, some months ago, at a Popish procession in Cincinnati, had the astonishing impudence to assault a Protestant and knock off his hat, because he chose to maintain his independence! How many hats will be knocked off when Rome gets to be more powerful? If this is the first lesson to Americans, what will be the second, and the last?

The Canon Law is Rome's *Magna Charta*. Robinson, the historian (a favorite author of Romanists), says, "*The Pope's public political end was to be absolute* ruler *of all the priesthood; and, through them, of all mankind.*" "It is a *Jewish Christianity*, having in it the seed of a hierarchy;" "they *sunk* the *people* to elevate the *order;*" "the order created a *master-like Aaron.*" "If this dispute," says he, "had been only about wearing the bells and pomegranates, as Aaron had done, and a breast-plate, that none but a Jew could read, it might have created *mirth;* but it took a very serious turn when it was *perceived that Aaron had under all his fine things* a KNIFE and a BLOOD BASIN."

Abbé De Pradt says: "Jesuitism is EMPIRE BY RELIGION. The general of the Jesuits is a veritable King." The Pope is *master* of the *general*. He says, "it is *organized* intolerance." Who is chief of this immense family, this militia present everywhere? THE POPE. *He counts more subjects than any sovereign ;* more than even *many* sovereigns together. IF THE WHOLE WORLD WERE CATHOLIC, THEN THE POPE WOULD COMMAND THE WHOLE WORLD."

"Catholicism," this Abbe De Pradt further says, "is not organized like other worships. *The latter have no common centre ; no exclusive source from whence flows power in every religious society.*" THEY HAVE NO ROME.

CHAPTER VI.

Now, my countrymen, by the very highest Roman Catholic authorities on earth, we have exposed the design and tendency of this corporation to subvert civil and religious liberty and law. Rome counts in her communion more than one hundred and fifty millions throughout the world. The entire Protestant world now exceeds but little upwards of one hundred and twenty millions. Rome has *one*, and *only* one, centre, and boasts of her *unity*, *indivisibility*, and *common principles* of the *great tyrant* who dwells in the "*Eternal City*." Protestants have no central head, and are never under such ecclesiastical rule. Yet, in the last three hundred years, where but with Protestants, and under Protestant governments, have *science*, enterprise, commerce, agriculture, order, law, and liberty, the inventions of mechanical genius, national and individual prosperity, flourished in all their beauty, grandeur, and successful triumphs? And here in the United States, where free institutions and liberty are best enjoyed, have not these developments been most gratifying and surprising?

The records of the world respond, *Nowhere beside.* Place not only the United States, but free England, Holland, or Scotland, in contrast with Catholic Italy, Catholic Spain, Catholic Germany, and Catholic Ireland, and what a striking contrast immediately presents itself! When Luther blew his trumpet, nations started up from the slumber of ages, burst the iron fetters which had chained them, and came forth into the light of heaven, and, rejoicing in its beams and the energies of their new manhood, stood erect, and commenced their march to national and individual independence, and the free enjoyment of the rights which God and nature gave them.

Who can estimate the value of this deliverance? It is beyond all price. Its magnificent results over Protestant nations are known and felt in free government, free conscience, free speech, free press, the diffusion of knowledge, the expansion of the human faculties, the happiness of families, the triumphs of peaceful arts and industry, and all the prosperity and glory which are shed on nations and their members.

America we hold to be *Bible ground*, and her institutions and principles are suited to all religious sects who do not claim to be infallible; but the system of Rome, by *its own documents*, avows its plan to *alter and prohibit books*, and YET KEEP THEIR TITLES; to *change the ideas of authors*; to *educate a political influence*, which, "*in ten, or, at most, twenty years*," *they have said, was to wield or control the destinies of this country;* and, in a word, "*to dictate to the souls* OF MYRIADS OF IMMORTAL BEINGS," and chain down the human faculties.

Our fathers declared in the Continental Congress that "THE CATHOLIC RELIGION HAD DELUGED ENGLAND IN BLOOD;" and they rose, in the might and spirit of unconquerable patriots, for the defence of their religious rights, that you, Americans, might be able now to vindicate and perpetuate them. Wait not till the Rubicon is passed! The Jesuits are within our lovely enclosures. What countries, where they have gained a foothold, have they not ruined? What monster errors do they not promulgate? What insidious plots do they not contrive? They are already combined with certain political leaders to distract this country. They are in our state politics. They are in our Washington counsels. Have they not already shocked the community by burning our Bibles? Have they not ejected it from our schools? Have they not defaced our school-books, and denounced our beautiful system of education, and American schools, as the "nurseries of hell"? Have they not attempted to gag free speech, — to seize the ballot-box, and assault our citizens in the exercise of their legal franchise? Have they not demanded the public funds, to support their sectarian education? And, with astonishing boldness, has not their leading prelate, acting in concert with all the popish bishops in this country, dictated to his political partisans in the legislature to alter the laws to suit his jesuitical and ambitious designs, to divert to his personal use, and in his legal right, the whole property of the church? Are not these men busy, and do they not act as spies in all our state and federal elections? And yet how feeble is the voice of Americans! how silent are many of the presses of the country! While these foreign agencies are at work; while dangers threaten from foes open and secret, alert and subtle, bound by oaths to make every interest, civil, political, and religious, subserve one grand end, — the supremacy of a foreign hierarchy in our midst, — these presses lift up no voice, speak in no indignant spirit of liberty. They are like a dead weight to the majestic wheel of the republic. They breathe not a whisper of warning against the designs of Catiline. They refuse to repel his insidious and impudent treacheries. They affect not to see, either through fear or through partisanship, the footsteps of the foreign intruder within the bowers of our happy homes; or the wily serpent coiling among the pleasant flowers, and stately foliage, and magnificent cypress, of our virgin scenery. They wink at the stratagems of Sylla, but condemn the merits of Fabius. They spurn the patriotic indignation of the Gracchi, and take to their embraces the plotting Tarquins. With the calculations of the political chess-board, their fame and independence are nicely balanced by a successful move, or aristocratically interwoven with the price of stocks in the market of the highest bidder. *Non tali auxilio.*

The patriotic heart of the nation demands no questionable Gloucesters, but magnanimous Sydneys, and heroic Hampdens, to defend the proud battlements of our liberties, and to stand in the breach on the invasion of the enemy. In every community, and often in responsible and prominent stations, there are men who either will not or cannot see danger till their house is in flames over their heads, or the assassin has effected his purpose. The time is approaching when no dubious action will be tolerated ; when the love of country, and the calls of patriotism, will awaken the most sluggish apathy. The field is chosen by the papacy. The plans are laid. The agents are commissioned not to faint or halt. America is to be the field on which the last great battle of the world is to be fought. The struggles of Rome will be in proportion to the value of the object, and the greatness and majestic splendor of the prize. Never were motives more impulsive and commanding ; never was an issue when the victory will be more coveted and magnificent, and the results so striking and extensive. But let this foreign influence beware ! The spirit which animated our ancestors glows with unabated fervor. In the words of the great orator of Yale, "Their sons scorn to be slaves," nor will they be circumvented or repelled in the background by monks and priestcraft. Let not the calm forebode the storm! The American "sky is charged with lightnings fiercer than ever flashed over that which canopies us all." Let not the fatal step be taken, nor the hand of the papal tyrant dare to press too closely on the American heart! While the "light of freedom is glowing with undiminished fires," may we hope to succeed in this grand battle of light against darkness, — of liberty against the combined forces of priests and despots!

ROMANISM OPPOSED TO OUR LIBERTIES.

CHAPTER I.

A recognition of the Protestant religion as the support of this government has been made by all who have administered it in the true spirit of republican freedom. Washington, Madison, Monroe, Adams, Jackson, and Harrison, offered supplications to God "to make our country continue the object of his divine care and gracious benediction." So do the principles of the American party date their origin with Luther, and were witnessed in the flames which made martyrs of Cranmer and Latimer. These principles came to our shores with the Protestant Huguenots of Florida, who were there murdered by the Spanish Inquisition for "seeking freedom to worship God." They afterwards passed over with the Mayflower, when the Pilgrims landed

Engraved by J.C.Buttre

Jacob Broom

OF PENNSYLVANIA

on Plymouth Rock. They appeared prominently in all the Revolutionary battles; they were embodied in the Declaration of Independence, which our fathers signed, and then sealed with their blood.

When it was resolved, in the second session of the Continental Congress, 1774, "to open to-morrow with prayer at the Carpenters' Hall," Rev. Mr. Duché, whom Mr. Adams called the most eloquent man in America, made the first prayer, in these precise words:

"O Lord, our Heavenly Father, high and mighty King of kings and Lord of lords, who dost from thy throne behold all the dwellers on earth, and reignest with power supreme and uncontrolled over all kingdoms, empires, and governments, look down in mercy, we beseech thee, on these American States, who have fled to thee from the rod of the oppressor, and thrown themselves on thy gracious protection, desiring to be henceforth dependent only on thee. To thee have they appealed for the righteousness of their cause; to thee do they now look up for that countenance and support which thou alone canst give. Take them, therefore, heavenly Father, under thy nurturing care; give them wisdom in council, and valor in the field; defeat the malicious designs of our cruel adversaries ; convince *them* of the unrighteousness of their cause ; and if they will still persist in their sanguinary purpose, O, let the voice of thine own unerring justice, sounding in their hearts, constrain them to drop the weapons of war from their unnerved hands in the day of battle. Be thou present, O God of wisdom, and direct the councils of this honorable assembly ; enable them to settle things on the best and surest foundation, that the scene of blood may be speedily closed, that order, harmony, and peace, may be effectually restored, and truth and justice, religion and piety, prevail and flourish amongst thy people. Preserve the health of their bodies and the vigor of their minds ; shower down on *them* and the *millions* they here represent such temporal blessings as thou seest expedient for them in this world, and crown them with everlasting glory in the world to come. All this we ask in the name and through the merits of Jesus Christ, thy Son and our Saviour. Amen ! "

At the close of the Revolution, 26th of August, 1783, Washington's first words, when he appeared before Congress, were a grateful acknowledgment to God, who had guided the Americans to battle and victory. And so he subsequently expressed himself.

when he resigned as commander in chief of the army, 23d of December, that same year. Upon the memorable event of his inaugural as President of the nation, he said:

"In this first official act, my fervent supplication is to that Almighty Being, that his benediction may consecrate to the liberties and happiness of the people of the United States a government instituted by themselves. No people can be bound to acknowledge and adore the *invisible* hand which conducts the affairs of men more than the people of the United States; and the destiny of the republican model of government is justly considered as deeply, perhaps *finally*, staked on the experiment intrusted to the hands of the American people."

When the convention sat to frame our constitution, and when all the governments of modern Europe had been examined without finding one suited to the condition of the American people, Dr. Franklin arose and addressed the president upon the importance of prayer; that, as "God governs the affairs of men," no blessing could be expected upon their deliberations without it; and that the constitution was the result of the infinite wisdom of the Almighty, and beyond the powers of any mortal assembly of men, is the indubitable conviction of the American people.

Thirteen years before the Declaration of Independence, Pownal, who had been Governor of three of the colonies, made this prophecy of America's destiny:

"A nation to whom all nations will come; a power whom all powers of Europe will court to civil and commercial alliances; a people to whom the remnants of all ruined people will fly; whom the oppressed and injured of every nation will seek for refuge," he exclaims, "ACTUATE YOUR SOVEREIGNTY, EXERCISE THE POWERS AND DUTIES OF YOUR THRONE."

And, now, without a monarch, an army, or an aristocracy, it will defy every Judas and Cain, foreign or native, who interposes between the rights, the honor, and the religion, of the American branch of the Anglo-Saxon race.

Our national interest and Christianity are inseparable; and as the people of the land of Bunker Hill, who built and paid for their churches, resisted the right of a foreign Andros to ring their bells, so will Americans, who claim the Protestant as their religion, resist the further aggression upon their schools, their property, and their institutions, by the political Romanism, of which they justly complain. At a recent meeting in Hope Chapel, New York city, Dr. O. A. Brownson, editor of the *Roman Catholic Review*, said: "We Catholics are here a *missionary* people. We are here to *Catholicize* the country. It remains for *us* Catholics to make it morally, intellectually, spiritually great. We are here God's chosen instruments for that purpose." Mr. McMasters, another fierce Romish editor, said: "Catholics were here not only to contribute to support their religion, and thereby their priests, but to make the people understand it. If they did not do so, they would be wiped out from the land in a sea of blood." How are the poor papists to understand it, Americans, when the priests keep them in ignorance, by shutting out the light of truth from their minds? The leading French journal of the 3rd of April, this year, speaking for the Romish church, says: "Railroads are not a progress; telegraphs are an analogous invention; the freedom of industry is not progress; machines derange all agricultural labor; industrial discoveries are a sign of abasement, not of grandeur." The following is from the *Univers*, their most influential paper in all

Europe: — "To make Rome the District of Columbia for the whole world, and the Pope the interpreter of the constitution of the United States." This declaration of the above journal expresses, of course, the avowed sentiments of the papists now in our republic.

Is it not time, Americans, to expose this worn-out foolery, when the great aim of this foreign concern is to say mass over our nation's soul? With *papal* baptism, *papal* matrimony, and papal rulers, what is to be the effect on our country, unless Protestantism counteract such teaching over the minds of the papal masses?

We have shown, in another chapter, that their device of baptism is a most entangling scheme to proselyte and extort money, and make its votaries slaves. That confession to the priests, in order to salvation, is an *invasion* upon personal liberty, and all sorts of human liberty. That the Church of Rome does interfere with *liberty of thought*, by denying the right to *read*, *buy*, or *circulate* books. And by its decrees in council it has taken the *Word of God out of its system*, and made it a criminal offence for any subject of their church to have *anything to do* with that holy book! By their Catechism of the Council of Trent, p. 313 this Romish system says, " *Without the presence of the parish priest, or some other priest commissioned by him, or by the ordinary, and two or three witnesses, there can be no marriage.*" They thereby declare that *none but Catholic priests can perform the marriage ceremony.* They have made this *civil* rite, then, a sacrament. They can dispense with prohibitions, or make them to suit all circumstances; and have, for political purposes, removed the impediment, and married brothers and sisters! The Church of Rome, therefore, begins with a *rite* to make *subjects*, at *birth;* to *secure* them through *marriage;* to *rule* them through life; and by indulgences and absolution in the *Confessional* to license practices of all iniquity; and sends them to Paradise, or denies it, in proportion to the amount of money paid.

We contend, as a Protestant people, that no power but the Word of God, or argument, and human persuasion, can be lawfully used to influence the conscience of any man. The constitution regards the *religion* of men so far as to require men to believe in God, and in the existence of future punishment and reward. Without this belief there is no sanctity to oaths. But the Romish confessional can absolve oaths, and render any law of our country a nullity which is opposed by the priest; and, consequently, the priest wields a secret power above our government and the laws of the land. There is not a thief, there is not a murderer, or a perjurer, or an incendiary, or a traitor, if he is a papist, but can go the very next day, or within a week, after the committal of the crime, and get absolution of the priest. If a papist swears in a court of justice on our Protestant Bible, he regards it as having no binding force on his conscience. Is not, then, the confessional a most dangerous and anti-republican power? The idea that religious opinions and secular trusts have no connection, and do not interfere with the discharge of public or official duty, has been a sad mistake with Protestants long enough; and to this mistake or error the rapid advancement of Romanism may partly be ascribed. Take *marriage* as an illustration. Protestants hold it in the light of a *civil* contract, of divine institution, *but not peculiar to any church.* Catholics make it a *sacrament.* The people, at first, look at this papal rite and obligation as of very small consequence, and would not regard it in connection with a man's fitness for office, whether connection with a man's fitness for office, whether his *opinion* was for or against it, as a sacrament. But, when it is understood that the descendants from every Protestant marriage in this country are pronounced by that church *illegitimate*, it becomes a matter of immense consequence to look at the effect of the system in connection with liberty.

By a treaty, or concordat, of the French government and the Pope, Pius VII., under Napoleon Bonaparte, in 1802, it was agreed to reëstablish the cures and sees, under certain conditions. The Pope declared himself very grateful, and publicly said he owed more to Napoleon than any other, next to God. But the laws of the French government in regard to marriage were distressing him, and in 1807 he sent a cardinal from Rome to Paris to negotiate the difficulty. Afterwards the discussion opened at Rome, when the doctrine that *no marriage was real or valid without the intervention of a priest* was decided. But, finding the French code was extending through Europe, he despatched instructions to his church to counteract the immoral doctrine of marriage as a civil right. The accompanying are extracts of the Pope's letter to Poland, in 1808, where an attempt was made by law to con form to this dogma. "Such a transaction," says the Pope (in this letter), "proposed by a Catholic prelate to a royal minister, upon a subject so sacred, considered in its consequences, in its whole tenor leads directly to consequences which sectaries have proposed to themselves, namely, to make Catholics and bishops, *and even* the Pope himself, confess that the power of governing men is indivisible. . . . . . For a Catholic bishop to acknowledge in Catholic marriages, civil publications, civil contracts, civil divorces, civil judgments, is to grant the prince power over the sacraments and discipline. It is to admit he can alter the forms and the rites; can derogate from the canons; can violate ecclesiastical liberty; can trouble conscience; that he has, by consequence, power over things ecclesiastical, essentially privileged, and dependent on the power of the Keys; which is as much as to say, he can put his hand in the censer, and make his laws prevail over the laws of the church. The bishop should either have *dissembled*, and *tolerated* a disorder imposed by irresistible force, or he should have informed the royal minister that the code, so far as respects marriage, cannot be applied to Catholic marriages in Catholic countries."

CHAPTER II.

THEN the Pope goes on to say: "If we examine the history of nations, we shall not find a Catholic prince suffering to be imposed on his subjects the obligation to publish their marriage, or discuss its validity or nullity before a judge of the district. If pastoral remonstrances proved useless, the bishop should still have continued to teach well the flock committed to his care, —

"1st. That there is no marriage if it is not contracted in the form which the church has established to render it valid.

"2d. That marriage once contracted according to its forms, no power on earth can sunder it.

"3d. That it remains indissoluble under all acts and circumstances.

"4th. In case of doubtful marriage, the church alone decides the validity or invalidity.

"5th. Marriage, without canonical impediment, is indissoluble, *whatever impediment the lay power may impose, without the consent of the Universal Church, or of its Supreme Head, the Roman Pontiff.*

"6th. That every marriage contracted, notwithstanding a canonical impediment, though abrogated by the sovereign, ought to be holden null and of no effect; *and that every Catholic is bound in conscience to regard such a marriage as void until made valid by a lawful dispensation of the church, if, indeed, the impediment which renders it null may be removed by a dispensation.*"

Americans, you all allow that marriage constitutes and *perpetuates* society; that it commends itself, as of the first importance, to the civil power. Are you willing, then, to surrender duties so momentous to the order and peace of families and our country, and enacted and sanctioned by our legislatures, to *foreign* priests, or to any priesthood whatever? The Romish system, by the Council of Trent, says: "Marriage contracted without the solemn forms of the church is void, which this council could not have done if it depended on the nature of two contracts, which depend on two dis tinct powers, — the one, civil, and dependent on civil laws; the other, religious, and dependent on the laws of the church." The belief that it *is necessary to go to the Pope of Rome to get a dispensation from a canonical impediment*, because a man regards marriage as a sacrament, and not a civil contract, and that his union by the civil law would be void, and his children illegitimate, without it, is a sufficient cause, we say, to disqualify any Romanist from holding a civil trust under our Protestant government, and cannot exist without affecting his conduct as a public officer, no matter what may be said or affirmed to the contrary. The system that blesses *horses* and *dogs* for money, in the name of the Holy Trinity, may well afford to curse American Protestant liberty. This law of Romish marriage, therefore, is most pernicious and anti-republican.

In 1654, after the final rising of the Council of Trent, Pius the Fourth issued a *creed*, which is received universally by the Roman Catholic Church, and is by a bull enforced upon the profession of *every doctor, teacher, and head of a university*. No election or promotion is valid without it. Another papal law requires the same profession of the heads of cathedrals, monastic institutions, and the military order, which law directly interferes with liberty. Milner, a popish writer, in his "End of Controversy," chap. xiv., says: "The same creed, namely, the Apostles' Creed, the Nicene Creed, the Athanasian Creed, and THE CREED OF POPE PIUS IV., DRAWN UP IN CONFORMITY *with the* Holy Council of Trent, and EVERYWHERE RECITED AND PROFESSED TO THE STRICT LETTER," &c. In addition to a *profession of faith, twelve* NEW ARTICLES, as foreign to the Christian creed as light from darkness, are subjoined. The following are extracts from each of these articles:

1. "I *admit* and embrace apostolical and ecclesiastical *traditions.*"

2. "I admit the Sacred Scriptures according to the sense which the Holy Mother Church held and does hold, to whom it belongs to judge of the true sense and interpretation of the Holy Scriptures; *nor will I ever interpret them otherwise than according to the unanimous consent of the fathers.*"

The first binds the soul to pagan traditions; the second, to the impossibility of *thinking* or *acting* as a responsible being!

3. "I profess that they are truly seven sacraments, instituted by Jesus Christ, for salvation, namely, *baptism, confirmation, eucharist, penance,*

extreme unction, orders, and matrimony ; and that they confer grace."

4. "*Without the sacrament of baptism, which is the sacrament of faith,* no one *can ever obtain justification.*"

That is, without the *priest* blesses the soul!

5. "*That in the mass there is offered to God a true, proper, propitiatory sacrifice for the living and the dead.*"

Every priest by this act is made to offer up a sacrifice of our blessed Saviour, directly violating that passage which says, "Christ was *once* offered up." If Christ was only *once* offered up (not by the priest, but by himself), how can he be offered up *again*, and that, too, by a priest? But this "sacrifice of the mass" is not Christianity: it is papal mystification and paganism, — an absurdity. None but a Catholic priest can offer up the sacrifice of the "mass," and turn a wafer into a God!!! Who can think of such blasphemy without a shudder? But this is not the worst of this turning a "wafer" into God. Rome *compels* physically all persons, whoever they be, to bow to, and worship, this wafer-God!!! Is not this *compulsory law* anti-republican?

6. This article speaks of *Purgatory*, — that is, a temporary punishment for the faithful on their way to heaven. "The souls therein are helped by the suffrages of the faithful." Prayers, well paid for, are one of the most *successful* of Rome's deceptions to enrich her treasury. The father, for the soul of his child or wife, employs *the official services of the priest*, *to deliver that soul* from the horrors of purgatorial torment! It makes slaves of the poor laity, whose hard earnings and scanty wages are exacted and given to this end; while the priests extort and secure *endowments* from the deceased wealthy, to save them from punishment!!

We find a church in Venice, in 1743, was in arrears for sixteen thousand four hundred masses; and Florentine tells of a Spanish priest who was paid for eleven thousand eight hundred masses which he never said! Thus do the priesthood of Rome traffic in souls; cheat the people of liberty; cheat them of their money; cheat them of their hopes; cheat them of their salvation! And this purgatorial lying, extortion, and compulsion, are anti-republican.

7 and 8. These articles profess belief in the doctrine of heathen worship of *saints*, and *images*, and

relics. — "the *image of Christ, of the Virgin Mother of God*," and of other saints. This belief is binding on all.

This is anti-Christian, and tends to make the people heathenish; and this pagan ignorance is inimical to the whole genius of our republican system.

9. Professes *faith in the power of indulgences*, which directly promotes and gives license for crimes. "I also *affirm that the power of indulgence was left* by Christ in the church, and that the use of them is most wholesome to a Christian people." They are very "wholesome" for the Pope and priests to fill their coffers with money, and to multiply crimes all over the land. They are sometimes called "*bills of exchange on purgatory*."

These indulgences are dispensed by the Pope *through the priests*. They are a bundle of licenses to commit all manner of iniquities. There is always a great *demand* for these little packages; and, depending on the *foreign* will of the Pope, they bring a fine price, and give the hierarchy an unbounded power over their people of the whole earth.

10. "*I acknowledge the Holy Catholic, Apostolic Roman Church for the Mother and Mistress of all churches; and I promise true obedience to the Bishop*

of Rome, successor to St. Peter, prince of the Apostles, Vicar of Christ," "THE MISTRESS OF ALL CHURCHES."

Is there anything to surpass this arrogant assumption of priestly power,—*this direct allegiance to the Pope?* What is it but a slavery, which our free spirits should denounce, and at which we should revolt? Is our country safe with such a decree?

11th. "I likewise, undoubtedly, receive and profess all other things, delivered, defined, and declared, by the sacred canons of the General Council." This is adopting all the *persecuting, immoral* legislation of the "Council of Trent," the "worst of all." Yet, every priest and every papist in our land is bound by *oath* to receive "all things defined, delivered, and declared," by that Council. "*And I condemn, reject, and anathematize, all things contrary thereto, and all heresies which the church has condemned, rejected, and anathematized.*" Here at one sweep they *curse* all *heretics*, or *Protestants*, wherever they are found.

12th. "*This true Catholic faith, without which no man can be saved, which I at present freely profess, and truly hold, the same I will take care of as far as in the lies, and shall be most constantly held and confessed by me,* whole and unviolated, with God's assistance, to the last breath of my life; and by all my subjects, or these, the care of whom, in my office, belongs to me, shall be held, taught, and preached." "I THE SAME, N, PROMISE, VOW, AND SWEAR, SO HELP ME GOD AND THESE HOLY GOSPELS." *This is the priest's article especially.* He is a *slave* to the Pope, and is himself a PARISH POPE TO THE PEOPLE.

Mark this, Americans: the Romish priest swears by an oath that *there is no salvation* to those who do not believe this creed; that is, who do not believe in the *supremacy of the Pope, indulgences, transubstantiation, purgatory, image worship, saint worship, persecution against Protestants, traditions,* &c. He swears also to *spread* these anti-Christian and persecuting doctrines among those *under his care,* and to do all he can to enforce them, without reference to *right* or liberty, to his life's end; to suppress freedom of thought and speech, and to make subjects for the Pope of Rome! Now, *Protestants,* all this is subversive of our free institutions. If the priests and the papists do not oppose, denounce, and persecute to death (whenever they can and dare), all Protestants, they swear *to a lie.*

We repeat, they are *bound,* by their *oath* to the Pope of Rome, to receive all the persecuting and tyrannical decrees of the general councils of that church. We say, they are *bound* to teach and diffuse principles utterly opposed to all the dear and cherished rights of American liberty to your children; and they ought not to be intrusted with the education of freemen, if you wish to preserve the precious and glorious privileges of our land. The whole body of papists, by the creed of Pius IV., is fastened and indissolubly *bound* up with the hierarchy of Rome! And how dangerous and inimical is it to the liberties of this republic!

CHAPTER III.

We will now give you the *precise* oath which binds every Roman Catholic bishop in the United States of America, and in the whole world, to the Pope of Rome and his throne. It is taken from Barrow's *unanswered* "Treatise on *Supremacy*," and is a COMPLETE FEUDAL OATH. Here it is:

"I, N, elect of the church of N, will henceforward be faithful *and obedient* to St. Peter, the Apostle, and to the Holy Roman Church, and to *our Lord*, the Lord N, Pope N, and to his successors canonically coming in. I will neither advise, *consent, or do anything*, that they may lose life or member, or that their persons may be seized, or *hands any wise laid upon them, under any pretence whatever.* The counsel which they shall intrust me withal, by themselves, their *messengers*, or letters, I will not knowingly reveal to any to their prejudice. *I will keep them to defend and keep the holy papacy*, and the ROYALTIES OF ST. PETER, saving my order, *against all men.* The legate of the apostolical see, going and coming, I will honorably treat, and help in his necessities. THE RIGHTS, HONORS, PRIVILEGES, AND AUTHORITY, OF THE HOLY ROMAN CHURCH OF OUR LORD THE POPE, and *his foresaid successors, I will endeavor to preserve, defend, increase, and advance. I will not be in any council, action, or treaty, in which shall be plotted against our said Lord, and the Romish church, anything to the hurt or prejudice of their persons, right, honor, state, or power ; and if I shall know any such thing to be treated or agitated by any whatsoever, I will hinder it to my power, and as soon as I can* will signify it to our said lord, or to some *other, by whom it may come to his knowledge.*

"*The rules of the holy fathers, the apostolic decrees, ordinances, or disposals, reservations, provisions, and mandates, I will observe with all my might, and cause to be observed by others.* HERETICS, SCHISMATICS, AND REBELS TO OUR SAID LORD, OR HIS FORESAID SUCCESSORS, I WILL TO MY POWER PERSECUTE AND OPPOSE. I will come to a council when I am called, unless I am hindered by a canonical impediment. I WILL BY MYSELF IN PERSON VISIT THE THRESHOLD OF THE APOSTLES EVERY THREE

YEARS, AND GIVE AN ACCOUNT TO OUR LORD AND HIS FORESAID SUCCESSORS OF ALL MY PASTORAL OFFICE, *and of all things any wise belonging to the state of my church, to the discipline of my clergy and people, and, lastly, of the salvation of souls committed to my trust; and will, in like manner, humbly receive and diligently execute the apostolic commands.*

"*And if I be detained by a lawful impediment, I will perform all things aforesaid by a certain messenger, hereto especially empowered a member of my chapter, or some other in ecclesiastical dignity, or else having a parsonage; or, in default of these, by a priest of the diocese; or, in default of one of the clergy (of the diocese), by some other secular or regular priest, of improved integrity and religion, fully instructed in all things above mentioned. And such impediment I will make out by lawful proofs, to be transmitted by the aforesaid messenger to the Cardinal proponent of the Holy Roman Church, in the congregation of the sacred council.*

"*The possessions belonging to my table I will neither sell, nor give away, nor mortgage, nor grant aneu in fee, nor any wise alienate,—no, not even with the consent of the chapter of my church,—without con sulting the Roman Pontiff.* And if I shall make any alienation, I will thereby incur the penalties contained in a certain constitution put forth about this matter. So HELP ME GOD, AND THESE HOLY GOSPELS."

Such is that servile and persecuting oath. This doctrine of the *supremacy* of the Pope and the *priesthood* makes *bond-slaves of all people who belong to them.* It makes a *God on earth* of the Pope at Rome. He is an ambitious *tyrant* over the PRIESTHOOD, and the priests are *tyrants* over the people.

No man can take this oath to the Pope, and be a *faithful* or *true* citizen of the United States, or a safe and *consistent* citizen of any country. *No Catholic bishop*, then, is an *honest* citizen of the United States; if he were, he would be a *perjurer.* In another chapter, we have shown, in the memorable contest between the Pope and the *republic of Venice*, that *the Jesuits all turned traitors, and fled from Venice, and went over to the Pope! The Jesuits, who are the Pope's greatest propagandists*, never did, according to all history and the authority of the *French Parliament*, dwell in any country, without destroying its *liberties* and its *morals.* The foreign hierarchy who control the Roman Catholic church in the United States to-day are Jesuits, from the leading bishops spread over the states, to the Irish priest who came by the last emigrant arrival.

It is in accordance with the American principle to examine everything presented to us. We are carrying forward the glorious emancipation Luther began. The liberty, *civil* and *religious*, we so earnestly cherish and develop, is Bible liberty, and its home is on American ground. Without note or comment, we send that blessed book abroad over the world, the emblem of this ennobling, sublime liberty, and the guardian evidence to all who breathe American air to stand erect as freemen, and to bow, unmolested by papal curses and bulls, in the worship of our God. This blessed volume has been translated into more than one hundred and sixty languages of the earth; and, without the cost of a single mass or prayer for a soul in purgatory, it is, through American means and Protestant teaching, enlightening, and comforting, and instructing, millions of the human family.

Two years ago, there was a consecration in St. Patrick's Cathedral, New York, of Bishops Bailey, McLaughlin, and Dr. Goesbriand, by the papal Nuncio, Monsignor *Bedini*. The Jesuits then took that oath in Latin, as we have given it in correct English; but the priests published a version in *English*, for the newspapers, and little pamphlets containing an account of the ceremonies; one of which pamphlets is now before us, and it contains a complete and wilful *forgery*. It omitted all the *persecuting* and *political* part, which the *oath* we give contains, and which is the *exact* one used here and at Rome this very day. They always *deny* this gross deception to Americans, and three fourths of the American Roman Catholic laity also deny it Why? Because these Jesuits find it expedient to *cheat* and *deceive* Protestants and their own papist subjects in this American land.

Cruelty is a *central principle* in the Church of Rome, and, therefore, anti-republican. It is very common, at present, with Roman Catholics, to deny that their church approves religious persecution, and in this assertion they are backed up by ignorant or designing Protestants, for political purposes solely. But there is no fact more clearly proved, both by history and the dogmas of their church everywhere contained in their canons and bulls, and carried out in practice to the present day. The prisons of Rome, and all the Italian prisons under the influence of the Pope, are, at this moment, filled with victims groaning under these horrid cruelties. The Inquisition, in some form, and every priest and his devotees, are agents to execute this intolerance.

The commentary of Menochius, which is a textbook at all Catholic colleges and seminaries of learning, declares, in connection with the parable of the wheat and the tares, that the Saviour "does not forbid heretics (or Protestants) to be taken away and put to death," and refers to Meldonatus on this special article of their belief. And these are the words of the authority alluded to: "They who deny that heretics are to be put to death ought much rather to deny that *thieves*, much rather that *murderers*, ought to be put to death; for heretics are the more pernicious than thieves or murderers, as it is a greater crime to steal and slay the souls of men than their bodies."

Bellarmine, the papal authority constantly appealed to, says: "Experience teaches us that there is no other remedy (than death); for the church has advanced by degrees, and tried every remedy. At first she only *excommunicated*, then *fined*, then *exiled*; at last she was compelled to have recourse to *death*.

* * * * * If you throw them (Protestants) into prison, or send them into exile, they corrupt their neighbors by their *language*, and those who are at a distance by their *books ;* therefore, *the only remedy is, to send them speedily to their proper place.*"

The following is the curse of Pope Benedict VIII. :

"May they suffer the curse of God and of the world ; may they suffer it in their body, may their mind become stupefied, may they meet with all bodily pains, and end in perdition.

"May they be damned with the cursed ones, and perish with the wicked.

"May they be cursed with the Jews, who did not believe in our Lord, and crucified him.

"May they be cursed with the heretics, Protestants, who attempt to overthrow the Holy Mother Church.

"May they be damned in the four parts of the world : cursed in the east, abandoned in the west, interdicted in the north, excommunicated in the south.

"May they be cursed in the day, excommunicated in the night.

"May they be damned in heaven, on earth, and in the regions below."

Says the historian Bruys: "Secular powers, if need be, may be compelled by church censures to *destroy all heretics* (Protestants) *marked by the church, out of the lands of their jurisdiction.*" — Labb., Tom. 13, p. 934. Bruys' Hist. of the Papacy, Tom. iii., p. 148.

The Council of Constance, 1414, in which Pope Martin presided, not only condemned and burned alive Huss and Jerome of Prague, but issued their terrific anathema against the millions of heretics all over Europe, and *commanded* all kings, emperors, and princes, forthwith to exterminate by fire and sword.

This dogma of persecution is introduced into the class-book at Maynooth Jesuit College, for which England contributes annually thirty thousand pounds sterling.—See Delahogue's Tract. Theolog., cap. 8. De Membris, p. 404, Dublin edit., 1795.

The oath which every Roman bishop swears contains this central principle of persecution.

The following propositions are taken from Dr. Den's System of Theology, a text-book for every papal theological seminary in the land:

1st. "Protestants are heretics, and as such are worse than Jews and Pagans."

2d. "They are, by baptism and blood, under the power of the Roman Catholic Church."

3d. "So far from granting toleration to Protestants, it is the duty of the church to exterminate the rites of their religion."

4th. "It is the duty of the Roman Catholic Church to compel heretics to submit to her faith."

5th. "That the punishments decreed by the Roman Catholic Church are confiscation of goods, exile, imprisonment, and death."

A converted Popish priest, in a late work, says:

"During the last three years I discharged the duty of a Romish clergyman, my heart often shuddered at the idea of entering the confessional. The recitals of the murderous acts I had often heard through this iniquitous tribunal had cost me many a restless night, and are still fixed with horror upon my memory. But the most awful of all considerations is this, — that through the confessional I have been *frequently apprised of intended assassinations*, and most diabolical conspiracies; and, still, from the ungodly injunctions of secrecy in the Romish creed, lest, as Peter Dens says, 'the confessional should become odious,' I dared not give the slightest intimation to the marked-out victims of slaughter."

Pope Urban II. says:

"We do not consider those as homicides who, burning with zeal for the Catholic church against excommunicated persons, happen to have killed any of them."

Pope Sixtus V., in a public address, applauded the assassination of Henry III. of France.

The Rhemish translators of the New Testament, on Rev. 17 : 6, "Drunken with the blood of the saints," say:

"Protestants foolishly expound it of Rome, for that they put heretics to death, and allow of their punishment in other countries; but their blood is not called the blood of saints no more than the blood of thieves, man-killers, and other malefactors, for the shedding of which, by order of justice, no commonwealth shall answer."

Bellarmine and Maldonatus, two of the highest authorities at Maynooth, teach the same doctrines. The proceedings at Rome in regard to the massacre of St. Bartholemew prove that Rome would have equally gloated over the Gunpowder Plot, if it had only been successful. She has never disavowed any of her atrocious principles, whilst the recent avowals of Dr. Cahill, the *Rambler*, and the *Shepherd of the Valley*, demonstrate that modern Papists are quite as bloodthirsty as their ancestors.

"The Inquisition was first established at Toulouse, in 1233. It subsequently spread in Spain, Portugal, and other countries, increasing in power and cruelty. The managers of the inquisitional courts were men of low origin and brutal nature, who had unlimited power from the Pope to put to death any person suspected of heresy; and heresy, in the Church of Rome, means nothing but opposing the pretensions of the Papacy. Under the tryannical sway of the Inquisition, parents were required to stifle all their natural affections, and children forgot their reverence, gratitude, and love. The immense power of the Inquisitor General we refer to. Among other practices of the Inquisition, it was common for persons to be seized and murdered in order to get possession of their property. It was in vain to search the world for an institution to compare with this in atrocity and merciless barbarity. 'Deliver yourself up a prisoner to the Inquisition,' filled the soul with horror, and made the frame motionless, for it was the prelude to the dungeon and death. The infamous practices of the inquisitional courts were made up of cruelty, blood, death!

"Romanism has not changed by the light and progress of civilization. In 1825, under Pope Leo XII., the work of the Inquisition was recommenced with great vigor. It was as dark, baneful, and bloody, as ever. From that period until the late revolution in Italy, scenes of horror transpired, the details of which are known only to their atrocious authors. In 1849, the Constituent Assembly determined that the tribunal should be abolished, and the building appropriated to some military purpose. In the buildings were the bones of human beings without number, thrown together in a manner to shock the feelings. There are to-day a thousand patriots suffering, in gloomy and filthy dungeons, all the horrors that the victims of the Inquisition endured. The truth is, that the spirit of deadly persecution is inherent in Romanism. It is one of its vital forces. While Romanism prides itself upon its immovability, progress is an integral part of Protestantism; and its onward march, however slow, is steady and direct."

To those who think that this spirit of intolerance is relaxed in our day, either in the United States or in other lands, we could present a volume of convincing and overwhelming facts to prove the contrary. But the following specimens will be sufficient:

A few years ago, a Protestant minister in the West, after preaching to his own congregation on the subject of Popery, was met by the priest of the town at the church door, and told by him that, "were it not for the laws of the country, he would cut his throat." "Yes," said the minister, "I know that already."

The Rev. Mr. Nast, of Cincinnati, who has been instrumental in the conversion of many German papists, by preaching, lecturing, and publishing a German paper, received a letter a few months since, stating that if he did not stop his efforts, they would do with their fists what their priests cannot do with their pens, "*knock your eyes out.*"

An Episcopal clergyman in the West stated that a member of his church married a Roman Catholic lady, who, by his influence, was converted to the Protestant faith. The father of the young lady called to inquire if it was so. "Yes," said the daughter, "it is." On leaving the house, he said to his son-in-law, "Sir, I will never be satisfied till I have washed my hands in your heart's blood."

Who was it, a few years since, that drove six hundred families from the Austrian empire into the Prussian territory, because they would not renounce the reformed religion? It was popish priests.

Who was it that drove the Rev. Mr. Rule from Cadiz? Papal authorities, directed to do so by the archbishop of the see.

Who flogged a man nearly to death for renouncing Popery, in the State of Pennsylvania? It was a popish priest. In the neighborhood of Doylestown, a German Catholic attended a funeral sermon of a Protestant minister, after which a priest called and asked him if he had become a Protestant. "If you have," said he, "you have committed a mortal sin; confess your sin to me." "I have confessed my sin to Christ," said the sick man, "and obtained absolution." The priest urged him with increasing warmth to confess; he declined. The priest then seized a chair, jumped on the bed, and pounded him with it till he broke it in pieces; he then took from his pocket a raw-hide, and began to scourge him, to compel him to confess. A stranger, passing by, hearing the noise, entered the house, and, finding the priest in the act of scourging the sick man, he seized him by the collar, and dragged him down stairs. Soon after, the man died. The priest was arrested and tried in Doylestown court-house, and fined fifty dollars and costs, and left the country.

Who was it that threatened the city of Boston? It was the lady superior of the convent, who, after that unclean and anti-republican cage had been attacked by rioters, said: "The bishop has more than twenty thousand Irishmen at his command, who will tear your houses over your heads, and you may read your riot-acts till your throats are sore!" We condemn the riot, but did that justify this diabolical and bloody threat of this female Jesuit?

Who was it that persecuted recently four hundred Madeira Protestants, and forced them to flee from their native country? The priests of the island.

A convert to Protestantism, travelling along the road leading to Scariff, Ireland, in the county of Clare, was accosted by some laborers in the field. After threatening him several times, they at length suffered him to pass, saying, "If you dare to come this way again, you bloody Sassenah rascal, we'll blow your brains out!" — *Limerick Standard.*

A savage-looking ruffian violently attacked the Rev. Mr. Marks, a Protestant clergyman, late of the Molyneux Asylum, in the public streets of Dublin, and, without provocation, knocked the reverend gentleman down. What next?— *Warder.*

On the evening of Wednesday last, 13th inst., as John Honner, a respectable Protestant, was returning home from the Macroon Sessions, he was savagely assaulted midway between Castletown and Enniskeane, by some person at present unknown; no less than sixteen wounds having been inflicted on his head and face, besides several others on his body and limbs; his skull was severely fractured. — *Cork Standard.*

The names of nearly one hundred persecuted Protestant clergymen are given in the Tipperary *Constitution.* The manner in which they were treated is thus marked: stoned to death; murdered; stoned; fired at; dangerously assaulted; abused and persecuted; plundered; interrupted and assaulted in the performance of duty; house attacked, demolished, or burned down; driven from his home, or his country.

Some time ago, M. Maurette, a French Roman priest, was brought to the knowledge of the truth as it is in Jesus, and, in consequence, abandoned the pale of the idolatrous and apostate church in which he had been brought up. Having convinced himself of the danger of continuing in Babylon, he wished to induce as many as possible of his countrymen to flee out of her infected communion. With this view, he published a statement of the reasons that had led him to adopt the Protestant faith, and plainly and forcibly exposed the superstition of Rome, by the usual arguments employed by the divines of the French Protestant church. For this he was condemned, on the 17th of May, 1844, by the Court of Assizes of L'Ariege, to a year's imprisonment, and a fine of six hundred francs!

You have all heard of the brutish papal persecutions at Damascus, where two or three of the unprotected sons of Abraham were recently flogged, soaked in large vessels of water, their eyes pressed out of their sockets with a machine, dragged about by the ears till the blood gushed out, thorns driven in between the nails and flesh of their fingers and toes, and candles put under their noses, burning their nostrils. This is Popery! After hearing of this act of persecution, and hundreds of others constantly taking place in papal countries, and our own country, who will believe that this unchangeable church has changed her system of butchery? What she has been she is now; and you, my Protestant brethren, would feel it if she had the power.

Now, with the fact of the presence of this mighty enemy in our beloved land, what more astonishing than the apathy and blindness of our statesmen, and the slumbering security in which our patriotic citizens, to whom liberty is so sweet and dear, fold their arms, and never dream of papal danger? Do they imagine that our country is too great, our resources too vast, our numbers too overwhelming, to feel the slightest apprehension on this subject? What was it but a spark that kindled up the conflagration of Rome, and that was to blow up the Parliament of England? What was it but a Guy Fawkes, employed by the Jesuit priests to make that fatal arrangement, to overturn Protestantism in England? What was it but one gilded bauble from the Pope that corrupted the royal monarch,

Henry II., to submit himself and kingdom to the dictation of the Vatican? What is it but Puseyism, now in the hands of the subtle and scheming Nuncio of Rome, aided by the University of Oxford, and the crafty spies and emissaries of Rome, that is undermining the foundation of Protestantism, and shaking the fancied stability of the throne of the Stuarts, in that land of the early Reformation, and heroic defenders of the bulwarks of liberty?

Do our listless Galbas imagine that the *two thousand papal bishops, priests, and Jesuits*, with their millions of obedient subjects, and multitudes of endowed nunneries, seminaries, and colleges, planted over our land like so many batteries, with their guns and ammunition ready for action, are sent here and put in operation merely for the idle amusement of that foreign potentate? Is the prize less tempting, by its surpassing beauty and magnificence, than other territories and states, at which its policy has been directed, and over which its skilful and deep-laid plots have triumphed? There are but a few of our people, comparatively, who are aware of the secret and mighty springs which are at work in the wheels within the wheels of this spiritual and political machine. Its central power is at Rome ; but its army of chameleon and vigilant spies are everywhere. Our people may despise its intrigues, and laugh at the warnings of more reflecting patriots, who stand like sentinels on the watch-towers of liberty ; but so reasoned the inhabitants of Troy, when the treacherous wooden horse entered within its gates and took the city.

A PROTESTANT EDUCATION FOR AMERICAN CITIZENS.

CHAPTER I.

AMERICANS, do you know that every time you unfurl the banner of your country, and rally to the defence of your republican school system, you insult the sensibilities of the anti-American party, foreign and native? Remember, the debt of gratitude has been fully paid to those who have aided you in cutting down your forests, levelling your mountains, opening your highways, digging your canals, settling your lands, and even in the blood shed for the common defence of the country. It is paid in the prosperity, the happiness, the success, of their posterity, for whom they labored, suffered, and endured. They looked to the good of their children; — you, Americans, have now to do

Engraved by J.C. Buttre

Erastus Brooks.

OF NEW YORK

the same. It is the duty of the father to protect himself and family from injurious influences; and it is a still more imperative duty for the nation to protect its people from the same. Then, shall we not be permitted to roll back the tide of priestcraft, and place in its way the great counter wave of American common and free school education? This is a question for wise men of all parties. This is the principle of that eclectic party which the people baptize in their own name to-day!

Remember, the greatest as well as the cheapest insurance upon this Union is its republican learning. You must educate those who are to make laws for yourselves and your children — who are to elect your judges and your rulers. The more schools you build, the fewer jails and alms-houses you will require. An extended and free education will give to America more private and public prosperity, more financial success, more political tranquillity, than all other means combined. And, if neglected, or surrendered into foreign hands, liberty cannot long linger upon your native soil. American citizens must be respected the world over; and it is their education which secures the rights of conscience, and of religious worship, and is the main guarantee of integrity and loyalty to their own country.

There is in the United States now an organization called "Christian Brothers." It has its seat in Italy, and under a special bull of the Pope is found in every city and neighborhood of our country where Popery has made a foot-print. This society obliges every "Christian Brother" to renounce his native country, friends, acquaintances, and even parents! And these are the "Brothers" who conduct the schools, colleges, nunneries, and monasteries, of Romanists, all over our land. They infuse into the youth of the country the poison of religious and national enmity, and there are thousands of their pupils in New York and other states, who, though born upon the soil, will proudly declare they are Roman Catholics, and *not Americans!* And, that there may be no mistake as to the rules and constitution of this secret society, to whom not only American Roman Catholics, but unsuspecting Protestants, commit the souls and bodies of their children, we give some of their "directions," obtained from that little printed volume, which is approved by the Pope, and sanctioned by all his bishops in our country, but concealed from the public eye. The author is John Baptist La Salle, an Abbot of Normandy, in France, assisted by Father Boudin, of the Society of Jesus, and rector of the Jesuits' Novitiate at Rouen.

NATIVE COUNTRY. — "Each brother is absolutely required to renounce his native country." (Pages 16 and 18 of the Rule of Government for the use of the Christian Brothers.)

DEPENDENCY. — "Absolute and blind obedience to the commands of the Brother Superior." (Ditto, page 43.)

SELF-DENIAL. — "We have to renounce our own judgment, because we are unable to judge things but in a worldly manner." (Ditto, page 91.)

DIFFIDENCE. — "When the 'Brothers' converse with persons, strangers to the Order, they will observe an absolute silence in all that regards the Institution. They are prohibited from letting anything transpire out of the Society. They shall never say in what localities, and how numerous, are the 'Brothers,' even if requested; but, in case they cannot avoid an answer, they will limit themselves to speak only of the spirit of the Institution." (Rules and Constitutions, page 34.)

PARENTS AND FRIENDS. — "They will break all affections which should bind them to the world, even with parents and friends.

"The 'Brother' shall never speak of his parents, nor of his native country, nor of what he has done, unless with persons such as the bishop, in case he should be interrogated." (Ditto, page 38.)

"The 'Brothers' are warned NOT TO ATTEND THE FUNERALS OF THEIR PARENTS, only in the church, in case they reside in the same locality. But the Superiors will see that even THIS DOES NOT OCCUR!" (Ditto, page 65.)

ESPIONAGE. — "If one of the fraternity should propose a new maxim, which was known to be false, or might cause serious consequences, the other 'Brothers' will combat it with silence, and report it immediately to the Brother Superior." (Ditto, page 32.)

HYPOCRISY. — "The 'Brothers' will carry their heads always straight, inclining it only in front, never turning behind, nor incline it on one side or on the other. Should necessity compel them to it, they will turn the whole body quickly and with gravity.

"They will avoid to show their forehead turned into ringlets, but the nose above all, in order that strangers may see in their faces an external wisdom, which might be the sign of spiritual virtue.

"They ought never to keep their lips neither too close, nor too open." (Ditto, pages 35, 36.)

The books of this society for the education of Americans are published under the authority of Archbishop Hughes, of New York, and endorsed by other bishops thus:

"I recommend the series of school-books compiled by the Christian Brothers, and published by (———), New York, and wish them to be used in every school in the diocese where there are no other Catholic school-books in the hands of the children.

"† J. B., *Archbishop of Cincinnati.*"

"We heartily recommend for the use of our Catholic

schools the books of the Christian Brothers, published by (——), New York. † JOHN, *Bishop of Albany.*"

"I earnestly recommend the books of the Christian Brothers, published by (——), for the use of our Catholic schools in this Diocese. † JOHN, *Bishop of Buffalo.*"

The last great Romish convention in Baltimore had for its true object nothing but to further the assault upon the education of the American masses.

Soon after its session, eight states of the Union made a simultaneous movement for a division of the public school funds for this purpose. In California alone, however, was the effort successful.

A pupil in a Roman Catholic school cannot, under the heaviest penalty, open the lids of a book, or look at a print or painting, which has not been sanctioned and approved by *the* church! Even the emblems on the tombs of masons in Jamaica have been effaced by stone-cutters, under the Jesuit priests, because that institution was hateful to the Pope.

Long before the murder of the Huguenots in Florida, under the Spanish Inquisition, the Pope had made disposal of the entire American continent. Pius the Fifth exercised this right to the monarchs of Spain; and the only way to possess it is that wisely adopted, in attempting to seduce the people through educational influences; in plain English, to keep them ignorant, as they do the masses in all Romish countries.

"We want to make Rome the District of Columbia for all Christendom," is the bold avowal of an editor of the Popish press. In the District of Columbia no citizen can even vote for the President of their country, while the Jesuit college of Georgetown furnishes the education to many of the officers of the government. And in the state department, especially, much facility is thus afforded for managers of that institution to know the private transactions of our national bureaus. Even the lion loves the lair of its nativity, and the wolf seeks the cavern where it was born; but here is a secret, invisible influence, training Americans upon their own soil to curse country, family, and government, because these shelter and protect from all tyrant foes.

Americans, there is a voice calling you to action now, stronger than that of court, jury, or country; it is the voice of God! It is time to rise and fix a higher value to the education of all the people, when men are dismissed for Americanism from office.

In Norfolk, Va., at the late election of Gov. Wise, it was publicly and semi-officially announced by the press that no one in the navy yard at that station could vote the American ticket, unless at the expense of his place; and fifteen hundred men were forced for their bread to vote against their sentiments, after making an example by removing three experienced mechanics, who had expressed their partiality for American principles before that election. In the treasury department, whether in the custom-houses, light-houses, or the erection of new light-houses, the same system has invariably been pursued. So, also, of the employés connected with the post-office and the transportation of mails; and all the patronage of the general government, and of the states which have sympathized with President Pierce's administration, the greatest crime has been faithfulness to the principles and policy of the government your fathers left you. They disclaimed all foreign interference in American affairs; they declared the Union must be preserved; that none but Americans should rule your country; that national treaties were inviolate;

that no union should exist between church and state; that personal morality was indispensable for office; and that we must have open Bibles in all our public schools.

In the legislature of Lower Canada, Normal schools have been abolished by Romanists, and none but those under the eye of the priests exist; so that mass, confession, the sacraments and dogmas of the Romish church, employ the whole time of the pupils. So will they have it in all the states of our Union, as soon as a sufficient number of Jesuits can be had to coöperate with corrupt politicians in our legislatures. Our public schools will be converted into *jails* for American women, and our Normal schools into Romish theological seminaries. Are we a people, Americans? Have we a country and government of our own? If so, can we, as Anglo-Saxon Protestants, sanction or endure to have mass said over our national soul by these meddling Jesuits, who thus insult our great nation with such worn-out foolery? Intelligence of the people is the foundation on which our institutions are based; and a practical Protestant education, therefore, is the essential element of our democratic freedom; hence, as a system of instruction, our Protestant free schools are inseparable from our liberties. This right to educate the people is the right of self-government, and our common schools are, in this sense, the means of self-preservation. No man is fit to be considered an intelligent voter, unless he is able to read the vote and the constitution from whence he derives the right of suffrage.

Americans boast of their free press; but how can that save their liberties, unless they have a free and enlightened people to read its products? What kind of an idea can we expect the masses to have of freedom, when, without an education of the mind, it implies in their judgment to do as they please? What kind of freedom is it which excludes the Bible from the people, and therefore forces the desecration of the Sabbath on the nation? In no country upon earth has liberty ever existed, where the Bible is hid from the education of the people. This has always kept republicanism out of France; the people cannot be fit for it without an open Bible in their schools and families. Sixteen years ago, the assault upon the American system of education openly commenced in the State of New York. At that time the Bible was found in all the public schools, and some portion of God's holy word was reverently read at the opening exercises every day. The Romish hierarchy became alarmed, and Bishop Hughes determined to prevent any Roman Catholic from entering these free schools. He went before the Common Council, and demanded a portion of the school fund to establish separate Roman Catholic schools, where no Bible could be read, and no God served but the Pope and his priests. The Council of New York city of course refused the application. He then had a petition numerously signed by his subjects, and sent it to the Legislature, asking that the power be taken away from the corporation of that city. The report and bill found the warmest coöperation in the executive of the state, and had it been sanctioned by the Legislature, more than one half of the Jesuit priesthood in New York would have been paid out of the school fund of that city! The rejection of this iniquity, by the people's representatives, exasperated the foreign hierarchy; and Bishop Hughes, as their leader, called a public meeting at Carroll Hall, to nominate a ticket to the next Assembly of the state. His political speech was vociferously cheered, and, as Americans caught the sound, it revived the spirit of the heroes of our liberties, and the American party, from that hour, was born to give salvation and deliverance to this people.

Our countrymen, give us your attention while we consider this solemn subject, in which, more than any other, you are deeply interested, and we will embrace in the next chapter *the Dangers of Education in Roman Catholic Seminaries.*

CHAPTER II.

THERE are now hundreds of Roman Catholic seminaries and colleges in full operation, and multiplying rapidly over our country. To monopolize instruction wherever they can, and to get the control of schools, that the whole may be reduced to the pliant domination of the Pope, — to this end the order of Jesuits was established. That they will involve this land in troubles and conflicts, is just as certain as that they are swarming over our country. Where is the American parent, let alone the Christian under vows, who, knowing the aim of the Jesuits, will turn over his child to be trained up by men who will use that child afterwards as their tool to ruin the liberty, civil and religious, which our fathers transmitted, a priceless boon, to us?

Will you lend me, therefore, Americans, your candid attention, while I present the *dangers* of intrusting your sons and daughters to be educated in Roman Catholic seminaries?

1st. Education in Roman Catholic seminaries is dangerous, because the method of instruction is superficial and anti-republican.

The character of the instruction imparted in these priestly schools is most superficial, and its whole tendency is anti-republican, and only calculated to weave around the mind the narrow and jesuitical prejudices inimical to freedom of thought and expanded intellect. Their method can never make good scholars, independent of the papal influence so sedulously thrown over them. They omit the modern improvements in some branches, and abridge to a narrow compass, to suit their purposes, some of the most important works. They emasculate every sentiment favorable to liberty, or our free Protestant institutions, — everything relating to the reformation by Luther, and to those heroic and noble founders of liberty who reared this beautiful and Protestant republic, or who have appeared at any time in the world; or, if their deeds or names are mentioned, they are depreciated and misrepresented. Books have been brought out from the schools, and publicly exposed, in the city of New York, some pages of which had been blackened over, or defaced and stricken out, by the priests and their teachers. Their system of elementary and scientific instruction is narrowed to conform to their ecclesiastical expurgation and repression of the youthful faculties. History is to them a dangerous subject, especially when the sons of Protestants are the pupils, and is, therefore, skimmed in a compend prepared by means well adapted to the end. Philosophy, natural, moral, and mental, is studied very superficially. So are the mathematics. The whole system of education is adapted to make only counterfeit republicans. With a very plausible appearance, they advertise "fashionable schools," where the "manners of the young ladies will be polished after the most approved patterns," and where the young gentlemen will be "educated in all manly arts and scientific attainments." With such professions and advertisements, they impose upon Protestants. It is the syren song of the sorceress, to charm the ear with seductive music, and beguile the unsuspecting listeners into their treacherous bosom. It is the white signal of a foe, — a trumpet blown from the Vatican across the Atlantic, to summon Americans to adorn their banner with the papal cross, and to bayonet their own bodies.

Unhappily, too many Protestants have contributed already to build up these seminaries of deadly mischief, and dangerous weapons of destruction. Have not the Protestants, in their liberality, been totally blind to the artful designs of the Romish priests and "Sisters of Charity," who have taken all pains to wave before their eyes these false colors, and to spread out, in flaming capitals, these flattering and gilded cards of a "solid and fashionable" education? In this mistaken liberality of Protestants, they have only been made unwitting tools to advance the grand policy of Rome to gain a controlling influence in the states, and to add subjects, power, and wealth, to their hierarchy.

2d. THESE SEMINARIES ARE DANGEROUS, BECAUSE THOSE WHO PRESIDE OVER THEM, AND ARE TEACHERS, ARE JESUITS AND JESUITESSES.

Since the order of the Jesuits was established by Pope Paul III., in 1540, they have usurped and controlled education in all the domains of the Papacy. But who are the Jesuits? They are the *body-guard* of the Pope. They poison the fountains of literature, and are everywhere the destroyers of youth. Pretending to favor intelligence, they are the agents of darkness, the corrupters of female virtue in the confessional, the libertines of monasteries, having the nuns for their concubines; the bane of families, society, governments, and the scourge of the world.

The Jesuitesses are the tools of the priests or Jesuits. They always follow them, and are placed over the nunnery schools. An able and reliable writer says:

"All who have acquired any knowledge of the interior working of the papal system are well aware how much use that system has already made of the agency of woman. This has been the case very specially where it could not put forth any very large measure of direct power; and to this the Jesuits have always devoted their utmost skill and treacherous craft. Their great aim is to gain the confidence of females in every rank of life, and of every shade of character, and to employ them all as agents. They may be ladies of rank, wealth, and beauty; and may use their personal influence in the very highest circles, around the throne, and behind the throne. They may be in the middle classes, and may manage to become acquainted with all the affairs of the busy and engrossing events of political and commercial life. They may be governesses and nursery-maids, and may insinuate their plausible wiles into the unsuspicious minds of even young children. They may be the seeming benefactresses of poverty and wretchedness, and may thus gain ascendency over the compassionate and the sentimental; or they may even haunt the scenes of deepest infamy, and ensnare youth into passion and crime. What they have to do, and are trained to do, is to acquire either an influence over men in all stations, so as to induce them to give countenance and support to Popery, or such a knowledge of all men's designs as to be able to betray them to their priestly and jesuitical advisers. This is done throughout all Europe, to an extent that scarcely any person can even imagine. By this secret, universal, and almost invisible agency, Rome contrives to know everything that is done, or said, or almost thought, by every man, in every circle; and can counterplot and overreach every attempt that can be made or framed against her wide enterprise of establishing universal dominion on the ruins of all true liberty, civil and sacred."

These agents are far more powerful when they are employed in education. Here they act, as in every other department, with the most crafty design, to captivate the young mind, and to attract young ladies into their seminaries, which are always an appendage to a convent or a nunnery. They are the spies of the priests. They are bound to carry out the designs of Romanism. With a bland and winning exterior, they conceal from the view of Protestants their real intentions. But behind this exterior, when Protestants and all outward responsibilities are withdrawn, they show their real traits to be the most imperious, cruel, and tyrannical.

The following testimony is from a competent witness, who has had good opportunities of watching them in France :

"A great number of Protestants speak of these Jesuit 'Sisters' as 'walking angels,' or representatives of the Virgin Mary. But I am convinced that, if many of the Protestant pastors of France were to contribute only a small part of the annoyances they have endured from those 'walking angels,' a huge volume of facts might be published, which would prove that the words *Protestant* and *demon* are synonymous in the opinion of a vast majority of these 'Sisters.' My dear departed friend, the Rev. A. Le Fourdrey, pastor at Brest, who visited the hospitals in that important seaport for twenty-two years, often told me that he never met with such an intolerant set of human beings as these 'Sisters.' Many of them, he has said, attend their patient till they find out that he is a Protestant; and then, unless they have some secret hope of converting him, very often their charity degenerates into brutality. It would, doubtless, open the eyes of Protestants, as to these 'Sisters,' were they only to become a little better acquainted with them. Could they only, for a moment, look upon their wrathful countenance when they see a person with a Bible in his hand, they would then, perhaps, understand the danger of these Jesuitesses;" and, we add, of sending the daughters of Protestant parents to their schools in the United States.

The daughters of Protestants who, unhappily,

enter these nunnery seminaries, see nothing but what is agreeable, polite, and perhaps delightful, until they are finally persuaded — for this is a constant end the Jesuitesses have in view — to take the white and black veil; and then, when shut out and imprisoned, under bars, and lock and key, they find, when too late, their sad mistake, and the awful deception which has been practised upon them. They find that these Jesuitesses, who appeared as angels of goodness, full of heavenly smiles, are but demure, unsocial, treacherous tyrants.

CHAPTER III.

3d. THESE SEMINARIES ARE DANGEROUS, BECAUSE THE BIBLE AND ALL CHRISTIAN INFLUENCES ARE REMOVED, AND THE IDOLATROUS RITES AND PAPAL MUMMERIES OF THE ROMISH CHURCH ARE SUBSTITUTED IN THEIR PLACE.

One of the first evidences that the pupil has passed from a Christian society and Protestant associations, after entering a Roman Catholic seminary, is the taking away of the Bible. This is invariably done to every pupil. Why is the Bible taken away? Does it deserve this treatment? Is it not the revelation from heaven to man, in which mercy, peace, and salvation, are made known to our world; the treasure of wisdom and truth; the only safeguard of man's rights, and of social, mental, moral, political, and religious liberty? Is not that mode of instruction to be suspected which leaves out its pure morality, its salutary motives, its sublime influence and precepts? Can that system

Engraved by J. C. Buttre

Millard Fillmore

PUBLISHED BY J.C.BUTTRE 48 FRANKLIN ST. N.Y.

be right which takes from the trunk of the pupil this blessed Book, and robs the owner, not only of property, but of the only guide of youth to hap piness and heaven? Is Rome afraid of the Bible? Yes, we have come to the difficulty. Rome is afraid of the Bible! Rome is from beneath,—the Bible is from above. The light of truth shines too clearly for its toleration. The worship of the Virgin Mary, the Pope, and his infallibility, his cardinals, and his supremacy, celibacy of the priests, purgatory, images, beads, relics, the mass, transub stantiation of a wafer, penances, and all the pomp ous ceremonies and pagan puerilities, have no place in this book of heaven. Popery is not found in the Bible; but the Bible opposes Popery, and all its works of darkness. It must not be in the possession of the pupil, for then the human impos-tures and lucrative incomes of the priests and Jesuitesses would be exposed. Having removed this grand obstacle to their success, the new pupils are directed to those popish observances to which they have been heretofore strangers. There is no consulting their inclinations, nor the inclinations of their parents. Unquestioned and absolute submission is required. They are compelled to conform to these religious and pagan ceremonies.

In the mean time, the pupil is totally unsuspecting of any design to alienate attachment to previous ideas and parental modes of thinking and worship, or to eradicate the lessons imbibed from Protestant education. Knowing nothing of Jesuitism, — its consummate art, its practised deceptions, its insidious approaches, and bland addresses, — the new pupil is easily deceived, and, by a gradual, continued process, becomes habituated to the impressions and instructions of the teachers, until, like a bird in the snare of the fowler, the web is woven and the innocent son, or daughter, becomes a Papist. The effect is, to bring the pupils to the feet of the monks and Jesuitesses, to reduce them under a yoke of superstitious dread and fear, to deprive the mind of all elastic energy, and to effeminate and dwarf the intellect and soul. Another effect is to alienate the affections from the parents, whom the daughter or son is taught to believe are heretics, and, therefore, unworthy of their confidence as guides in this world, much less as guides to the next. Have you ever reflected, parents, upon the effect of these papal delusions?

—the poison which is inhaled? The danger to which your children are exposed, in this respect, in these seminaries, is confirmed by numerous and incontro vertible testimonies; and, could the examples and the statements be set before you in all the truth and vividness of the reality, you would shrink from these institutions with horror.

"Experience," says a writer, "furnishes many signal and mournful examples of the perversion of the minds of ingenuous youth, when committed to the instruction of Romanists. Never shall I forget one remarkable instance, which occurred many years ago, not only within the bounds of my own knowledge, but in one of the families of my own pastoral charge. An amiable, elegant, and highly-promising youth was sent to a Roman Catholic seminary, for the single object of learning, to rather more advantage than was otherwise practicable, a polite living language. He attained his purpose, but at a dreadful expense. He very speedily became a zealous Papist; began in a few weeks to address and reproach his parents, by letter, as blinded heretics, out of the way of salvation; was deaf to every remonstrance, both from them and their pastor, and remains to the present day a devoted, incorrigible Romanist. And similar to this is the mournful story of hundreds of the sons and daughters of Protestant parents in our land, who have inconsiderately and cruelly committed their children to papal training, and found, when too late, that they had contracted a moral contagion never to be eradicated."

"I am well acquainted," says Dr. Sandwith, "with a gentleman of great influence, and great ability, who has seen much of the world, and in the course of his travels on the Continent was so impressed with the importance of a knowledge of the continental languages, that, in an evil hour, he brought home a Roman Catholic governess to instruct his children in that accomplishment. Now, the effect of that did not appear at first. His children had been generally taught the principles of Protestantism, and for a while all went on smoothly. But, so insidious is the progress of Popery, the foundations of Protestantism in that family were being sapped while no external effect appeared; but, after a while, his wife went over to the Roman Catholic church, and then I need not say in what danger the whole family were placed. Thus is Roman Catholicism ever seeking to undermine and overthrow Protestantism; by industriously introducing Roman Catholic governesses and Roman Catholic servants into Protestant families, the mischief is accomplished ere we are aware. It is well for us to be on our guard."

The opposition of Popery to Protestantism is well known. Every Papist, as well as the priests, is bound by the decrees of the Council of Trent to oppose, to the utmost of his power, "heretics," that is, Protestants. Hence Papists, in the United States, are laid under a solemn obligation, at the peril of excommunication, never to enter a Protestant church. The system of education, infusing into the minds of pupils this bitter hostility to Protestants, is, in the most dangerous sense, anti-republican. "Spreading over our cities, towns, and rural districts, enjoying all the advantages of native citizens, *they are not with us, but against us.* While our Protestant people had charitably supposed that Romanism had undergone some modification for the better, yet *it is unchanged in all its essential points. It has lost none of its virulence and enmity to Protestants.*" Hence, on "Maunday Thursday," once every year, in Rome, and in all Catholic churches of the United States, Protestants, here and all over the world, are solemnly, with "bell and candle," *cursed and damned.* Archbishop Hughes, in his organ, the *Freeman's Journal*, tells us, "*Protestantism is dangerous to the country. All who love truth and sustain right must seek the counterbalancing power to disunion in the Catholic population of the country.*" The dogmas enjoining this unchristian hatred and unmitigated bigotry to Protestants, and to all who entertain different sentiments, are spread all over the canons of the Romish church, and have been acted out in every period of its history. A gentleman writing from Italy states the following fact :

"An English lady lost a daughter at Rome, and on the tomb, which was in the English Protestant cemetery, she wished to have the verse from St. Matthew, 'Blessed are the pure in heart, for they shall see God,' inscribed; but an officer of the Pope, connected with the censorship, entered the workshop of the statuary who was working at the tomb, and forbade him inscribing more than the first half of the verse, as he said it was neither right nor just that heretics should see the Lord."

Thousands of Protestants in the United States are ignorant of the workings of this system; that it is a system chiefly of proselytism to gain their sons and daughters over to Rome, to secure, as far as possible, the control of their faculties, and, as a consequence, to ruin their moral and mental qualities, and all their dearest hopes of heaven.

4th. THEY ARE DANGEROUS, BECAUSE ROMANISM IN ITS INSTRUCTIONS AND FRUITS IS IMMORAL.

The moral profligacy of the Romish priests and nuns has for ages characterized the histories of that church, and filled with "astonishment, loathing, and horror, the Christian world." The evidence on this subject is clear and overwhelming. The Popes of Rome, from Gregory VIII., through all the succeeding centuries, with scarcely an exception, were notorious for peculation, extortion, gluttony, concubinage, murder, perjury, theft, lying, forgery, and other crimes, which served to show more than anything else to what shameless degradation these lordly pontiffs could descend, and how much they have deserved the universal execration of mankind. Parallel with these, and in natural consistency with their immoral tenets and instructions, have been the vices and awful corruptions of monasteries and nunneries.

Unless we are prepared to discard the accumulating testimony of a thousand years; unless we are willing to set at naught the suffrages of the greatest and best men that ever adorned the church of God; nay, unless we are prepared to reject the confessions of some of the most respectable Romanists themselves, — we cannot evade the evidence that many, very many, of those boasted seats of celibacy and peculiar devotedness, have been, in reality, sinks of deep and awful licentiousness. Indeed, if it were not so, considering what human nature is, and considering the nature and management of those institutions, it would encroach on the province of miracle.

CHAPTER IV.

The tree is known by its fruits; the fruits are known by the tree. The fruits of priestly education are strikingly seen in all Roman Catholic countries. What a picture do Austria, Rome, Spain, Portugal, Belgium, Roman Catholic Ireland, Mexico, Cuba, Central America, and the South American states, present! The annals of the world, in no countries, can present such an amount of pauperism, ignorance, crimes, and licentiousness. By official documents, submitted to the House of Commons, in 1854, there were, in Catholic Ireland, 700 cases of murders in three years, or 54 to every million of inhabitants, besides filth, ignorance, vices, and other crimes of every phase and degree. In papal France, the existence and fruits of the Romish religion, with priestly instruction, have produced a nation of infidels; while, in the city of Paris alone, according to the census in 1854, there were 29,066 legitimate, and 19,000 illegitimate children. In the city of Vienna, regarded as the model city of the Papacy, there were 8,081 legitimate, and 10,000 illegitimate ; — more than half. But priestly education in Rome itself, the very fountain of the Papacy, shows its striking effects. On the authority of Metamier, out of 4,543 births, 3,160 were foundlings, three fourths of whom die in the Romish asylums, while misery, rags, beggary, indolence, and every species of vice and immorality, abound. And this in the consecrated city of the Pope, with its 10,000 papal priests, monks, nuns, and in a population of only 130,000! Mirabeau says :

"A peasant who knows how to read, in papal countries, is a rare being. There is often only one school for a whole bailiwick ; and, moreover, the schoolmasters are ignorant and ill-paid. The priests govern the whole nation ; and they wish this state of things to last, as it is advantageous to them. They increase superstition all they can, and this superstition is destructive of every kind of industry. The infinite numbers of fêtes, pilgrimages, and processions, keep up idleness and misery. In the island of Sicily alone, there are 28,000 monks and 18,000 nuns—in all, 46,000 useless individuals out of a population of 1,650,000 souls ; that is to say, one idle monk amongst every 35 inhabitants. It is a phenomenon to find a person among the lower classes who can either read or write, throughout the insular and continental part of the kingdom of Naples. This is, I say, from personal cognizance. As a necessary consequence, the people are a prey to the most absurd superstitions; credulous believers in the sacrilegious farces called miracles, such as the liquefaction of the blood of St. Januarius, and other similar tricks of priestly legerdemain, and the blind instruments of scheming priests."

Dr. Giustiniani, in a late work, described the immoral lives of the priests in Rome as a thing so common that it excites little surprise, except with strangers. He speaks of the moral corruptions of auricular confession, the depth of pollutions which characterize this feature of priestly power. "But why," says he, "should I speak of this moral depravity of Popery in Rome? It is everywhere the same. It appears differently, but never changes its character. In America, where female virtue is the characteristic of the nation, it is under the control of the priest. If a Roman Catholic lady, the wife of a free American, should choose to have the priest in her bedroom, she has only to pretend to be indisposed, and, asking for the spiritual father, the confessor, no other person, not even the husband, dare enter. In Rome, it would be at the risk of his life; in America, at the risk of being excommunicated, and deprived of all spiritual privileges of the church, and even excluded from heaven." Such, parents, all over the papal world, are the baneful and dangerous effects of coming in contact with priests and Popery. Can you consent to place your children under their influence and power? Are you willing to hazard their mental and moral training to such hands?—to hazard all that is dear in life?

5th. ROMAN CATHOLIC SEMINARIES ARE DANGEROUS, BECAUSE THEY DENY LIBERTY OF OPINION, AND SUBJUGATE THE CONSCIENCE.

The conscience belongs to the individual, and is responsible to no human being, but to God alone. In the Declaration of Independence and the federal constitution, no more sacred principle was enunciated than the *liberty of private judgment, or opinion, and freedom of conscience.* This right is inherited by creation; no human or ecclesiastical governments can confer it or take it away. It is the birthright of the individual, and inalienable. But the hierarchy of Rome, in its insatiable thirst for power and blasphemous presumption, claims the *conscience* of every human being. We need not ask where it derived this claim; for the demand is so absurd that nature, reason, and heaven, at once belie it, and declare its foul usurpation. It, of course, like every other tyrannical usurpation of that corrupt church, only proves its astonishing impudence in making the demand. But, nevertheless, it issues its dogmas and decrees to this effect, and from the eleventh century to this hour has subjugated the *conscience* of its votaries. They must think as the church—that is, the priests—think. They must not dare to assume the exercise of reason and freedom of conscience in any matters of faith, or in what concerns the priesthood ; for the priests alone, not the Bible, nor heaven, enact their rules and publish their dogmas by which they claim the conscience. Pope Pius IX., only a few years ago, denounced the liberty of the press, and all Bible societies ; and Archbishop Hughes confines the same liberty of conscience to the interior of the soul. "There is not," says he, "a single religious book, of common reputation, in the Roman Catholic church, which does not make unlimited obedience to a priestly confessor the safest and most perfect way to salvation."

Are you ready, parents, to commit your daughters to the guidance and care of Jesuits and Jesuitesses, whose one great aim is to teach them to renounce the native sentiment of liberty, to proselyte them to their faith, and to get hold of the conscience? Do you consent that they should surrender this right, this American principle, the grand principle of their indefeasible inheritance? But, by placing them in Romish seminaries, you place them in a situation where, from all past experience, not one in twenty, if one at all, ever escapes the snare. The conductors of these establishments make to you very fair promises, and will deny any attempt at creating a sectarian feeling, with a view to detach their affections from the ties of family or home, or to alienate their free Protestant preferences; but it is the art of their profession to deceive, and their very oath and their invariable practice contradict these statements. One of the maxims of Jesuits is, to prevaricate, to affirm, or deny, as the case requires. Another maxim is, "the end justifies the means;" and as any means for their interest are justified, so truth or lying is equally ready at their command. And so common is this vice of lying, not only among the Jesuits, but among the more ignorant Papists, that the remark of the fact is proverbial among Protestants. And the wonder ceases when it is known that the maxims of the Jesuits inculcate duplicity and deceit in all their phases. For the proof of this, we need only refer to their rules and instructions contained in their published books, and in the "Moral Theologies" of Ligori, Escobar, Bellarmine, and Dens, which are the text-books for candidates preparing for the priesthood in the Roman Catholic college at Maynooth, Ireland, and in all similar institutions in Europe and America.

6th. THESE SEMINARIES ARE DANGEROUS, BECAUSE, UNDER THEIR PLAUSIBLE DISGUISE, ROME HOPES TO REPEL THE CHARGE THAT SHE IS HOSTILE TO KNOWLEDGE, AND THUS ENTICE PROTESTANT SONS AND DAUGHTERS TO BECOME THE VICTIMS OF THEIR TREACHEROUS PURPOSES.

This proposition, that Rome is hostile to knowledge, would seem paradoxical, since the Romish church boasts of being the channel of the transmission of learning for six hundred years before the invention of printing in the fifteenth century, and exhibits such zealous endeavors to set up schools and colleges in the United States. But we shall show that these pretensions of Rome are but deception; that they are intended to create a false impression over the minds both of Papists and Protestants in the United States. That *Rome is the enemy of knowledge*, that is, opposed to the general diffusion of it among the body of the people, is a truth conclusively established by such facts and considerations as the following, namely: There have been other channels beside Rome to transmit the learning of previous centuries, namely, the Greek church, whose patriarchs, through the whole existence of the Romish church, have been cotemporary and in regular parallel succession with the Popes, down to the present day. The Greek church is as old as the Roman; and so is the Waldensian church, which, through all the persecuting wars which Rome waged against her during the dark ages, still preserved her separate identity. The Popes, certainly, have carefully preserved whatever works of great writers she possessed, for the simple reason that they very rigorously locked their books up in the libraries, not allowing any one to open a single volume,— they were forbidden books. It was no difficulty, it can easily be imagined, for the Popes to preserve their books for centuries, as we shall show in the next chapter.

CHAPTER V.

Cardinal Wiseman, in his lecture, delivered in Leeds, said that science, literature, and the arts, never flourished more luxuriantly than under the papal system, and that the Romish church is the mother of all wisdom. In proof of this proposition, he refers to Italy. He said, in substance, Italy is the first country in Europe in point of talent and genius, and it is also the foremost country of the papal dominion; therefore, the papal domination is the immediate creator and patron of lofty genius in science, literature, and art. That is evidently false; for Ireland is the greatest country in the United Kingdom for talent, producing the best order of poets, orators, and scientific and literary men. But Ribbon Societies are an exclusively Irish institution; therefore Ribbon Societies produce the best orators, poets, statesmen, and literary people, of all the United Kingdom. Is not that as good an argument as Cardinal Wiseman's? If in Italy there is still great genius, it is not because

Italy is under papal dominion, but it is because Italy is Italy, and she produces great genius not by the ruling of the Pope, but because it is, as it were, the natural product of her sun and soil. It was not a Pope that called forth the genius of a Cicero, a Virgil, a Livy, and a Horace, and all the ancient poets and orators. Her genius is not from the Pope, but it is in spite of the Pope and Popery. Therefore, the great men of that country appertain to Italy, and not to the Vatican. In Rome itself, the Popes, in many instances, have been destroyers instead of conservators of the glorious works of antiquity. Pope Barberini destroyed the Coliseum, in order to build palaces for his bastard children with the venerable marbles of that once splendid edifice; whilst Urban robbed the Pantheon of many of its glories. What has the Roman Catholic church done to compare with the memorials of the ancient Roman civilization? The dome — the great beauty of the Basilica of St. Peter — is the dome of the ancient Pantheon; that is, the idea was taken by Michael Angelo from that building. Certainly, the Popes, not for the sake of the people, but for their own advantage, built many very fine churches, and they employed able artists to beautify them. Wiseman spoke of Dante, Petrarch, Boccacio, and Galileo, in support of his proposition. But Dante was persecuted by the Popes, and his works were forbidden to be read until two centuries ago; the Jesuits even now exclude his writings from their schools. Petrarch was forbidden to be read, too, because he wrote two sonnets satirizing a Pope. Boccacio is also denounced; in fact, all the great writers of Italy have been placed in the Inquisitorial *Index Expurgatorius.* That is the patronage of the Roman church for men of letters.

The figure of St. Peter, which Rome boasts of being such a noble specimen of art, and which is placed for admiring reverence in her temple, is an ancient bronze Jupiter. The splendid ruins of art left by pagan Rome to papal Rome only served to the latter as quarries. By accident of position, papal Rome became trustee; but a more reckless and scandalous trustee there never was than the Vatican proved for ages. The fairest columns of the Ionic and Corinthian orders were torn down from their porticos, and broken up for building material. The marbles of Paros and Numidia were burned for lime. Ever since the admiration of strangers for what remained, after ages of such waste, awoke Rome to the value of her treasures, she has been their careful custodian. But, without doubt, all the destruction wrought upon the monuments of antiquity by all the Goths and Vandals that ever set foot in Rome was a bagatelle to the dilapidation carried on by the Popes. Let this boast, therefore, of Cardinal Wiseman, and the priestly and lay lecturers in the United States, of Rome's being the warm and liberal patron of expansive genius and learning, no longer impose upon superficial minds and credulous Protestants. Rome has always shackled the human faculties; always cramped human genius; always kept the Scriptures shut up from the people; always performed much of her service in an unknown tongue; always opposed liberal investigations of either morals, philosophy, or theology.

Did she not condemn Galileo for asserting a true problem of science? Did not her hostility to the culture of the masses, and closing the fountains of literature, and discouraging light and knowledge, create the "Dark Ages"? *Did she not thunder forth her bull against the inventor of the art of printing, and tremble when the first Bible appeared in type?* Did she not frame the *Index Expurgatorius*, which put an interdict upon many of the most splendid works of learning, and which is still in full force, with many additions of the most valuable and popular books, such a Milton, Macaulay's History, Irving's Life of Washington, and numerous other kindred works, which contain liberal ideas, and advocate the freedom of man? What anathemas and execrations did she pour out upon the illustrious reformer, Luther, for advocating free inquiry, and opening the sources of knowledge! And have not her priests and most prominent writers, participating in this spirit of defamation, assailed that defender, and all the reformers who shone as bright lights amid Rome's moral and intellectual darkness, and emitted their fruitful venom? Have not the priests and Romish presses in our country denounced liberal inquiry and Protestant education, which favors the free and manly improvement of the mind, and the development of all its rational and noble faculties?

Macaulay, in his History, observes that, "The loveliest provinces in Europe have, under the rule of Rome, been sunk in poverty, in political servitude, and in intellectual torpor; while Protestant countries, once proverbial for their sterility and barbarism, have been turned by skill and industry into gardens, and can boast of a long list of heroes, statesmen, philosophers, and poets." Yes, Rome is an enemy to the human race, and seeks to hide the "key of knowledge" from all within her withering influence. We could write not merely a few brief paragraphs, but a volume, to illustrate this truth. The following specimens, among numberless others which are passing in the world, to establish the proof of our proposition, we present to the reader.

"*The Univers*, the most celebrated organ of the Jesuits in France," says the *Congregationalist*, "is speaking openly against the use of the living languages or popular idioms in the sciences, letters, and arts, as well as in theology, and regrets that books are not now written in Latin, as in the middle ages. All knowledge must be confined to a few select minds, in order that the priests may retain an unbroken hold on the multitude; wide and thorough discussions on any subject are dangerous, because they liberalize the mind, and cherish the thirst for intellectual improvement that ill comports with the great aims of Romanism, — to bind the world over to ignorance, for the sake of pecuniary accumulation. The time was, till the seventeenth century, when books on medicine, history, the natural sciences, astronomy, and politics, were written in Latin, and the common people were excluded from all knowledge, except of the catechism, which the curate taught them; the return of such times is equivalent to the return of 'the golden age' in the eyes of the Jesuit fathers, and for it they are laboring, though in their labors at sowing the wind, they are preparing to reap the whirlwind."

Sir Walter Scott, in his "Life of Napoleon," alluding to Spain, says, "The education of the nobility was committed to the priests, who took care to give them no lights beyond Catholic bigotry."

M. Leone, an Italian, settled in England, now engaged on the great work of the codification of the commercial laws of Great Britain, paid a visit to Italy during the Italian republic.

"On the fall of the pontifical government," said he, "the republicans immediately established schools in every town, and village, and rural district. There were day-schools, and night-schools, and Sabbath-schools. I was inexpressibly delighted at the wonderful change. But, ah! back came the Pope; and in a week, in one short week, every one of these schools was closed! Italy is again sunk in its old torpor and stagnation, and one black cloud of barbaric ignorance extends from the Mediterranean to the Adriatic! I sat down," says he, "on the steps of the Temple of Vesta, which, though crumbling with age, is one of the most beautiful of the ruins of Rome. Three boys, the eldest fifteen years of age, came about me, to beg a few baicchi. I took an opportunity of putting a few questions to them, judging them a fair sample of the Roman youth. The following dialogue occurred:

"'Can you tell me,' I asked, 'who made the world?

The question started a subject on which they seemed never to have thought before. They stood in a muse for some seconds; and then all three looked around them, as if they expected to see the world's Maker, or to read his name somewhere. At last the youngest and smartest of the three spoke briskly up, 'The masons, Signore.' It was now my turn to feel the excitement of a new idea. Yet I thought I could see the train of thought that led to the answer. The masons had made the baths of Caracalla; the masons had made the Coliseum, and those other stupendous structures which in bulk rival the hills, and seem as eternal as the earth on which they rest; and why might not the masons have made the whole affair? I might have puzzled the boy by asking, 'But who made the masons?' My object, however, was simply to ascertain the amount of his knowledge. I demurred to the proposition that the masons had made the world, and desired them to try again. They did try again; and at last the eldest of the three found his way to the right answer, — 'God.' 'Have you ever heard of Christ?' I asked. 'Yes.' 'Who is he? Can you tell me anything about him?' I could elicit nothing under these heads. 'Whose Son is he?' I then asked. 'He is Mary's Son,' was the reply. 'Where is Christ?' I inquired. 'He is on the Cross,' replied the boy, folding his arms, and making the representation of a crucifix. 'Was Christ ever on earth?' I asked. He did not know. 'Are you aware of anything he ever did?' He had never heard of anything that Christ had done. I saw that he was thinking of those hideous representations which are to be seen in all the churches of Rome, of a man hanging on a cross. That was the Christ of the boys. Of Christ the Son of the living God, — of Christ the Saviour of sinners, and of his death as an atonement for human guilt, — they had never heard. In a city swarming with professed ministers of the Gospel, these boys knew no more of Christianity than if they had been Hottentots."

And now, in the view of all these clear and positive evidences, from her history and uniform practice, that Rome is hostile to knowledge, we ask, how is it that Rome is so zealously engaged in setting up schools and seminaries in the United States? The answer is ready at hand: It is to create an impression on the minds of our Protestant people that she is a warm friend to education. In this land of light and intelligence, she is necessarily forced to put on an *appearance* of being that patron, to avoid the imputation of the opposite charge, which she, with adroit Jesuitism, knows would be injurious to her interests, and might entirely frustrate all her plans of papal aggrandizement and influence. She must, therefore, assume this pretension, and *appear* to be the friend of education. But, in the midst of all these attempts to delude superficial Protestants, the "cloven foot" protrudes, the symbolic type of its owner. She arrogantly approaches the state superintendent and committees of schools, and demands the *exclusion of the Bible* from Protestant schools. These Protestant officers, not being adepts in the crafty schemes of this enemy of our noble system of education, thoughtlessly complied, in some instances, with the demand, and thus betrayed the high trust reposed in them. The next subtle design was, to demand of the Legislature to divide the school funds of the state, to favor her Jesuit sectarian plan of separate schools for her sectarian ends. In this she has not yet succeeded. Other demands she has made, all going to establish the fact that Rome is hostile to knowledge, and, with a seeming zeal, establishes schools and seminaries, to entice Protestant parents to send their daughters and sons into them, more effectually to accomplish her objects.

In conclusion, let me appeal to all classes of our people. Patriots, do you love your country? Do you value the priceless legacy transmitted by the fathers of the Revolution? Do you appreciate and rejoice in its Protestant laws, institutions, and government; in its charter of independence; in the value of its American system of education, and in its model schools, which approach nearer to perfection than any yet devised by the skill, wisdom, experience, and genius, of man? Are you awake to guard inviolate these inestimable privileges and sentinels of liberty from the touch of ruthless hands, and from the spoliation and corruptions of the invader? Then never let the public funds be used for sectarian, foreign purposes; and give no countenance to papal approaches, whose hierarchy is the bane of knowledge, and in deadly hostility to this free republic. The following document, from the Roman Catholic journal at Buffalo, will show the confidence with which that hierarchy is at work in the United States:

"Whoever undervalues the spiritual power of the church in the United States wanders in a fearful labyrinth. We have not only seven archbishops, thirty-three bishops, and seventeen hundred and four priests, all in the service of the Pope and the church, but we have also thirty-one colleges, thirty-seven seminaries, and a hundred and seventeen female academies, all founded by the Jesuits, bringing danger and death to unbelief and mischief, to American Know-nothing-ism, and un-American radicalism. And the hierarchal band which, like a golden thread, surrounds forty-one dioceses and two apostolic vicarites, and stretches from the Atlantic Ocean to the still waters of the Pacific, and maintains an invisible secret magnetic connection with Rome, — this hierarchy is to us a sure guarantee that the church, perhaps after severe struggles and sufferings, will one day come off victorious over all the sects of America. It is computed that there are, at present, more than two millions of Catholic inhabitants in the United States who are baptized and confirmed Catholic soldiers of the Lord, and who, at the first summons, will assemble in rank and file; then will men not undervalue the power of the Catholic church in the United States. I will scatter sand in no one's eyes, and therefore I stand forth openly, and directly declare that the power and the influence of the Catholic church are stronger than many believe. Whoever doubts this must be either a fool, or blind."

In this document, my countrymen, weigh the expressions, "the secret magnetic connection with Rome," and that these papal seminaries and colleges are "*all founded by the Jesuits;*" and then consider the dangers which hover over our land.

Fathers, mothers, do you love your children? Can you intrust the dearest objects upon which your parental hopes, and the joys of the family roof, centre, to the supervision and charge of Jesuits and Jesuitesses? Why do the conductors of these papal seminaries manifest such a remarkable zeal in pursuit of females, and especially the daughters of Protestant parents? They know that, in gaining them, they can secure the most powerful influence, and often gratify their avaricious desires in greater profits; but the one great end they have in view is, to proselyte them to their faith. Remember, they give a special preference to Protestants. They select the most wealthy and beautiful, and persuade them to the confessional and into the convent; and, when once secured there, they become the slaves of a tyrannic priesthood. O, could you comprehend their designs, — could you penetrate into one tithe of their art, and ruinous plots against the life, honor, and liberty, of your daughters, — you would start back aghast at the insidious and fatal sacrifice of the objects and images of your affection. Could the secrets of the confessionals be uncovered, there is not a priest that could stay in the city of New York, or Baltimore, or Philadelphia, one week. Pause, then, parents, I beg of you, while your daughters are safe on this side of an admission into these pestiferous and ruinous establishments!

Edwin O. Perrin

OF TENNESSEE

HON. EDWIN O. PERRIN.

The father of this American, the late Judge Perrin, of Maryland, became one of the earliest settlers of Ohio, and at Springfield, in that state, the subject of this sketch was born. The death of his father, and the consequent deprivation of young Perrin's patrimony by the injudicious management of his estate, obliged him, like most of the public men of our country, to become the architect of his own fortune. After acquiring a suitable education by his industry and energy, he adopted the law as his profession, and studied with Judge Mason, of Ohio. Mr. Perrin subsequently removed to Memphis, Tennessee, where he married Miss Stanton, sister of the Hons. Richard and Frederick P. Stanton, late Representatives in Congress from Kentucky and Tennessee and who, estimable for every excellence and virtue, is also admired for her intelligence, beauty, and accomplishments.

Under the administration of Gen. Taylor, Mr. Perrin was appointed navy agent of Memphis, and discharged the duties of that office with fidelity and faithfulness, until the accession of Franklin Pierce, who found Mr. Perrin's political principles good cause for removal. He then removed to the city of New York to pursue his profession, and united with the great American party in the attempt to restore the country to its pristine integrity and purity. In the elections of 1855 he became the eloquent defender of American principles upon the hustings, and the people greeted him with enthusiasm wherever he was heard in that cause. A company of volunteers, soon after the success of the American ticket in New York, was organized as the "Perrin Guard," in that city; and in contending for the prize of a magnificent silver basket, presented by Mr. Perrin, the captain of that company said: "Our distinguished guest, Edwin O. Perrin: One of Tennessee's ablest orators. We extend to him a cordial welcome to the home of his adoption, the Empire City of the Empire State. Long may he live to defend with eloquent tongue our common country and our country's cause! Having adopted his name, let us emulate his devotion!" Mr. Perrin closed his speech with the following:

"The Volunteer Soldiery of New York: A standing army in time of peace, and no running army in time of war. Their discipline and courage at home have only been equalled by their patriotism and bravery abroad. May the junior American corps prove worthy descendants of their gallant seniors; maintaining for the future what *they* have so gallantly achieved in the past."

After the nomination of the American Presidential ticket, Mr. Perrin appeared again in the political field, to press with eloquence and earnestness the election of Millard Fillmore to the chief magistracy of the nation. Like the heroes of our Revolutionary battles, he put aside all other pursuits for the American cause, and is now winning "golden opinions," throughout the State of New York, for the intelligent persuasions and thrilling appeals he is making to the patriotism of the people, and which are the more effectively enforced because of the impregnable defences which surround and elevate his character.

The genius and oratory of Mr. Perrin, are not only eminently original, but the peculiarity of his style gives him great individuality. He is animated and bold, and attracts and captivates his audience by his wit and humor. The extract, from a well-known democratic organ of the State of New York, will show the estimate in which he is held, in this connection, without regard to party consideration :

The Fillmore men had a large meeting at the Court-house in this city last Saturday evening. Every seat and vacant place was filled. Hon. E. O. Perrin was the speaker. Mr. Perrin was formerly from Tennessee, but is now a resident of this State. He is a young man, not far, we should say, from thirty years of age, yet he is one of the most eloquent orators, and captivating speakers we ever heard in our life. We have listened to the graceful oratory of Henry Clay; we have been riveted to our seat by the fascinating voice, pleasing gestures, and sublime eloquence of Wm. C. Preston, of South Carolina; we have heard the gifted Breckinridge, and been carried away captive on the wings of his matchless eloquence; we have been one of a thousand who have been moved first to tears, and then provoked to laughter, by the overwhelming and powerful eloquence of Gough—yet, none of these men, in our judgment, surpasses, in fluency of expression, in the eloquency of words, in beautiful imagery, and, in fact, in all those elements that go to make a popular and eloquent orator, Hon. E. O. Perrin, the eloquent Tennessean. To such of our readers who may think us over-enthusiastic, we can only say, go and hear Mr. Perrin, and judge as to his eloquence for yourselves. He is full of humor as well as pathos; he can, in a moment, change "from grave to gay, from lively to severe." His style and manner more closely resemble Gough than do any other man's we ever heard. We cannot, of course, give a synopsis of Mr. Perrin's speech. In conclusion, he paid a glowing tribute to Clay and Webster, and closed with a grand, beautiful, and eloquent appeal in behalf of the Constitution and the Union of the States.

Mr. Perrin's mother was a daughter of Mr. Maddox Fisher, of Lexington, Kentucky. She was born and reared almost beneath the shades of Ashland, and remained through life the devoted friend of the honored statesman and patriot, of whom every Kentuckian is proud. The press has, within the last year, often styled Mr. Perrin the "young man eloquent!" and a commendable public spirit has not been wanting in attesting their appreciation of the worth and estimate of their distinguished fellow-citizen. We have no specimen of Mr. Perrin's published speeches before us, save a Masonic address, which would be more interesting to the *craft* than to the public generally.

Sidney Kopman

OF NEW YORK

MR. SIDNEY KOPMAN.

The father of Sidney Kopman was the late Louis Kopman, of New York. He was introduced into the United States by Robert Southey, the poet, and William Roscoe, the historian, of Liverpool, and was eminent in his day as one of the largest importers of British goods in New York and Savannah, Georgia. Mr. Kopman was a scholar, an accomplished gentleman, and an unobtrusive Christian, in communion with the Church of England; and after enjoying for more than eighty years the most faultless reputation in every relation in life, he has transmitted these excellences of character to his son, whose portrait appears in these pages.

Mr. Sidney Kopman was born in New York, and was educated to the mercantile profession; and, after a long experience as clerk in his own city, he became a merchant in Memphis, Tennessee. During the period of the Mexican war, he acted as the efficient chief clerk to Capt. Wm. K. Latimer, of the United States Navy, at the Pensacola Navy Yard. He there founded a lodge of the benevolent society of Odd Fellows, and for many years has been an active and prominent member of the Masonic fraternity. He contributed the leading editorials of the *Pensecola Gazette*, when in Florida.

After the Mexican war closed, Mr. Kopman was among the first to make a commercial exploration to California, by the way of Cape Horn. In this perilous voyage of six months, he most miraculously escaped shipwreck at Terra del Fuego, the extreme point of Patagonia. He was at Juan Fernandez, visited the Island of Madeira, was present at the opening of the Chilian congress, and slept two weeks upon the Andes Mountains. He was presented, with several other Americans, to the Emperor of Brazil, at Rio Janeiro, and penetrated the interior of that state to visit the diamond mines; and, finally, after the completion of a most hazardous voyage of twenty-three thousand miles, with the attendant evils, at one time, of a threatened famine, he settled down in San Francisco and Sacramento, California, for some months, to make a survey of the country, and then return to New York, by the way of Mexico.

The Mercantile Library of his native city, New York, was for many years an object of the deepest solicitude to Mr. Kopman, and to whose energy and action, as a member of that association, may be attributed much of the present position and standing of the institution. He has recently been elected an honorary member of the historical society at Madison, Wisconsin.

Mr. Kopman early enlisted in the great national movement to regenerate the country, and has been one of the most earnest and active members of the American party. In the formation of organizations in the country, he has efficiently contributed in the three past years, by inducing prominent men, who have visited New York, to unite with the American order, which prepared the way for their individual coöperation when they returned to their own homes. From four to five hundred members, who are now exerting an extended influence in their respective localities, gave their first adhesion to the cause under the earnest pleadings of this true American; while the author cannot neglect to acknowledge the valuable data furnished by Mr. Kopman in connection with this work.

Few possess more extended literary acquirements, or a better-cultivated taste, than Mr. Kopman; and his remarkable gift of remembering all that he has read would not make it inappropriate to style him a moving *cyclopedia* of useful knowledge. But the crowning virtue of the man is in the beauty of his character, his high moral rectitude, and his pure integrity.

Within a few days of the sailing of the Arctic Expedition, in 1853, under the command of Dr. Elisha K. Kane, it was made known in New York city, by Mr. Kopman, that Doctor Kane was a member of the Masonic fraternity; and the most prompt and efficient efforts were made by him to testify the appreciation of the Order, for the services of this daring and enthusiastic American who had undertaken the perilous search for a long lost brother!

The announcement made by Mr. Kopman, that Doctor Kane was a Free Mason, created extraordinary feeling among the fraternity of New York; and the Arcana Lodge, of which Mr. Kopman was a member, was the first to propose a public demonstration by the craft of that city, in honor of the labors of Dr. Kane in the cause of science and humanity! The estimate placed upon this evidence of interest is best exhibited by Doctor Kane's own letter to Mr. Kopman:

PHILADELPHIA, *May 12th*, 1853.

DEAR SIR AND BROTHER:—I have received your eloquent letter, inclosing the resolutions of the Free and Accepted Masons, of Arcana Lodge. These resolutions, expressive of the sympathy of our brethren with the objects of the Expedition, under my command, are to me especially pleasing. I shall communicate them, formally, to the officers and men, as an indication of valued sympathy at home, and a useful stimulus in the search after our lost brother, Sir John Franklin.

I have the honor to be, faithfully,

Your friend and brother,

E. K. KANE.

SIDNEY KOPMAN, Esq.,
Secretary of Arcana Lodge, New York city.

The Grand Lodge, of New York, was convened, and, on the evening previous to the sailing of the Expedition, Doctor Kane met its officers and members, by invitation, at the Medical College, in Crosby street; and the press, after these interesting ceremonies, announced the fact, that he was an honored member of that "Ancient Order." Next morning the Expedition sailed! The waters around New York, as the "Advance" passed out of the Narrows, were crowded with sailing craft, all bearing the flags and emblems of Masonry, and bidding "God speed" to the honored Commander, and brave and noble crew, who seemed, even then, prepared for that almost superhuman endurance to which danger and privation did actually call them.*

* Subsequently, Mr. Kopman resigned his office in Arcana Lodge, when the most flattering eulogium was passed upon him by his brethren, for "the interest he had manifested, and the energy and zeal he had displayed, in aiding the Lodge to attain its present position and standing."

GENERAL NATHAN RANNEY.

The subject of this sketch was born in Bethlehem, in the State of Connecticut, the 27th of April, 1797. In the war with England, 1812, he entered the army of the United States, though but sixteen years of age; and his determined bravery, and fearlessness in the discharge of his duties, made him prominent in every battle, and exposed him to every danger in the thickest of the fight. But, his only purpose in enlisting in the war being a patriotic one, he was steadfast in his refusal of all promotion tendered him, and adhered to his original intention of remaining in the service during the five years for which he had enlisted. It cannot be doubted that, had his ambition led him to a different decision, he would long since have occupied the highest rank among the gallant men of the army.

In 1819, Gen. Ranney located in St. Louis, Missouri, where, as a prominent member of society and an enterprising merchant, he has eminently assisted in the opening prosperity of St. Louis, and possesses a hold upon the confidence and esteem of the community equal to that enjoyed by any other resident.

In 1827, he became a member of the Presbyterian Church. And so faithful, active, and consistent, has he proved, in the discharge of every Christian duty belonging to his religious profession, that he has held the important and responsible position of elder, almost ever since, in the congregation with which he worships. "All that I am is through the blessing of God," has been the glorious sentiment which has emulated this noble American to action, and given him a name that kings, with their sceptres, might wisely envy.

In 1855, the convention of the soldiers of 1812 met in Philadelphia. Gen. Ranney addressed that assembly in these words:

"FELLOW-CITIZENS AND FELLOW-SOLDIERS: Much has been said in relation to the militia of this country, and their services in the late war with Great Britain. They are, indeed, the bulwark and safety of our country; but, while just honors have been paid to them, the gallant spirits who fought by their side with equal honor and equal success — the soldiers of the regular army of 1812 — were not mentioned. I propose, on this occasion, to make a few remarks in relation to the regular soldiers of that eventful war.

"It will be recollected by most of you, perhaps, that the soldiers and officers of 1812 came from the first families of the land. They entered the army, not as mercenaries, but from patriotic motives, with a determination to serve their country, and drive back the myrmidons of Britain from our sacred soil. [Applause.] I will give you briefly the history of one of those soldiers, which, with some modifications, may be the history of every soldier in the regular army.

"There was a lad belonging to one of the most respectable families of the United States, who, at the age of sixteen years, was the favored of his family. At that age he left his home and his school, and enlisted as a private in the 29th Regiment for five years. His father's brother, who was a colonel in the army, obtained an order for the boy's discharge. The discharge came, and was refused. [Great applause.] A commission was also offered him, and that, too, was refused. This lad served under General Wool. He was one of the three hundred who met Governor Provost eighteen miles from Plattsburg, and who cut their way, inch by inch, until they reached the banks of the Saranac. He was one of thirty who crossed the Saranac and set fire with hay and tar to the underbrush of dry pine directly under the guns of the British battery, and returned across the Saranac by floating a hundred yards down that stream, and fainting from the loss of blood. He was but one of a regiment through whose instrumentality, in part, the British lion was made to turn in defeat from the American eagle. [Applause.] This same person, in the darkness of night, led twenty men into a British town of five hundred inhabitants, and where British guards were stationed to defend it, and took three distinguished prisoners, and carried them safely into the American camp, with loss of only one man wounded. He was made a sergeant, and afterwards a provost-marshal, that being the highest non-commissioned officer in the army. But he did not seek the life of a soldier as a profession. He determined to serve his country as a patriot, and when national honor and national rights were vindicated to return into civil life. Now, in the far West, the lad then, but man now, has reared an interesting family, and maintains a good name there, and commands the respect and honor of his fellow-men. [Voices —"Give us his name!"] I'll come to that by and by. I know, fellow-soldiers, that so dearly does that man love the quiet and unostentatious position which he now occupies, that were Congress at this day to offer to confer upon him a title of Lieutenant-General of our army, or any other trust of a like character, that he would refuse it. If he has served his country, it alone is satisfaction. He has but discharged his duty. [Applause.]

Fellow-soldiers, many of us will never meet each other again on this side of Jordan. This meeting is interesting to me — more so than any which it has been my fortune to ever attend, since the scenes of that war. We have all fought our last fight — but we have still the warfare of life before us. Let us, then, so contend that we shall win a crown of victory, and be led by the eternal Captain of our salvation to our last, our eternal home in heaven! [Great applause, and cries of 'Tell us the name of that boy.']

Fellow-soldiers, he stands now before you. [Renewed applause, and nine cheers for General Ranney.]"

In 1836, General Ranney was induced to accept the post of Brigadier-General in the Missouri militia; which he filled with honor to himself, and entire acceptability to those under his command. This constitutes the only military situation he has consented to occupy in his adopted state.

In politics, he was an original Jackson democrat, and until the American party was organized he was well known as a leader in the ranks of the democracy of the state. He was among the first to enrol his name upon the records of the party to which he is now attached, and of which he is a firm, bold, and eloquent advocate. He feels, as do his brethren everywhere, all over America, that the safety of the Union and of the nation depends upon guarding the ballot-box from the inroads that are being made upon it by the influx of foreigners; opposition to extremists both of the South and the North; a conservative, peace-loving, and country-loving band of patriots, who are ready and willing to sacrifice themselves for the good of their native land. In his youth, he fought for his country; in his manhood, he has prayed for it; and in his old age, he is ready to die for it.

The same influences which led Gen. Ranney to battle for his country when a youth of only sixteen summers have again brought him into the present American revolution; and to an immense gathering of freemen in the rotunda of the court-house of St. Louis, in March, 1856, who had convened to ratify the American nominations for President and Vice President, he spoke as follows:

"AMERICANS: We are here, not as Northern men from the North, not as Southern men from the South, but as

Union men of the United States. We meet to give a hearty sanction to the Philadelphia nomination of President and Vice President.

"We have had but one Washington and Jackson, one Webster and Clay, and but one Calhoun.

"Fillmore and Donelson are good men,—the best in the Union. A better, a stronger, a more suitable nomination, cannot be made by any party, nor one better calculated to succeed. Three times in my life I have rejoiced with exceeding great joy; first when, in 1814, at Plattsburgh, one thousand four hundred Americans defeated fourteen thousand of Lord Wellington's best troops."

* * * * *

"The constitution must be preserved from violation. The one billion five hundred million dollars of slave property is nothing, compared with the worth of the Union. Ay, can the ten thousand millions of property in the world purchase of us the fame of Washington, or the memory of Yorktown, of Monmouth, of Saratoga, or of Plattsburgh and New Orleans? No! the Union *must*—it shall—it will be saved! The nation looks to us for its safety. The good men of the North will help us, and our prospects are good. We take no step backward; our platform is the constitution and the rights of the states.

"The Christian who throws away his Bible has no religion. The American who throws away the constitution has *no country*. Americans, let our party do right, and act right, if the heavens fall!

"The third time of my joy was at the nomination of Fillmore and Donelson. My reasons are, that the nominees are worthy; that the country looked for such men, with the determination to elect them."

On the 4th of June, 1856, the American party of Missouri held a mass meeting at *Hannibal*, in that state. Gen. Ranney was present to enforce the principle that "Americans alone should rule America." And he did it with a *will*, which found its way with electric power into the hearts of thousands. He told the people that

"For more than thirty years he was a consistent, an unflinching democrat, and that he had acted with them in good faith as long as they had continued honest and pure in principles; but two years ago his conviction was certain that the democratic party had changed, had become corrupt; and he had done what every honest man should do,— thrown himself body and soul into the great American cause; that he had become a member of the only party truly national, and truly devoted to the preservation of this Union."

At a convention held in Burlington, Iowa, in October, 1851, a member from St. Louis, in a set speech, declared that "while the rains of heaven were refreshing and fructifying the earth, and swelling the tide of the Mississippi, *he thanked his God that not one drop came from* SOUTH CAROLINA!!!"

Gen. Ranney, his personal friend, born in New England, but loving the whole Union, rebuked him, with this significant language, for his wanton attack upon a sister state: "Why, sir," said he, "attempt to goad men on to madness, who were placed under different circumstances with ourselves, and of which we know but little?"

He then referred to the glorious history of this chivalric and heroic state,— to the memory of Marion, Sumpter, Greene, and others; to the battles of Yorktown, Cowpens, and the Eutaw Springs, and asked the President, in a mild but emphatic manner, if all these were to be forgotten. He stated that there was one delegate in that assembly whose body had been scarred, and whose limbs had been disfigured, while fighting side by side with the Carolinian against our ancient foe in the war of 1812.

He also referred to the choicest blood of South Carolina

which had enriched the plains of Mexico, and said, "Mr. President, shall we be no longer allowed to revere and honor these events, and be compelled to steel our hearts against the noble actors in them?

"Sir, the rains of heaven, falling upon the eastern slope of the Alleghany Mountains, refreshing and fructifying the soil of South Carolina, ran some of it down her rivers, and some of these 'drops' helped to swell the tide of the sea that floated the Constitution, the Guerriere, the Wasp, and the Hornet, and enabled the American navy to obtain victory and renown."

Said Gen. Ranney, "Is this gallant state to be made accountable for all the vagaries of some of her Hotspurs, and mistaken friends?

"Why not attack good old New England, the land of churches and school-houses, and make her accountable for the infamy of the Hartford Convention, and the infernal acts of her hosts of abolitionists, who cast aside the laws of the land, and the authority of the Bible, and ridicule our holy religion? No, Mr. President," said Gen. Ranney, "I love New England, and I love South Carolina; and, with all their faults, I will love them still."

As president of the Missouri Bible Society, Gen. Ranney is also known for his distinguished efforts to advance the circulation of the Word of God, as well as diffuse its spirit among his fellow-men.

Gen. Ranney is the artificer of his own fortune, and his industry, intelligence, and energy, have more than supplied any deficiency of early culture; while the history of his life is replete with every virtue, and, without flaw or blemish, may well serve as a model for every American patriot.

www.ingramcontent.com/pod-product-compliance
Lightning Source LLC
LaVergne TN
LVHW021224110826
845150LV00002B/242
9781425564049